Franc

ois Xavier Schouppe

Purgatory

Illustrated by the lives and legends of the saints

François Xavier Schouppe
Purgatory
Illustrated by the lives and legends of the saints
ISBN/EAN: 9783337150013
Printed in Europe, USA, Canada, Australia, Japan
Cover: Foto ©ninafisch / pixelio.de

More available books at **www.hansebooks.com**

PURGATORY

ILLUSTRATED BY THE LIVES AND
LEGENDS OF THE SAINTS

BY

REV. F. X. SCHOUPPE, S.J.

TRANSLATED FROM THE FRENCH

LONDON: BURNS & OATES, LIMITED
NEW YORK, CINCINNATI, CHICAGO: BENZIGER BROTHERS

THE
DOGMA OF PURGATORY.

AUTHOR'S PREFACE.

Object of the Work—To what Class of Readers it is Addressed—What we are Obliged to Believe, what we may Piously Believe, and what we are at Liberty not to Admit—Visions and Apparitions—Blind Credulity and Exaggerated Incredulity.

THE Dogma of Purgatory is too much forgotten by the majority of the faithful; the Church Suffering, where they have so many brethren to succour, whither they foresee that they themselves must one day go, seems a strange land to them.

This truly deplorable forgetfulness was a great sorrow to St. Francis de Sales. "Alas!" said this pious doctor of the Church, "we do not sufficiently remember our dear departed; their memory seems to perish with the sound of the funeral-bells."

The principal causes of this are ignorance and lack of faith; our notions on the subject of Purgatory are too vague, our faith is too feeble.

In order, then, that our ideas may become more distinct and our faith enlivened, we must take a closer view of this life beyond the tomb, this intermediate state of the just souls, not yet worthy to enter the Heavenly Jerusalem.

This is the object of the present work : we propose not to prove the existence of Purgatory to sceptical minds, but to make it better known to the pious faithful who believe with a divine faith this dogma revealed of God. It is to them, properly speaking, that this book is addressed, to give them a less confused idea of Purgatory. I say purposely a *clearer* idea than people generally have, by placing this great truth in the strongest possible light.

To produce this effect we possess three very distinct sources of light : first, the dogmatic doctrine of the Church ; then the doctrine as explained by the doctors of the Church ; in the third place, the revelations and apparitions of the saints, which serve to confirm the teachings of the doctors.

1. The dogmatic doctrine of the Church on the subject of Purgatory comprises two articles, of which we shall speak later on.[1] These two articles are of faith, and must be believed by every Catholic.

2. The teaching of the doctors and theologians, or rather their opinions on several questions relative to Purgatory, and their explanations of them, are not imposed as articles of faith ;[2] we are free to reject them without ceasing to be Catholic. Nevertheless, it would be imprudent, and even rash, to reject them, and it is the spirit of the Church to follow the opinions commonly held by the doctors.

3. The revelations of the saints, called also *particular* revelations, do not belong to the deposit of faith confided by Jesus Church to His Church ; they are historical facts, based upon human testimony. It is permitted to believe them, and piety finds wholesome food in them. We may,

---

[1] See Chap. iii.   [2] See also lower down, Chap. iii.

however, disbelieve them without sinning against faith; but they are authenticated, and we cannot reject them without offending against reason; because sound reason demands that all men should give assent to truth when it is sufficiently demonstrated.

To illustrate this subject more clearly, let us, in the first place, explain the nature of the revelations of which we speak.

Particular revelations are of two kinds: the one consists in visions, the other in apparitions. They are called *particular*, because they differ from those found in Holy Scripture, not forming part of the doctrine revealed for mankind, and not being proposed by the Church to our belief as dogmas of faith.

Visions, properly so called, are subjective lights, infused by God into the understanding of His creatures, in order to discover to them His mysteries. Such are the visions of the prophets, those of St. Paul, of St. Bridget, and many other saints. These visions usually take place when the subject is in a state of ecstasy; they consist in certain mysterious representations, which appear to the eyes of the soul, and which must not always be taken literally. Frequently they are figures, symbolic images, which represent in a manner proportionate to the capacity of our understanding, things purely spiritual, of which ordinary language is incapable of conveying an idea.

Apparitions, at least, frequently are objective phenomena which have a real exterior object. Such was the apparition of Moses and Elias on Mount Thabor; that of Samuel evoked by the Witch of Endor; that of the Angel Raphael to Tobias; those of many other angels; in fine, such are the apparitions of the souls in Purgatory.

That the spirits of the dead sometimes appear to the living, is a fact that cannot be denied. Does not the

Gospel clearly suppose it? When the risen Jesus appeared for the first time to His assembled apostles, *they supposed they saw a spirit.* Our Saviour, far from saying that spirits appear not, spoke to them thus: *Why are you troubled, and why do thoughts arise in your hearts? See My hands and My feet, that it is I Myself; handle and see; for a spirit has not flesh and bones, as you see Me to have* (Luke xxiv. 37, &c.).

Apparitions of the souls that are in Purgatory are of frequent occurrence. We find them in great numbers in the "Lives of the Saints;" they happen sometimes to the ordinary faithful. We have collected those which appear best qualified to instruct or to edify, and we now present them to the reader. But, it may be asked, are all these facts historically certain? We have selected the best authenticated.[1] If, among the number, the reader finds any which he thinks could not stand the rigour of criticism, he need not admit them. In order to avoid an excessive severity, one which is akin to incredulity, it is good to remark that, generally speaking, apparitions of souls occur, and that they frequently occur cannot be doubted. "Ap-

---

[1] It is from the lives of the saints, honoured as such by the Church, and other illustrious servants of God, that we have taken the greater part of the examples herein cited. The reader who wishes to investigate these facts, in order to give them their just value, may without difficulty have recourse to the originals by the aid of our references. If the incident is drawn from the life of a saint, we indicate the day on which his name is entered on the martyrology, which is sufficient for consulting the *Acta Sanctorum.* If we mention any venerable personage, such as Father Joseph Anchieta, Apostle and Thaumaturgus of Brazil, whose life is not inserted in the volumes of the Bollandists, they must then have recourse to biographies and particular histories. For the examples borrowed from Father Rossignoli, *Merveilles Divine dans les Ames du Purgatoire* (trans. Postel; Tournai, Casterman), we content ourselves by marking the number of the *Merveille*, because the author has there indicated one or more sources whence he himself has drawn.

paritions of this kind," says the Abbé Ribet,[1] "are not uncommon. God permits them for the relief of souls in order to excite our compassion, and also to make us sensible of how terrible are the rigours of His Justice against those faults which we consider trivial." St. Gregory in his "Dialogues" cites several examples, of which, it is true, we may dispute the full authenticity; but which, in the mouth of this holy doctor, prove at least that he believed in the possibility of the existence of these phenomena. A great number of other authors, not less reliable than St. Gregory, both on account of sanctity and learning, relate similar instances. Moreover, incidents of this sort abound in the lives of the saints. To be convinced of this, it suffices to peruse the *Acta Sanctorum*.

The Church Suffering has ever implored the suffrages of the Church Militant; and this intercourse, bearing the impress of sadness, yet also full of instruction, is for the one a source of inexhaustible relief, and for the other a powerful incitement to sanctity.

The vision of Purgatory has been granted to many holy souls. St. Catherine de Ricci descended in spirit into Purgatory every Sunday night; St. Lidwina, during her raptures, penetrated into this place of expiation, and, conducted by her angel-guardian, visited the souls in their torments. In like manner, an angel led Blessed Osanne of Mantua through this dismal abyss.

Blessed Veronica of Binasco, St. Frances of Rome, and many others had visions exactly similar, with impressions of terror.

More frequently it is the souls themselves that appear to the living and implore their intercession. Many appeared in this manner to Blessed Margaret Mary Alacoque, and to

---

[1] *La Mystique Divine, distinguée des Contrefaçons Diaboliques et des Analogies Humaines.* Paris, Poussielgue.

a great number of other holy persons. The souls departed frequently besought the intercession of Denis the Carthusian. This great servant of God was one day asked how many times the holy souls appeared to him? "Oh! hundreds of times," he replied.

St. Catherine of Sienna, in order to spare her father the pains of Purgatory, offered herself to the Divine Justice to suffer in his stead during her whole life. God accepted her offer, inflicted the most excruciating torments upon her, which lasted until her death, and admitted the soul of her father into eternal glory. In return this blessed soul frequently appeared to his daughter to thank her, and to make to her many useful revelations.

When the souls in Purgatory appear to the living, they always present themselves in an attitude which excites compassion; now with the features which they had during life or at their death, with a sad countenance and imploring looks, in garments of mourning, with an expression of extreme suffering; then like a mist, a light, a shadow, or some kind of fantastic figure, accompanied by a sign or word by which they may be recognised. At other times they betray their presence by moans, sobs, sighs, or hurried respiration and plaintive accents. They often appear enveloped in flames. When they speak, it is to manifest their sufferings, to deplore their past faults, to ask suffrages, or even to address reproaches to those who ought to succour them. Another kind of revelation, adds the same author, is made by invisible blows which the living receive, by the violent shutting of doors, the rattling of chains, and the sounds of voices.

These facts are too multiplied to admit of doubt; the only difficulty is to establish their connection with the world of expiation. But when these manifestations coincide with the death of persons dear to us, when they cease, after prayers and reparations have been made to God in their behalf, is it not reasonable to see therein signs by which the souls make known their distress?

In the various phenomena to which we have just drawn attention we recognise the souls in Purgatory. But there is a case when the apparition should be held in suspicion; it is when a notorious sinner, unexpectedly carried away by a sudden death, comes to implore the prayers of the living that he may be delivered from Purgatory. The devil is interested in making us believe that we can live in the greatest disorders until the moment of our death and yet escape Hell. However, even in such instances, it is not forbidden to think that the soul which appears has repented, and that it is in the temporary flames of expiation; nor, consequently, is it forbidden to pray for it, but it is proper to observe the greatest caution in regard to visions of this kind, and the credit which we give to them.[1]

The details into which we have entered suffice to justify in the eyes of the reader the quotation of facts which he will find in the course of this work.

Let us add that the Christian must guard against too great incredulity in supernatural facts connected with dogmas of faith. St. Paul tells us that *Charity believeth all things*,[2] that is to say, as interpreters explain it, all that which we may prudently believe, and of which the belief will not be prejudicial. If it is true that prudence rejects a blind and superstitious credulity, it is also true that we must avoid another extreme, that with which our Saviour reproached the Apostle St. Thomas. "*You believe*," He said to him, "*because you have seen and touched;* it were better to have believed the testimony of your brethren. In exacting more, you have been guilty of incredulity; this is a fault that all My disciples should avoid. *Blessed are they that have*

---

[1] Ribet, *Mystique Divine*, vol. ii. chap. x.   [2] 1 Cor. xiii. 7.

not seen, and have believed. Be not faithless, but believing" (John xx. 27).

The theologian who expounds dogmas of faith must be severe in the choice of his proofs; the historian must proceed with rigorous circumspection in the narration of facts, but the ascetic writer, who cites examples to illustrate truths and edify the faithful, is not held to this strict rigour. The best authorised persons in the Church, such as St. Gregory, St. Bernard, St. Frances de Sales, St. Alphonsus Liguori, Bellarmine, and many others, as much distinguished for their learning as for their piety, when writing their excellent works knew nothing of the fastidious requirements of the present day—requirements which in nowise constitute progress.

In fact, if the spirit of our fathers in the faith was more simple, what is the cause of the disappearance of that ancient simplicity in the present time? Is it not the Protestant Rationalism with which, in our day, so many of our Catholics are infected? Is it not the spirit of reasoning and criticism that emanated from the Lutheran Reformation, propagated by French Philosophism, which, leading them to consider the things of God from a purely human point of view, makes them cold, and alienates them from the Spirit of God? The Venerable Louis of Blois, speaking of the "Revelations of St. Gertrude," says: "This book contains treasures. Proud and carnal men," he adds, "who understand nothing of the Spirit of God, treat as reveries the writings of the holy virgin Gertrude, of St. Mechtilde, St. Hildegarde, and others; it is because they are ignorant of the familiarity with which God communicates Himself to humble, simple, and loving souls, and how in these intimate communications He is pleased to illumine these souls with the pure light of truth, without any shadow of error."[1]

---

[1] Louis of Blois, *Epist. ad Florentium.*

These words of Louis of Blois are serious. We did not wish to incur the reproach of this great master in the spiritual life, and, whilst avoiding a blameworthy credulity, we have collected with a certain kind of liberty those which seem to us at once the best authenticated and the most instructive. May they increase in those who read them devotion towards the faithful departed. May they profoundly inspire all who read them with a holy and salutary fear of Purgatory.

TRANSLATOR'S PREFACE

The author of this work is the well-known writer, Rev. Father F. X. Schouppe, of the Society of Jesus. The reverend author scarcely needs any introduction to English readers, as several of his valuable works have been already translated from French into English. To the reverend clergy the author is best known through his works on Dogmatic Theology and Sacred Scripture, which, in the judgment of competent critics, possess the very highest order of merit. In this work on Purgatory they will find the same fulness and solidity of thought and judgment, joined with wonderful clearness and simplicity of diction, which distinguish the above works. We are confident that the reverend clergy will hail with delight the appearance of this work in an English garb, and will give it their esteemed encouragement.

A profound theologian and Scriptural scholar, acquainted as only very few are with the writings of the Fathers, the author was specially equipped for writing a work of this kind. A faithful and devoted son of the Church, his works are ever guided by a Catholic instinct, which keeps them in harmony with Catholic faith and Catholic practice.

The subject of this book is at once dear and interesting to every Catholic heart. About the existence of this intermediate state Catholics have no more doubt than of the existence of Heaven or Hell. The Church, by her authoritative teaching, has decided the matter for all time. "The Catholic Church," says the Council of Trent, "instructed by the Holy Ghost, has, from the sacred writings and the ancient tradition of the Fathers, taught in sacred councils, and very recently in the Œcumenical Synod, that there is a Purgatory, and that the souls there detained are helped by the suffrages of the faithful, but principally by the acceptable sacrifice of the altar" (Sess. 25).

The pious reader cannot fail to have his faith nourished and strengthened after reading a chapter of this book; and realising how much help and comfort he can bring to the poor souls, his charity will prompt him to come to their assistance and rescue. Their cries, wafted hither on the wings of faith from the shore of eternity, will not appeal to him in vain. A new interest will spring up within him for that realm of pain yet also of hope, where those not wholly pure are cleansed and prepared for everlasting joys.

This work has been translated into English at the earnest request of the author. Wishing that devotion for the holy souls might grow and flourish in many hearts, he considered that his purpose would be best attained by having this work translated into English, for the benefit of English-speaking readers. It may also interest the readers of this book to know that the learned author is at present labouring for the salvation of souls among the pagan people of India.

The translator has specially aimed at giving the exact sense of the author, without any attempt at style or literary finish. Such an attempt, she believes, would detract from the value of the work as a whole.

For the rest, should this work contribute even in a small measure to the greater glory of God and of Holy Church;

should it make the doctrine of Purgatory better understood; should it convince its readers of the excellence of devotion for the holy souls, and inspire at least some of them with a holy zeal to practise it, then indeed would the ambition of the author and translator be realised.

J. J. S.

CONTENTS

	PAGE
AUTHOR'S PREFACE	v
TRANSLATOR'S PREFACE	xv

Part I.

PURGATORY, THE MYSTERY OF JUSTICE.

CHAPTER I.

Purgatory in the Divine Plan 1

CHAPTER II.

Prayer for the Dead—Fear and Confidence 2

CHAPTER III.

The Word Purgatory—Catholic Doctrine—Council of Trent—Controverted Questions 4

CHAPTER IV.

Location of Purgatory—Doctrine of Theologians—Catechism of the Council of Trent—St. Thomas 5

CHAPTER V.

Location of Purgatory—Revelations of the Saints—St. Teresa—St. Louis Bertrand—St. Mary Magdalen de Pazzi . . 8

CHAPTER VI.

Location of Purgatory—St. Frances of Rome—St. Magdalen de Pazzi 11

CHAPTER VII.

Location of Purgatory—St. Lidwina of Schiedam . . . 16

CHAPTER VIII.

Location of Purgatory—St. Gregory the Great—The Deacon Paschasius and the Priest—Blessed Stephen, the Franciscan, and the Religious in his Stall—Theophilus Renaud and the Sick Woman of Dôle 19

CHAPTER IX.

The Pains of Purgatory, their Nature, their Rigour—Doctrine of Theologians—Bellarmine—St. Francis of Sales—Fear and Confidence 24

CHAPTER X.

Pains of Purgatory—The Pain of Loss—St. Catherine of Genoa—St. Teresa—Father Nieremberg 28

CHAPTER XI.

The Pain of Sense—Torment of Fire and Torment of Cold—Venerable Bede and Drithelm 30

CHAPTER XII.

Pains of Purgatory—Bellarmine and St. Christine the Admirable   34

CONTENTS. xxi

CHAPTER XIII.

PAGE

Pains of Purgatory—Brother Antony Pereyra—The Venerable Angela Tholomei 37

CHAPTER XIV.

Pains of Purgatory—Apparition of Foligno—The Dominican Religious of Zamorra 41

CHAPTER XV.

Pains of Purgatory—The Brother of St. Magdalen de Pazzi—Stanislaus Chocosca—Blessed Catherine of Racconigi . 45

CHAPTER XVI.

Pains of Purgatory—St. Antoninus and the Sick Religious—Father Rossignoli on a Quarter of an Hour in Purgatory—Brother Angelicus 47

CHAPTER XVII.

Pains of Purgatory—Blessed Quinziani—The Emperor Maurice 50

CHAPTER XVIII.

Pains of Purgatory—St. Perpetua—St. Gertrude—St. Catherine of Genoa—Brother John de Via 53

CHAPTER XIX.

Pains of Purgatory—St. Magdalen of Pazzi and Sister Benedicta—St. Gertrude—Blessed Margaret Mary and Mother de Montoux 57

CHAPTER XX.

Diversity of the Pains—King Sancho and Queen Guda—St. Lidwina and the Soul Transpierced—Blessed Margaret Mary and the Bed of Fire 60

CHAPTER XXI.

Diversity of the Pains—Blasio Raised from the Dead by St. Bernardine—Venerable Frances of Pampeluna and the Pen of Fire—St. Corpreus and King Malachi 64

CHAPTER XXII.

Duration of Purgatory—Opinions of the Doctors—Bellarmine—Calculations of Father Mumford. 68

CHAPTER XXIII.

Duration of Purgatory—St. Lutgarde, the Abbot of Citeaux, and Pope Innocent III.—John de Lierre 71

CHAPTER XXIV.

Duration of Purgatory—The Duellist—Father Schoofs and the Apparition at Antwerp 75

CHAPTER XXV.

Duration of Purgatory—The Abbey of Latrobe—A Hundred Years of Suffering for Delay in the Reception of the Last Sacraments 79

CHAPTER XXVI.

Duration of Purgatory—Venerable Catherine Paluzzi and Sister Bernardine—Brothers Finetti and Rudolfini—St. Peter Claver and the two Poor Women 82

CHAPTER XXVII.

The Cause of Suffering—Matter of the Expiation of Purgatory—Doctrine of Suarez—St. Catherine of Genoa . . . 85

CHAPTER XXVIII.

Matter of Expiation—The Remains of Mortal Sin—Lord Stourton—Sins of Lust not fully Expiated upon Earth —St. Lidwina 88

CHAPTER XXIX.

Matter of Expiation—Worldliness—St. Bridget—The Young Person—The Soldier—Blessed Mary Villani and the Worldly Lady 90

CHAPTER XXX.

Matter of Expiation—Sins of Youth—St. Catherine of Sweden and the Princess Gida 93

CHAPTER XXXI.

Matter of Expiation—Scandal Given—Immodest Paintings— Father Zucci and the Novice 95

CHAPTER XXXII.

Matter of Expiation—The Life of Pleasure—The Pursuit of Comfort—Venerable Frances of Pampeluna and the Man of the World—St. Elizabeth and the Queen, her Mother . 98

CHAPTER XXXIII.

Matter of Expiation—Tepidity—St. Bernard and the Religious of Citeaux—Venerable Mother Agnes and Sister de Haut Villars—Father Surin and the Religious of Loudun . . 100

CHAPTER XXXIV.

Matter of Expiation—Negligence in Holy Communion—Louis of Blois—St. Magdalen de Pazzi and the Departed Soul in Adoration 10

CHAPTER XXXV.

Matter of Expiation—Want of Respect in Prayer—Mother Agnes of Jesus and Sister Angelique—St. Severin of Cologne—Venerable Frances of Pampeluna and the Priests—Father Streit, S.J. 106

CHAPTER XXXVI.

Matter of Expiation and Chastisement—Immortification of the Senses—Father Francis of Aix—Immortification of the Tongue—Durand 109

CHAPTER XXXVII.

Matter of Expiation—Intemperance of the Tongue—The Dominican Father—Sisters Gertrude and Margaret—St. Hugh of Cluny and the Infringer of the Rule of Silence . 111

CHAPTER XXXVIII.

Matter of Expiation—Failure in Matters of Justice—Father d'Espinoza and the Payments—Blessed Margaret of Cortona and the Assassinated Merchants 113

CHAPTER XXXIX.

Matter of Expiation—Sins against Charity—Blessed Margaret Mary—Two Persons of Rank in the Pains of Purgatory—Several Souls Punished for Discord 115

CHAPTER XL.

Matter of Expiation—Lack of Charity and of Respect towards our Neighbour—St. Louis Bertrand and the Departed Soul asking Pardon—Father Nieremberg—Blessed Margaret Mary and the Benedictine Religious 117

CONTENTS.

CHAPTER XLI.

Matter of Expiation—Abuse of Grace—St. Magdalen de Pazzi and the Dead Religious—Blessed Margaret Mary and the three Souls in Purgatory 121

Part II.

PURGATORY, THE MYSTERY OF MERCY.

CHAPTER I.

Fear and Confidence—The Mercy of God—St. Lidwina and the Priest—Venerable Claude de la Colombière . . . 124

CHAPTER II.

Confidence—Mercy of God towards Souls—He Consoles them —St. Catherine of Genoa—The Brother of St. Magdalen de Pazzi 129

CHAPTER III.

Consolations of the Souls—St. Stanislaus of Cracow and the Resuscitated Peter Miles 131

CHAPTER IV.

Consolations of Souls—St. Catherine de Ricci and the Soul of a Prince 133

CHAPTER V.

Consolations of Souls—The Blessed Virgin—Revelations of St. Bridget — Father Jerome Carvalho — Blessed Renier of Citeaux 135

CHAPTER VI.

Consolations of Purgatory—The Blessed Virgin Mary—Privilege of Saturday—Venerable Paula of St. Teresa—St. Peter Damian and the Deceased Marozi 137

CHAPTER VII.

Consolations of Purgatory—The Angels—St. Bridget—Venerable Paula of St. Teresa—Brother Peter of Basto . . 139

CHAPTER VIII.

Consolations of Purgatory—The Angels—Blessed Emilia of Vercelli—The Saints in Heaven 144

CHAPTER IX.

Assistance given the Holy Souls—Suffrages—Meritorious, Impetratory, and Satisfactory Works—God's Mercy—St. Gertrude—Judas Machabeus 146

CHAPTER X.

Assistance given to the Holy Souls—Holy Mass—St. Augustine and St. Monica 149

CHAPTER XI.

Assistance rendered to the Souls — Holy Mass — Jubilee of Leo XIII.—Solemn Commemoration of the Dead on the Last Sunday in September 152

CHAPTER XII.

Means of Assisting the Souls in Purgatory—Holy Mass—The Religious of Citeaux delivered by the Sacred Host—Blessed Henry Suzo 155

CONTENTS. xxvii

CHAPTER XIII.

PAGE

Relief of the Souls—Holy Mass—St. Elizabeth and Queen Constance—St. Nicholas of Tolentino and Pellegrino d'Osimo . 158

CHAPTER XIV.

Relief of the Holy Souls—Holy Mass—Father Gerard—The Thirty Masses of St. Gregory 161

CHAPTER XV.

Relief of the Holy Souls — Eugenie Wybo — Lacordaire and the Polish Prince 164

CHAPTER XVI.

Relief of the Holy Souls—Liturgy of the Church—Commemoration of the Dead—St. Odilo 168

CHAPTER XVII.

Relief of the Souls—The Sacrifice of the Mass—Brother John of Alvernia at the Altar—St. Magdalen de Pazzi—St. Malachy and his Sister 170

CHAPTER XVIII.

Relief of the Souls—Holy Mass—St. Malachy at Clairvaux —Sister Zénaïde—Venerable Joseph Anchieta and the Requiem Mass. 173

CHAPTER XIX.

Relief of the Souls through the Holy Sacrifice of the Mass— Venerable Mother Agnes and Sister Seraphique—Margaret of Austria—The Archduke Charles—Father Mancinelli . 176

CHAPTER XX.

Relief of the Souls through the Holy Sacrifice of the Mass—St. Teresa and Bernardine de Mendoza—Multiplicity of Masses—Pomp of the Obsequies 179

CHAPTER XXI.

Relief of the Souls—Prayer—Brother Corrado d'Offida—The Golden Fish-hook and the Silver Thread 182

CHAPTER XXII.

Relief of the Holy Souls—The Holy Rosary—Father Nieremberg—Mother Frances of the Blessed Sacrament and the Rosary 184

CHAPTER XXIII.

Relief of the Holy Souls—Fasts, Penances, and Mortifications, however Trifling—A Glass of Cold Water—Blessed Margaret Mary 186

CHAPTER XXIV.

Relief of the Holy Souls—Holy Communion—St. Magdalen de Pazzi delivering her Brother—General Communion in the Church 188

CHAPTER XXV.

Relief of the Holy Souls—The Stations of the Cross—Venerable Mary of Antigua 191

CHAPTER XXVI.

Relief of the Holy Souls—Indulgences—Blessed Mary of Quito and the Heaps of Gold 193

CHAPTER XXVII.

Relief of the Holy Souls—Indulgences—Mother Frances of Pampeluna and the Bishop de Ribera—St. Magdalen de Pazzi—St. Teresa 196

CHAPTER XXVIII.

Relief of the Holy Souls—Indulgences—Indulgenced Prayers . 198

CHAPTER XXIX.

Relief of the Holy Souls—Alms—Raban-Maur and Edelard at the Monastery of Fulda 200

CHAPTER XXX.

Relief of the Holy Souls—Alms-giving—Christian Mercy—St. Francis de Sales and the Widow at Padua 203

CHAPTER XXXI.

Relief of the Holy Souls—The Heroic Act of Charity towards the Holy Souls—Father Mumford—Denis the Carthusian and St. Gertrude 205

CHAPTER XXXII.

Relief of the Holy Souls—Which of them should be the Objects of our Charity—All the Faithful Departed—St. Andrew Avellino—Sinners Dying without the Sacraments—St. Francis de Sales 208

CHAPTER XXXIII.

Relief of the Holy Souls—For whom are we to Pray?—Great Sinners—Father Ravignan and General Exelmans—The Widow in Mourning and the Venerable Curé of Ars—Sister Catherine of St. Augustine and the Sinner Dead in the Grotto 211

CHAPTER XXXIV.

Motives for Assisting the Holy Souls—Excellence of this Work —St. Francis de Sales—St. Thomas of Aquin—St. Bridget   215

CHAPTER XXXV.

Motives for aiding the Holy Souls—Excellence of the Work— Controversy between Brother Benedict and Brother Bertrand 218

CHAPTER XXXVI.

Motives for Assisting the Holy Souls—Intimate Ties which Unite us to them—Filial Piety—Cimon of Athens and his Father in Prison—St. John of God Saving the Sick from the Conflagration 221

CHAPTER XXXVII.

Motives for Assisting the Holy Souls—Facility in Relieving them—The Example of the Saints and of all Fervent Christians—The Servant of God, Mary Villani—The Burned Forehead 223

CHAPTER XXXVIII.

Motives for Assisting the Holy Souls—Examples of Holy Persons — Father James Laynez — Father Fabricius — Father Nieremberg a Victim of his Charity 226

CHAPTER XXXIX.

Motives an Incentive to Devotion towards the Holy Souls—Examples of Generosity—St. Peter Damian and his Father—A Young Annamite—The Doorkeeper at the Seminary and the Propagation of the Faith 229

CHAPTER XL.

Motives for Assisting the Holy Souls — Obligation not only of Charity but also of Justice — Pious Legacies — Father Rossignoli and the Devastated Property— St. Thomas of Cantimpré and the Soldier of Charlemagne . . . 232

CHAPTER XLI.

Motives of Justice—St. Bernardine of Sienna and the Unfaithful Widow—Disguised Restitutions—Neglect to Execute the Last Will 236

CHAPTER XLII.

Motives of Justice—Barren Tears—Thomas of Cantimpré and his Grandmother—Blessed Margaret of Cortona . . 239

CHAPTER XLIII.

Motives of Justice—Prayer for Departed Parents—St. Catherine of Sienna and her Father Jacomo 242

CHAPTER XLIV.

Motives an Incentive to Devotion towards the Holy Souls—St. John of God—Give Alms for your Own Sake—St. Bridget —Blessed Peter Lefèvre 245

CHAPTER XLV.

Advantages of the Devotion towards the Holy Souls — Their Gratitude—St. Margaret of Cortona—St. Philip Neri— Cardinal Baronius and the Dying Woman 248

CHAPTER XLVI.

Advantages—Gratitude of the Souls—The Return of an Exiled Priest—Father Mumford and the Printer, Willian Freyssen 250

CHAPTER XLVII.

Advantages—Temporal Favours—The Abbé Postel and the Servant of Paris 254

CHAPTER XLVIII.

Advantages—Temporal Favours—The Neapolitan Woman and the Mysterious Note 257

CHAPTER XLIX.

Advantages—Spiritual and Temporal Favours—Christopher Sandoval at Louvain—The Lawyer Renouncing the World —Brother Lacci and Dr. Verdiano 259

CHAPTER L.

Advantages—Prayers of the Souls for us—Suarez—St. Bridget St. Catherine of Bologna—Venerable Vianney . . . 263

CHAPTER LI.

Advantages—Gratitude of the Divine Spouse of Souls—Venerable Archangela Panigarola and her Father, Gothard . . 266

CHAPTER LII.

Advantages—Charity towards the Souls Recompensed by Jesus Christ—St. Catherine of Sienna and Palmerine—St. Magdalen de Pazzi and her Mother 268

CHAPTER LIII.

Advantages—Charity towards the Dead Rewarded—St. Thomas of Aquin, his Sister and Brother Romano—The Archpriest Ponzoni and Don Alphonso Sanchez—Blessed Margaret Mary and Mother Greffier 271

CHAPTER LIV.

Advantages— Salutary Thoughts — Make Satisfaction in this Life rather than in the Next—St. Augustine and St. Louis Bertrand—Brother Lourenco—Father Michel de la Fontaine 276

CHAPTER LV.

Advantages—Salutary Instruction—Blessed Mary of the Angels —St. Peter Claver and the Sick Negro—The Negro and the Rosary 279

CHAPTER LVI.

Advantages – Salutary Instructions—St. Magdalen de Pazzi and Sister Benedicta—Father Paul Hoffée—Venerable Father de la Colombière—Father Louis Corbinelli . . . 281

CHAPTER LVII.

Advantages—Stimulant to Fervour—Cautions to us—Probability of going to Purgatory—Means of Escaping it—Employment of those Means—St. Catherine of Genoa . . . 285

CHAPTER LVIII.

Means to avoid Purgatory—Great Devotion to the Blessed Virgin — Father Jerome Carvalho — St. Bridget — The Scapular of Mount Carmel 288

CHAPTER LIX.

Means to Avoid Purgatory—Privileges of the Holy Scapula— Venerable Father de la Colombière—The Hospital at Toulon—The Sabbatine—St. Teresa—A Lady at Otranto . 291

c

CHAPTER LX.

Means to Avoid Purgatory—Charity and Mercy—The Prophet Daniel and the King of Babylon—St. Peter Damian and John Patrizzi 295

CHAPTER LXI.

Means to Avoid Purgatory—Blessed Margaret Mary and the Suffering Souls—The Novice and her Father—A Soul that had Suffered without Complaint 298

CHAPTER LXII.

Means to Avoid Purgatory—Christian Mortification—St. John Berchmans—Blessed Emily of Vercelli and the Religious who was Weary of Choir 300

CHAPTER LXIII.

Means to Avoid Purgatory—The Sacraments—Receiving them Promptly—Medicinal Effect of Extreme Unction—St. Alphonsus Liguori 303

CHAPTER LXIV.

Means to Avoid Purgatory—Confidence in God—St. Francis de Sales—St. Philip Neri and Sister Scholastica . . . 306

CHAPTER LXV.

Means to Avoid Purgatory—Holy Acceptation of Death—Father Aquitanus—St. Alphonsus Liguori—Venerable Frances of Pampeluna and the Person who was not Resigned to Die—Father Vincent Caraffa and the Condemned Man—Sister Mary of St. Joseph and Mother Isabella—St. John of the Cross—Sweetness of the Death of the Saints . . . 308

PROTESTATION OF THE AUTHOR

In conformity to the decree of Urban VIII., Sanctissimum, *of March 13, 1525, we declare that if in this work we have cited facts represented to be supernatural, nothing but a personal and private authority is to be attached to our opinion; the discernment of facts of this kind belongs to the supreme authority of the Church.*

Part First.

PURGATORY, THE MYSTERY OF JUSTICE.

CHAPTER I.

Purgatory in the Divine Plan.

PURGATORY occupies an important place in our holy religion: it forms one of the principal parts of the work of Jesus Christ, and plays an essential *rôle* in the economy of the salvation of man.

Let us call to mind that the Holy Church of God, considered as a whole, is composed of three parts: The Church Militant, the Church Triumphant, and the Church Suffering, or Purgatory. This triple Church constitutes the mystical body of Jesus Christ, and the souls in Purgatory are no less His members than are the faithful upon earth and the elect in Heaven. In the Gospel, the Church is ordinarily called the *Kingdom of Heaven;* now Purgatory, just as the heavenly and terrestrial Church, is a province of this vast kingdom.

The three sister Churches have incessant relations with each other, a continual communication which we call the *Communion of Saints.* These relations have no other object than to conduct souls to eternal glory, the final term to which all the elect tend. The three Churches mutually assist in peopling Heaven, which is the permanent city, the glorious Jerusalem.

What then is the work which we, members of the Church Militant, have to do for the souls in Purgatory? We have to alleviate their sufferings. God has placed in our hands the key of this mysterious prison: it is *prayer for the dead*, devotion to the souls in Purgatory.

CHAPTER II.

Prayer for the Dead—Fear and Confidence.

PRAYER for the departed, sacrifices, and suffrages for the dead form a part of Christian worship, and devotion towards the souls in Purgatory is a devotion which the Holy Ghost infuses with charity into the hearts of the faithful. *It is a holy and wholesome thought*, says Holy Scripture, *to pray for the dead, that they may be loosed from sins.*[1]

In order to be perfect, devotion to the souls in Purgatory must be animated both by a spirit of fear and a spirit of confidence. On the one hand, the Sanctity of God and His Justice inspires us with a salutary fear; on the other, His infinite Mercy gives us boundless confidence.

God is Sanctity itself, much more so than the sun is light, and no shadow of sin can endure before His face. *Thine eyes are pure*, says the prophet, *and thou canst not look on iniquity.*[2] When iniquity manifests itself in creatures, the Sanctity of God exacts expiation, and when this expiation is made in all the rigour of justice, it is terrible. It is for this reason that the Scripture says again, *Holy and terrible*

---

[1] Machab. xii. 46.   [2] Habac. i. 13.

is His name ;[1] as though it would say, His Justice is terrible because His Sanctity is infinite.

The Justice of God is terrible, and it punishes with extreme rigour even the most trivial faults. The reason is, that these faults, light in our eyes, are in nowise so before God. The least sin displeases Him infinitely, and, on account of the infinite Sanctity which is offended, the slightest transgression assumes enormous proportions, and demands enormous atonement. This explains the terrible severity of the pains of the other life, and should penetrate us with a holy fear.

This fear of Purgatory is a salutary fear; its effect is, not only to animate us with a charitable compassion towards the poor suffering souls, but also with a vigilant zeal for our own spiritual welfare. Think of the fire of Purgatory, and you will endeavour to avoid the least faults; think of the fire of Purgatory, and you will practise penance, that you may satisfy Divine Justice in this world rather than in the next.

Let us, however, guard against excessive fear, and not lose confidence. Let us not forget the Mercy of God, which is not less infinite than His Justice. *Thy mercy, Lord, is great above the Heavens,* says the prophet;[2] and elsewhere, *The Lord is gracious and merciful: patient, and plenteous in mercy.*[3] This ineffable mercy should calm the most lively apprehensions, and fill us with a holy confidence, according to the words, *In te, Domine, speravi, non confundar in æternum*—" In Thee, O Lord, I have hoped; let me never be put to confusion."[4]

If we are animated with this double sentiment, if our confidence in God's Mercy is equal to the fear with which His Justice inspires us, we shall have the true spirit of devotion to the souls in Purgatory.

This double sentiment springs naturally from the dogma of Purgatory rightly understood—a dogma which contains

[1] Ps. cx.   [2] Ps. cvii.   [3] Ps. cxliv.   [4] Ps. lxx.

the double mystery of Justice and Mercy : of Justice which punishes, of Mercy which pardons. It is from this double point of view that we are about to consider Purgatory and illustrate its doctrine.

CHAPTER III.

The Word Purgatory—Catholic Doctrine—Council of Trent —Controverted Questions.

THE word *Purgatory* is sometimes taken to mean a place, sometimes as an intermediate state between Hell and Heaven. It is, properly speaking, *the condition of souls* which, at the moment of death, are in the state of grace, but which have not completely expiated their faults, nor attained the degree of purity necessary to enjoy the vision of God.

Purgatory is, then, a transitory state which terminates in a life of everlasting happiness. It is not a trial by which merit may be gained or lost, but a state of atonement and expiation. The soul has arrived at the term of its earthly career; that life was a time of trial, a time of merit for the soul, a time of mercy on the part of God. This time once expired, nothing but justice is to be expected from God, whilst the soul can neither gain nor lose merit. She remains in the state in which death found her; and since it found her in the state of sanctifying grace, she is certain of never forfeiting that happy state, and of arriving at the eternal possession of God. Nevertheless, since she is burdened with certain debts of temporal punishment, she must satisfy Divine Justice by enduring this punishment in all its rigour.

Such is the signification of the word *Purgatory*, and the condition of the souls which are there.

On this subject the Church proposes *two truths* clearly defined as dogmas of faith : first, *that there is a Purgatory;* second, *that the souls which are in Purgatory may be assisted by the suffrages of the faithful, especially by the Holy Sacrifice of the Mass.*

Besides these two *dogmatic points*, there are several doctrinal questions which the Church has not decided, and which are more or less clearly solved by the Doctors. These questions relate (1) to the location of Purgatory; (2) to the nature of the sufferings; (3) to the number and condition of the souls which are in Purgatory; (4) to the certainty which they have of their beatitude; (5) to the duration of their sufferings; (6) to the intervention of the living in their behalf, and the application of the suffrages of the Church.

CHAPTER IV.

Location of Purgatory—Doctrine of Theologians—Catechism of the Council of Trent—St. Thomas.

ALTHOUGH faith tells us nothing definite regarding the location of Purgatory, the most common opinion, that which most accords with the language of Scripture, and which is the most generally received among theologians, places it in the bowels of the earth, not far from the Hell of the reprobates. Theologians are almost unanimous, says Bellarmin,[1] in teaching that Purgatory, at least the *ordinary* place of expiation, is situated in the interior of the earth, that the souls in Purgatory and the reprobate are in the same subterranean space in the deep abyss which the Scripture calls *Hell.*

When we say in the Apostles' Creed that after His

[1] Catech. Rom., chap. vi. § 1.

death *Jesus Christ descended into Hell*, the name Hell, says the Catechism of the Council of Trent, signifies those hidden places where the souls are detained which have not yet reached eternal beatitude. But these prisons are of different kinds. One is a dark and gloomy dungeon, where the damned are continually tormented by evil spirits, and by a fire which is never extinguished. This place, which is Hell properly so called, is also named *Gehenna* and abyss.

There is another Hell, which contains the fire of Purgatory. There the souls of the just suffer for a certain time, that they may become entirely purified before being admitted into their heavenly fatherland, where nothing defiled can ever enter.

A third Hell was that into which the souls of the saints who died before the coming of Jesus Christ were received, and in which they enjoyed peaceful repose, exempt from pain, consoled and sustained by the hope of their redemption. They were those holy souls which awaited Jesus Christ in Abraham's bosom, and which were delivered when Christ descended into Hell. Our Saviour suddenly diffused among them a brilliant light, which filled them with infinite joy, and gave them sovereign beatitude, which is the vision of God. Then was fulfilled the promise of Jesus to the good thief: *This day thou shalt be with me in Paradise.*

"A very probable opinion," says St. Thomas,[1] "and one which, moreover, corresponds with the words of the saints in particular revelation is, that Purgatory has a double place for expiation. The first will be destined for the generality of souls, and is situated below, near to Hell; the second will be for particular cases, and it is from thence that so many apparitions occur."

The holy Doctor admits, then, like so many others who share his opinions, that sometimes Divine Justice assigns

[1] Supplem., part. iii. ques. ult.

a special place of purification to certain souls, and even permits them to appear either to instruct the living or to procure for the departed the suffrages of which they stand in need; sometimes also for other motives worthy of the wisdom and mercy of God.

Such is the general view concerning the location of Purgatory. Since we are not writing a controversial treatise, we add neither proofs nor refutations; these can be seen in authors such as Suarez and Bellarmin. We will content ourselves by remarking that the opinion concerning a subterranean Hell has nothing to fear from modern science. A science purely natural is incompetent in questions which belong, as does this one, to the supernatural order. Moreover, we know that spirits may be in a place occupied by bodies, as though these bodies did not exist. Whatever, then, the interior of the earth may be, whether it be entirely of fire, as geologists commonly say, or whether it be in any other state, there is nothing to prevent its serving as a sojourn of spirits, even of spirits clothed with a risen body. The Apostle St. Paul teaches us that the air is filled with a multitude of evil spirits: *We have to combat,* says he, *against the spirits of wickedness in the high places.*[1]

On the other hand, we know that the good angels who protect us are no less numerous in the world. Now, if angels and other spirits can inhabit our atmosphere, whilst the physical world is not in the least degree changed, why cannot the souls of the dead dwell in the bosom of the earth?

[1] Ephes. vi. 12.

CHAPTER V.

Location of Purgatory—Revelations of the Saints—St. Teresa —St. Louis Bertrand—St. Mary Magdalen de Pazzi.

ST. TERESA had great charity towards the souls in Purgatory, and assisted them as much as lay in her power by her prayers and good works. In recompense, God frequently showed her the souls she had delivered; she saw them at the moment of their release from suffering and of their entrance into Heaven. Now, they generally came forth from the bosom of the earth. "*I received tidings,*" she writes, "of the death of a Religious who had formerly been Provincial of that province, and afterwards of another. I was acquainted with him, and he had rendered me great service. This intelligence caused me great uneasiness. Although this man was commendable for many virtues, I was apprehensive for the salvation of his soul, because he had been Superior for the space of twenty years, and I always fear much for those who are charged with the care of souls. Much grieved, I went to an oratory; there I conjured our Divine Lord to apply to this Religious the little good I had done during my life, and to supply the rest by His infinite merits, in order that this soul might be freed from Purgatory.

"Whilst I besought this grace with all the fervour of which I was capable, I saw on my right side this soul come forth from the depths of the earth and ascend into Heaven in transports of joy. Although this priest was advanced in years, he appeared to me with the features of man who had not yet attained the age of thirty, and with a countenance resplendent with light.

"This vision, though very short, left me inundated with joy, and without a shadow of doubt as to the truth of what I had seen. As I was separated by a great distance from the place where this servant of God had ended his days, it was some time before I learned the particulars of his edifying death; all those who were witnesses of it could not behold without admiration how he preserved consciousness to the last moment, the tears he shed, and the sentiments of humility with which he surrendered his soul to God.

"A Religious of my community, a great servant of God, had been dead not quite two days. We were saying the Office for the Dead for her in choir, a sister was reading the lesson, and I was standing to say the versicle. When half of the lesson had been said, I saw the soul of this Religious come forth from the depths of the earth, like the one of which I have just spoken, and go to Heaven.

"In this same monastery there died, at the age of eighteen or twenty years, another Religious, a true model of fervour, regularity, and virtue. Her life had been but a tissue of maladies and sufferings patiently endured. I had no doubt, after having seen her live thus, that she had more than sufficient merits to exempt her from Purgatory. Nevertheless, whilst I was at office, before she was interred, and about a quarter of an hour after her death, I saw her soul likewise issue from the earth and rise to Heaven." Behold what St. Teresa writes.

A like instance is recorded in the Life of St. Louis Bertrand, of the Order of St. Dominic. This Life, written by Father Antist, a Religious of the same Order, and who lived with the saint, is inserted in the *Acta Sanctorum* on the 10th of October. In the year 1557, whilst St. Louis Bertrand resided at the convent of Valentia, the pest broke out in that city. The terrible plague spread rapidly, threatening to exterminate the inhabitants, and each one trembled for his life. A Religious of the community, wishing to prepare himself fervently for death, made a general confession of his whole life to the saint; and on leaving him said, "Father, if it should now please God to call me, I shall return and make known to you my condition in the other life." He died a short time afterwards, and the following night he appeared to the saint. He told him that he was detained in Purgatory on account of a few slight faults which remained to be expiated, and begged the saint to recommend him to the community. St. Louis communicated the request immediately to the Prior, who hastened to recommend the soul of the departed to the prayers and Holy Sacrifices of the brethren assembled in chapter.

Six days later, a man of the town, who knew nothing of what had passed at the convent, came to make his confession to Father Louis, and told him "that the soul of Father Clement had appeared to him. He saw, he said, the earth open, and the soul of the deceased Father come forth all glorious; it resembled, he added, a resplendent star, which rose through the air towards Heaven."

We read in the Life of St. Magdalen de Pazzi,[1] written by her confessor, Father Cepari, of the Company of Jesus, that this servant of God was made witness of the deliverance of a soul under the following circumstances:—One of her sisters in religion had died some time previous, when the saint being one day in prayer before the Blessed Sacrament, saw issue from the earth the soul of that sister, still captive in the dungeons of Purgatory. She was enveloped in a mantle of flames, under which a robe of dazzling whiteness protected her from the fierce heat of the fire; and she remained an entire hour at the foot of the altar, adoring in inexpressible annihilation the hidden God of the Eucharist.

This hour of adoration, which Magdalen saw her perform, was the last of her penance; that hour passed, she arose and took her flight to Heaven.

[1] May 25.

CHAPTER VI.

*Location of Purgatory—St. Frances of Rome—
St. Magdalen de Pazzi.*

IT has pleased God to show in spirit the gloomy abodes of Purgatory to some privileged souls, who were to reveal the sorrowful mysteries thereof for the edification of the faithful. Of this number was the illustrious St. Frances,[1] foundress of the Oblates, who died in Rome in 1440. God favoured her with great lights concerning the state of souls in the other life. She saw Hell and its horrible torments; she saw also the interior of Purgatory, and the mysterious order —I had almost said hierarchy of expiations—which reigns in this portion of the Church of Jesus Christ.

In obedience to her superiors, who thought themselves bound to impose this obligation upon her, she made known all that God had manifested to her; and her visions, written at the request of the venerable Canon Matteotti, her spiritual director, have all the authenticity that can be desired in such matters. Now, the servant of God declared that, after having endured with unspeakable horror the vision of Hell, she came out of that abyss and was conducted by her celestial guide into the regions of Purgatory. There reigned neither horror nor disorder, nor despair nor eternal darkness; there divine hope diffused its light, and she was told that this place of purification was called also *sojourn of hope*. She saw there souls which suffered cruelly, but angels visited and assisted them in their sufferings.

"Purgatory, she said, is divided into three distinct parts, which are as the three large provinces of that kingdom of suffering. They are situated the one beneath the other, and occupied by souls of different orders. These souls are

[1] March 9.

buried more deeply in proportion as they are more defiled and farther removed from the time of their deliverance.

The lowest region is filled with a fierce fire, but which is not dark like that of Hell; it is a vast burning sea, throwing forth immense flames. Innumerable souls are plunged into its depths: they are those who have rendered themselves guilty of mortal sin, which they have duly confessed, but not sufficiently expiated during life. The servant of God then learned that, for all forgiven mortal sin, there remains to be undergone a suffering of seven years. This term cannot evidently be taken to mean a definite measure, since mortal sins differ in enormity, but as an average penalty. Although the souls are enveloped in the same flames, their sufferings are not the same; they differ according to the number and nature of their former sins.

In this lower Purgatory the saint beheld laics and persons consecrated to God. The laics were those who, after a life of sin, had had the happiness of being sincerely converted; the persons consecrated to God were those who had not lived according to the sanctity of their state. At that same moment she saw descend the soul of a priest whom she knew, but whose name she does not reveal. She remarked that he had his face covered with a veil which concealed a stain. Although he had led an edifying life, this priest had not always observed strict temperance, and had sought too eagerly the satisfactions of the table.

The saint was then conducted into the intermediate Purgatory, destined for souls which had deserved less rigorous chastisement. It had three distinct compartments; one resembled an immense dungeon of ice, the cold of which was indescribably intense; the second, on the contrary, was like a huge caldron of boiling oil and pitch; the third had the appearance of a pond of liquid metal resembling molten gold or silver.

The upper Purgatory, which the saint does not describe, is the temporary abode of souls which suffer little, except the pain of loss, and approach the happy moment of their deliverance.

Such, in substance, is the vision of St. Frances relative to Purgatory.

The following is an account of that of St. Magdalen de Pazzi, a Florentine Carmelite, as it is related in her Life by Father Cepare. It gives more of a picture of ̄Purgatory, whilst the preceding vision but traces its outlines.

Some time before her death, which took place in 1607, the servant of God, Magdalen de Pazzi, being one evening with several other Religious in the garden of the convent, was ravished in ecstasy, and saw Purgatory open before her. At the same time, as she made known later, a voice invited her to visit all the prisons of Divine Justice, and to see how truly worthy of compassion are the souls detained there.

At this moment she was heard to say, "Yes, I will go." She consented to undertake this painful journey. In fact, she walked for two hours round the garden, which was very large, pausing from time to time. Each time she interrupted her walk, she contemplated attentively the sufferings which were shown to her. She was then seen to wring her hands in compassion, her face became pale, her body bent under the weight of suffering, in presence of the terrible spectacle with which she was confronted.

She began to cry aloud in lamentation, "Mercy, my God, mercy! Descend, O Precious Blood, and deliver these souls from their prison. Poor souls! you suffer so cruelly, and yet you are content and cheerful. The dungeons of the martyrs in comparison with these were gardens of delight. Nevertheless there are others still deeper. How happy should I esteem myself were I not obliged to go down into them."

She did descend, however, for she was forced to continue her way. But when she had taken a few steps, she stopped terror-stricken, and, sighing deeply, she cried, "What! Religious also in this dismal abode! Good God! how they are tormented! Ah, Lord!" She does not explain the nature of their sufferings; but the horror which she manifested in contemplating them caused her to sigh at each step. She passed from thence into less gloomy places. They were the dungeons of simple souls, and of children in whom ignorance and lack of reason extenuated many faults. Their torments appeared to her much more endurable than those of the others. Nothing but ice and fire were there. She noticed that these souls had their angel-guardians with them, who fortified them greatly by their presence; but she saw also demons whose dreadful forms increased their sufferings.

Advancing a few paces, she saw souls still more unfortunate, and she was heard to cry out, "Oh! how horrible is this place; it is full of hideous demons and incredible torments! Who, O my God, are the victims of these cruel tortures? Alas! they are being pierced with sharp swords, they are being cut into pieces." She was answered that they were the souls whose conduct had been tainted with hypocrisy.

Advancing a little, she saw a great multitude of souls which were bruised, as it were, and crushed under a press; and she understood that they were those souls which had been addicted to impatience and disobedience during life. Whilst contemplating them, her looks, her sighs, her whole attitude betokened compassion and terror.

A moment later her agitation increased, and she uttered a dreadful cry. It was the dungeon of lies which now lay open before her. After having attentively considered it, she cried aloud, "Liars are confined in a place in the vicinity of Hell, and their sufferings are exceedingly great. Molten lead is poured into their mouths; I see them burn, and at the same time tremble with cold."

She then went to the prison of those souls which had sinned through weakness, and she was heard to exclaim,

"Alas! I had thought to find you among those who have sinned through ignorance, but I am mistaken; you burn with an intenser fire."

Farther on, she perceived souls which had been too much attached to the goods of this world, and had sinned by avarice.

"What blindness," said she, "thus eagerly to seek a perishable fortune! Those whom formerly riches could not sufficiently satiate, are here gorged with torments. They are smelted like metal in the furnace."

From thence she passed into the place where those souls were imprisoned which had formerly been stained with impurity. She saw them in so filthy and pestilential a dungeon that the sight produced nausea. She turned away quickly from that loathsome spectacle. Seeing the ambitious and the proud, she said, "Behold those who wished to shine before men; now they are condemned to live in this frightful obscurity."

Then she was shown those souls which had been guilty of ingratitude towards God. They were a prey to unutterable torments, and, as it were, drowned in a lake of molten lead, for having by their ingratitude dried up the source of piety.

Finally, in a last dungeon, she was shown souls that had not been given to any particular vice, but which, through lack of proper vigilance over themselves, had committed all kinds of trivial faults. She remarked that these souls had share in the chastisements of all vices. in a moderate degree, because those faults committed only from time to time rendered them less guilty than those committed through habit.

After this last station the saint left the garden, begging God never again to make her witness of so heartrending a spectacle: she felt that she had not strength to endure it. Her ecstasy still continued, and, conversing with Jesus, she said to Him, "Tell me, Lord, what was your design in discovering to me those terrible prisons, of which I knew so little, and comprehended still less? Ah! I now see; you wished to give me the knowledge of your infinite sanctity, and to make me detest more and more the least stain of sin, which is so abominable in your eyes."

CHAPTER VII.

Location of Purgatory—St. Lidwina of Schiedam.

LET us narrate a third vision relating to the interior of Purgatory, that of St. Lidwina of Schiedam,[1] who died April 11, 1433, and whose history, written by a contemporary priest, has the most perfect authenticity. This admirable virgin, a true prodigy of Christian patience, was a prey to all the pains of the most cruel maladies for the period of thirty-eight years. Her sufferings rendering sleep impossible to her, she passed long nights in prayer, and then, frequently wrapt in spirit, she was conducted by her angel-guardian into the mysterious regions of Purgatory. There she saw dwellings, prisons, divers dungeons, one more dismal than the other; she met, too, souls that she knew, and she was shown their various punishments.

It may be asked, " What was the nature of those ecstatic journeys?" and it is difficult to explain; but we may conclude from certain other circumstances that there was more reality in them than we might be led to believe. The holy invalid made similar journeys and pilgrimages upon earth, to the holy places in Palestine, to the churches of Rome, and to monasteries in the vicinity. She had an exact knowledge of the places which she had thus traversed. A Religious of the monastery of St. Elizabeth, conversing one day with her, and speaking of the cells, of the chapter-room, of the refectory, &c., of his community, she gave him as

[1] April 14.

exact and detailed a description of his house as though she had passed her life there. The Religious having expressed his surprise, "Know, Father," said she, "that I have been through your monastery; I have visited the cells, I have seen the angel-guardians of all those who occupy them." One of the journeys which our saint made to Purgatory occurred as follows:—

An unfortunate sinner, entangled in the corruptions of the world, was finally converted. Thanks to the prayers and urgent exhortations of Lidwina, he made a sincere confession of all his sins and received absolution, but had little time to practise penance, for shortly after he died of the plague.

The saint offered up many prayers and sufferings for his soul; and some time afterwards, having been taken by her angel-guardian into Purgatory, she desired to know if he was still there, and in what condition. "He is there," said her angel, "and he suffers much. Would you be willing to endure some pain in order to diminish his?" "Certainly," she replied, "I am ready to suffer anything to assist him." Instantly her angel conducted her into a place of frightful torture. "Is this, then, Hell, my brother?" asked the holy maiden, seized with horror. "No, sister," answered the angel, "but this part of Purgatory is bordering upon Hell." Looking around on all sides, she saw what resembled an immense prison, surrounded with walls of a prodigious height, the blackness of which, together with the monstrous stones, inspired her with horror. Approaching this dismal enclosure, she heard a confused noise of lamenting voices, cries of fury, chains, instruments of torture, violent blows which the executioners discharged upon their victims. This noise was such that all the tumult of the world, in tempest or battle, could bear no comparison to it. "What, then, is that horrible place?" asked St. Lidwina of her good angel. "Do you wish me to show it to you?" "No, I beseech you," said she, recoiling with terror; "the

B

noise which I hear is so frightful that I can no longer bear it; how, then, could I endure the sight of those horrors?"

Continuing her mysterious route, she saw an angel seated sadly on the curb of a well. "Who is that angel?" she asked of her guide. "It is," he replied, "the angel-guardian of the sinner in whose lot you are interested. His soul is in this well, where it has a special Purgatory." At these words, Lidwina cast an inquiring glance at her angel; she desired to see that soul which was dear to her, and endeavour to release it from that frightful pit. Her angel, who understood her, having taken off the cover of the well, a cloud of flames, together with the most plaintive cries, came forth.

"Do you recognise that voice?" said the angel to her. "Alas! yes," answered the servant of God. "Do you desire to see that soul?" he continued. On her replying in the affirmative, he called him by his name; and immediately our virgin saw appear at the mouth of the pit a spirit all on fire, resembling incandescent metal, which said to her in a voice scarcely audible, "O Lidwina, servant of God, who will give me to contemplate the face of the Most High?"

The sight of this soul, a prey to the most terrible torment of fire, gave our saint such a shock that the cincture which she wore around her body was rent in twain; and, no longer able to endure the sight, she awoke suddenly from her ecstasy.

The persons present, perceiving her fear, asked her its cause. "Alas!" she replied, "how frightful are the prisons of Purgatory! It was to assist the souls that I consented to descend thither. Without this motive, if the whole world were given to me, I would not undergo the terror which that horrible spectacle inspired."

Some days later, the same angel whom she had seen so dejected appeared to her with a joyful countenance; he told her that the soul of his protégé had left the pit and passed into the ordinary Purgatory. This partial alleviation did not suffice the charity of Lidwina; she continued to pray for the poor patient, and to apply to him the merits of her sufferings, until she saw the gates of Heaven opened to him.

CHAPTER VIII.

Location of Purgatory—St. Gregory the Great—The Deacon Paschasius and the Priest of Centumcellæ—Blessed Stephen, a Franciscan, and the Religious in his Stall—Theophilus Renaud and the Sick Woman of Dôle.

ACCORDING to St. Thomas and other doctors, as we have previously seen, Divine Justice, in particular cases, assigns a special place upon earth for certain souls. This opinion we find confirmed by several facts, among which we quote the two mentioned by St. Gregory the Great in his "Dialogues."[1] "Whilst I was young and still a layman, I heard told to the seniors, who were well-informed men, how the Deacon Paschasius appeared to Germain, Bishop of Capua. Paschasius, Deacon of the Apostolic See, whose books on the Holy Ghost are still extant, was a man of eminent sanctity, devoted to works of charity, zealous for the relief of the poor, and most forgetful of self. A dispute having arisen concerning a pontifical election, Paschasius separated himself from the Bishops, and joined the party disapproved by the Episcopacy. Soon after this he died, with a reputation for sanctity which God confirmed by a miracle: an instantaneous cure was effected on the day of the funeral by the simple touch of his dalmatic. Long after this, Germain, Bishop of Capua, was sent by the physicians

[1] Dialog., iv. 40.

to the baths of St. Angelo. What was his astonishment to find the same Deacon Paschasius employed in the most menial offices at the baths! "I here expiate," said the apparition, "the wrong I did by adhering to the wrong party. I beseech of you, pray to the Lord for me: you will know that you have been heard when you shall no longer see me in these places."

Germain began to pray for the deceased, and after a few days, returning to the baths, sought in vain for Paschasius, who had disappeared. "He had but to undergo a temporary punishment," says St. Gregory, "because he had sinned through ignorance, and not through malice."

The same Pope speaks of a priest of Centumcellæ, now Civita Vecchia, who also went to the warm baths. A man presented himself to serve him in the most menial offices, and for several days waited upon him with the most extreme kindness, and even eagerness. The good priest, thinking that he ought to reward so much attention, came the next day with two loaves of blessed bread, and, after having received the usual assistance of his kind servant, offered him the loaves. The servant, with a sad countenance, replied, "Why, Father, do you offer me this bread? I cannot eat it. I, whom you see, was formerly the master of this place, and, after my death, I was sent back to the condition in which you see me for the expiation of my faults. If you wish to do me good, ah! offer up for me the Bread of the Eucharist."

At these words he suddenly disappeared, and he, whom the priest had thought to be a man, showed by vanishing that he was but a spirit.

For a whole week the good priest devoted himself to works of penance, and each day offered up the Sacred Host in favour of the departed one: then, having returned to the same baths, he no longer found his faithful servant, and concluded that he had been delivered.

It seems that Divine Justice sometimes condemns souls

to undergo their punishment in the same place where they have committed their sins. We read in the chronicles of the Friars Minors,[1] that Blessed Stephen, Religious of that Order, had a singular devotion to the Blessed Sacrament, so that he passed a part of the night in adoration before it. On one occasion, being alone in the chapel, the darkness broken only by the faint glimmer of the little lamp, he suddenly perceived a Religious in one of the stalls. Stephen approached him, and asked if he had permission to leave his cell at such an hour. "I am a deceased Religious," he replied. "Here, by a decree of God's Justice, must I undergo my Purgatory, because here I sinned by tepidity and negligence at the Divine Office. The Lord permits me to make known my state to you, that you may assist me by your prayers."

Touched with these words, B. Stephen immediately knelt down to recite the *De Profundis* and other prayers; and he noticed that whilst he prayed, the features of the deceased bore an expression of joy. Several times, during the following nights, he saw the apparition in the same manner, but more happy each time as it approached the term of its deliverance. Finally, after the last prayer of B. Stephen, it arose all radiant from the stall, expressed its gratitude to its liberator, and disappeared in the brightness of glory. The following incident is so marvellous, that we should hesitate to reproduce it, says Canon Postel, had it not been narrated by Father Theophilus Renaud, theologian and controversialist, who relates it as an event which happened in his time, and almost under his very eyes.

The Abbé Louvet adds, that the Vicar-General of the Archbishop of Besançon, after having examined all the details, recognised its truth. In the year 1629, at Dôle, in Franche-Compte, Hugette Roy, a woman of the middle station in life, was confined to bed by inflammation of the lungs, which endangered her life. The physician consider-

[1] Book iv. chap. xxx. ; cf. Rossignoli, *Merveilles du Purgatoire*.

ing it necessary to bleed her, in his awkwardness cut an artery in the left arm, which speedily reduced her to the last extremity. The following day, at dawn, she saw enter into her chamber a young girl clad in white, of most modest deportment, who asked her if she was willing to accept her services and to be nursed by her. The sick person, delighted with the offer, answered that nothing could give her greater pleasure; and instantly the stranger lighted the fire, approached Hugette, and placed her gently on the bed, and then continued to watch by her and serve her like the most devoted infirmarian. But, oh wonder! contact with the hands of the unknown one was so beneficial that the dying person found herself greatly relieved, and soon felt entirely cured. Then she would absolutely know who the amiable stranger was, and called her that she might question her; but she withdrew, saying that she would return in the evening. In the meantime astonishment and curiosity were extreme when the tidings of this sudden cure spread abroad, and nothing was spoken of in Dôle but this mysterious event.

When the unknown visitor returned in the evening, she said to Hugette, without trying to disguise herself, "Know, my dear niece, that I am your aunt, Leonarde Collin, who died seventeen years ago, leaving you an inheritance from her little property. Thanks to the Divine bounty, I am saved, and it was the Blessed Virgin, to whom I had great devotion, who obtained for me this happiness. Without her I was lost. When death suddenly struck me, I was in the state of mortal sin, but the merciful Virgin Mary obtained for me perfect contrition, and thus saved me from eternal damnation. Since that time I am in Purgatory, and our Lord permits me to finish my expiation by serving you during fourteen days. At the end of that time I shall be delivered from my pains if, on your part, you have the charity to make three pilgrimages for me to three holy sanctuaries of the Blessed Virgin."

Hugette, astonished, knew not what to think of this language. Not being able to believe the reality of the apparition, and fearing some snare of the evil spirit, she consulted her confessor, Father Antony Roland, a Jesuit, who advised her to threaten the unknown person with the exorcisms of the Church. This menace did not disturb her; she replied tranquilly, that she feared not the prayers of the Church. "They have no power," she added, "but against the demons and the damned; none whatever against predestined souls, who are in the grace of God as I am." Hugette was not yet convinced. "How," said she to the young girl, "can you be my Aunt Leonarde? She was old and worn, disagreeable and whimsical, whilst you are young, gentle, and obliging?" "Ah, my dear niece," replied the apparition, "my real body is in the tomb, where it will remain until the resurrection; this one which you see is one miraculously formed from the air to allow me to speak to you, to serve you, and obtain your suffrages. As regards my irritable disposition, seventeen years of terrible suffering have taught me patience and meekness. Know, also, that in Purgatory we are confirmed in grace, marked with the seal of the elect, and therefore exempt from all vice."

After such explanation, incredulity was impossible. Hugette, at once astounded and grateful, received with joy the services rendered during the fourteen days designated. She alone could see and hear the deceased, who came at certain hours and then disappeared. As soon as her strength permitted, she devoutly made the pilgrimages which were asked of her.

At the end of fourteen days the apparition ceased. Leonarde appeared for the last time to announce her deliverance; she was then in a state of incomparable glory, brilliant as a star, and her countenance bore an expression of the most perfect beatitude. In her turn, she testified her gratitude to her niece, promised to pray for her and her whole family, and advised her ever to remember, amid the sufferings of this life, the end of our existence, which is the salvation of our soul.

CHAPTER IX.

The Pains of Purgatory, their Nature, their Rigour—Doctrine of Theologians—Bellarmine—St. Francis of Sales—Fear and Confidence.

THERE is in Purgatory, as in Hell, a double pain—the pain of loss and the pain of sense.

The pain of loss consists in being deprived for a time of the sight of God, who is the Supreme Good, the beatific end for which our souls are made, as our eyes are for the light. It is a moral thirst which torments the soul. The pain of sense, or sensible suffering, is the same as that which we experience in our flesh. Its nature is not defined by faith, but it is the common opinion of the Doctors that it consists in fire and other species of suffering. The fire of Purgatory, say the Fathers, is that of Hell, of which the rich glutton speaks, *Quia crucior in hac flamma,* "I suffer," he says, "cruelly in these flames."

As regards the severity of these pains, since they are inflicted by Infinite Justice, they are proportioned to the nature, gravity, and number of sins committed. Each one receives according to his works, each one must acquit himself of the debts with which he sees himself charged before God. Now these debts differ greatly in quality. Some, which have accumulated during a long life, have reached the ten thousand talents of the Gospel, that is to say, millions and ten of millions; whilst others are reduced to a few farthings, the trifling remainder of that which has not been expiated on earth. It follows from this that the souls undergo various kinds of sufferings, that there are innumerable degrees of expiation in Purgatory, and that some are incomparably more severe than others. However, speaking in general, the doctors agree in saying that the pains are most excruciating. The same fire, says St. Gregory, torments the damned and purifies the elect.[1] "Almost all theologians," says Bellarmine, "teach that the reprobate and the souls in Purgatory suffer the action of the same fire."[2]

It must be held as certain, writes the same Bellarmine,[3] that there is no proportion between the sufferings of this life and those of Purgatory. St. Augustine declares precisely the same in his commentary on Psalm xxxi.: *Lord*, he says, *chastise me not in Thy wrath*, and reject me not with those to whom Thou hast said, *Go into eternal fire;* but chastise me not in Thine anger: purify me rather in such manner in this life that I need not to be purified by fire in the next. Yes, I fear that fire which has been enkindled for those *who will be saved*, it is true, but *yet so as by fire*.[4] They will be saved, no doubt, after the trial of fire, but that trial will be terrible, that torment will be more intolerable than all the most excruciating sufferings in this world. Behold what St. Augustine says, and what St. Gregory, Venerable Bede, St. Anselm, and St. Bernard have said after him. St. Thomas goes even further; he maintains that the least pain of Purgatory surpasses all the sufferings of this life, whatsoever they may be. Pain, says B. Peter Lefèvre, is deeper and more acute when it directly attacks the soul and the mind than when it reaches them only through the medium of the body. The mortal body, and the senses themselves, absorb and intercept a part of the physical, and even of moral pain.[5]

---

[1] In Ps. xxxvii.   [2] *De Purgat.*, i. 2. cap. 6.
[3] *De Gemitu Columbæ*, lib. ii. cap. ix.
[4] 1 Cor. iii. 15.
[5] *Sentim. du B. Lefèvre sur la Purg.* Mess. du S. Cœur, Nov. 1873.

The author of the "Imitation" explains this doctrine by a practical and striking sentence. Speaking in general of the sufferings of the other life: *There*, he says, *one hour of torment will be more terrible than a hundred years of rigorous penance done here.*[1]

To prove this doctrine, it is affirmed that all the souls in Purgatory suffer the pain of loss. Now this pain surpasses the keenest suffering. But to speak of the pain of sense alone, we know what a terrible thing fire is, how feeble so ever the flame which we enkindle in our houses, and what pain is caused by the slightest burn; how much more terrible must be that fire which is fed neither with wood nor oil, and which can never be extinguished! Enkindled by the breath of God to be the instrument of His Justice, it seizes upon souls and torments them with incomparable activity. That which we have already said, and what we have still to say, is well qualified to inspire us with that salutary fear recommended to us by Jesus Christ. But, lest certain readers, forgetful of the Christian confidence which must temper our fears, should give themselves up to excessive fear, let us modify the preceding doctrine by that of another Doctor of the Church, St. Francis of Sales, who presents the sufferings of Purgatory soothed by the consolations which accompany them.

"We may," says this holy and amiable director of souls, "draw from the thought of Purgatory more consolation than apprehension. The greater part of those who dread Purgatory so much think more of their own interests than of the interests of God's glory; this proceeds from the fact that they think only of the sufferings without considering the peace and happiness which are there enjoyed by the holy souls. It is true that the torments are so great that the most acute sufferings of this life bear no comparison to them; but the interior satisfaction which is there enjoyed

---

[1] Imitation, lib. i. chap. xxiv.

is such that no prosperity nor contentment upon earth can equal it.

The souls are in a continual union with God. They are perfectly resigned to His will, or rather their will is so transformed into that of God that they cannot will but what God wills ; so that if Paradise were to be opened to them, they would precipitate themselves into Hell rather than appear before God with the stains with which they see themselves disfigured. They purify themselves willingly and lovingly, because such is the Divine good pleasure.

They wish to be there in the state wherein God pleases, and as long as it shall please Him. They cannot sin, nor can they experience the least movement of impatience, nor commit the slightest imperfection. They love God more than they love themselves, and more than all things else; they love Him with a perfect, pure, and disinterested love. They are consoled by angels. They are assured of their eternal salvation, and filled with a hope that can never be disappointed in its expectations. Their bitterest anguish is soothed by a certain profound peace. It is a species of Hell as regards the suffering; it is a Paradise as regards the delight infused into their hearts by charity—Charity, stronger than death and more powerful than Hell; Charity, whose lamps are all fire and flame (Cantic. viii.). "Happy state!" continues the holy Bishop, "more desirable than appalling, since its flames are flames of love and charity." [1]

Such are the teachings of the doctors, from which it follows that if the pains of Purgatory are rigorous, they are not without consolation. When imposing His cross upon us in this life, God pours upon it the unction of His grace, and in purifying the souls in Purgatory like gold in the crucible, He tempers their flames by ineffable consolations. We must not lose sight of this consoling element, this bright side of the often gloomy picture which we are going to examine.

[1] *Esprit de St. François de Sales*, chap. ix. p. 16.

CHAPTER X.

Pains of Purgatory—The Pain of Loss—St. Catherine of Genoa—St. Teresa—Father Nieremberg.

AFTER having heard the theologians and doctors of the Church, let us listen to doctors of another kind; they are saints who speak of the sufferings of the other life, and who relate what God has made known to them by supernatural communication. St. Catherine of Genoa in her treatise on Purgatory[1] says, "The souls endure a torment so extreme that no tongue can describe it, nor could the understanding conceive the least notion of it, if God did not make it known by a particular grace." "No tongue," she adds, "can express, no mind form any idea of what Purgatory is. As to the suffering, it is equal to that of Hell."

St. Teresa, in the "Castle of the Soul,"[2] speaking of the pain of loss, expresses herself thus :—" The pain of loss, or the privation of the sight of God, exceeds all the most excruciating sufferings we can imagine, because the souls urged on towards God as to the centre of their aspiration, are continually repulsed by His Justice. Picture to yourself a shipwrecked mariner who, after having long battled with the waves, comes at last within reach of the shore, only to find himself constantly thrust back by an invisible hand. What torturing agonies! Yet those of the souls in Purgatory are a thousand times greater."

Father Nieremberg, of the Company of Jesus, who died in the odour of sanctity at Madrid in 1658, relates a fact that occurred at Treves, and which was recognised, says Father Rossignoli,[3] by the Vicar-General of the diocese as possessing all the characteristics of truth.

---

[1] Chap. ii. viii.   [2] Part sixth, chap. xi.
[3] *Merveilles,* 69.

On the Feast of All Saints, a young girl of rare piety saw appear before her a lady of her acquaintance who had died some time previous. The apparition was clad in white, with a veil of the same colour on her head, and holding in her hand a long rosary, a token of the tender devotion she had always professed towards the Queen of Heaven. She implored the charity of her pious friend, saying that she had made a vow to have three masses celebrated at the altar of the Blessed Virgin, and that, not having been able to accomplish her vow, this debt added to her sufferings. She then begged her to pay it in her place. The young person willingly granted the alms asked of her, and when the three masses had been celebrated, the deceased again appeared, expressing her joy and gratitude. She ever continued to appear each month of November, and almost always in the church. Her friend saw her there in adoration before the Blessed Sacrament, overwhelmed with an awe of which nothing can give an idea; not yet being able to see God face to face, she seemed to wish to indemnify herself by contemplating Him at least under the Eucharistic species. During the Holy Sacrifice of the Mass, at the moment of the elevation, her face became so radiant that she might have been taken for a seraph descended from Heaven. The young girl, filled with admiration, declared that she had never seen anything so beautiful.

Meanwhile time passed, and, notwithstanding the masses and prayers offered for her, that holy soul remained in her exile, far from the Eternal Tabernacles. On December 3, Feast of St. Francis Xavier, her protectress going to receive Communion at the Church of the Jesuits, the apparition accompanied her to the Holy Table, and then remained at her side during the whole time of thanksgiving, as though to participate in the happiness of Holy Communion and enjoy the presence of Jesus Christ.

On December 8, Feast of the Immaculate Conception, she

again returned, but so brilliant that her friend could not look at her. She visibly approached the term of her expiation. Finally, on December 10, during Holy Mass, she appeared in a still more wonderful state. After making a profound genuflexion before the altar, she thanked the pious girl for her prayers, and rose to Heaven in company with her guardian angel.

Some time previous, this holy soul had made known that she suffered nothing more than the pain of loss, or the privation of God; but she added that *that privation caused her intolerable torture.* This revelation justifies the words of St. Chrysostom in his 47th Homily: "*Imagine,*" he says, "*all the torments of the world, you will not find one equal to the privation of the beatific vision of God.*"

In fact, the torture of the pain of loss, of which we now treat, is, according to all the saints and all the doctors, much more acute than the pain of sense. It is true that, in the present life, we cannot understand this, because we have too little knowledge of the Sovereign Good for which we are created; but, in the other life, that ineffable Good seems to souls what bread is to a man famished with hunger, or fresh water to one dying with thirst, like health to a sick person tortured by long suffering; it excites the most ardent desires, which torment without being able to satisfy them.

CHAPTER XI.

The Pain of Sense—Torment of Fire and Torment of Cold— Venerable Bede and Drithelme.

If the pain of loss makes but a feeble impression upon us, it is far different with the pain of sense; the torment of fire, the torture of a sharp and intense cold, affrights our sensibility. This is why Divine Mercy, wishing to excite a holy fear in our souls, speaks but little of the pain of loss, but we are continually shown the fire, the cold, and other torments, which constitute the pain of sense. This is what we see in the Gospel, and in particular revelations, by which God is pleased to manifest to His servants from time to time the mysteries of the other life. Let us mention one of these revelations. In the first place, let us see what the pious and learned Cardinal Bellarmine quotes from the Venerable Bede. England has been witness in our own days, writes Bede, to a singular prodigy, which may be compared to the miracles of the first ages of the Church. To excite the living to fear the death of the soul, God permitted that a man, after having slept the sleep of death, should return to life and reveal what he had seen in the other world. The frightful, unheard-of details which he relates, and his life of extraordinary penance, which corresponded with his words, produced a lively impression throughout the country. I will now resume the principal circumstances of this history.

There was in Northumberland a man named Drithelm, who, with his family, led a most Christian life. He fell sick, and his malady increasing day by day, he was soon reduced to extremity, and died, to the great desolation and grief of his wife and children. The latter passed the night in tears by the remains, but the following day, before his interment, they saw him suddenly return to life, arise, and place himself in a sitting posture. At this sight they were seized with such fear that they all took to flight, with the exception of the wife, who, trembling, remained alone with her risen husband. He reassured her immediately: "Fear not," he said; "it is God who restores to me my life; He wishes to show in my person a man raised from the dead. I have yet long to live upon earth, but my new life will be very different from the one I led heretofore." Then he arose full of health, went straight to the chapel or church of the place, and there remained long in prayer. He returned home only to take leave of those who had been dear to him upon earth, to whom he declared that he would live only to prepare himself for death, and advised them to do likewise. Then, having divided his property into three parts, he gave one to his children, another to his wife, and reserved the third part to give in alms. When he had distributed all to the poor, and had reduced himself to extreme indigence, he went and knocked at the door of a monastery, and begged the Abbot to receive him as a penitent Religious, who would be a servant to all the others.

The Abbot gave him a retired cell, which he occupied for the rest of his life. Three exercises divided his time— prayer, the hardest labour, and extraordinary penances. The most rigorous fasts he accounted as nothing. In winter he was seen to plunge himself into frozen water, and remain there for hours and hours in prayer, whilst he recited the whole Psalter of David.

The mortified life of Drithelm, his downcast eyes, even his features, indicated a soul struck with fear of the judgments of God. He kept a perpetual silence, but on being pressed to relate, for the edification of others, what God had manifested to him after his death, he thus described his vision:—

"On leaving my body, I was received by a benevolent person, who took me under his guidance. His face was brilliant, and he appeared surrounded with light. He arrived at a large deep valley of immense extent, all fire on one side, all ice and snow on the other; on the one hand braziers and caldrons of flame, on the other the most intense cold and the blast of a glacial wind.

"This mysterious valley was filled with innumerable souls, which, tossed as by a furious tempest, threw themselves from one side to the other. When they could no longer endure the violence of the fire, they sought relief amidst the ice and snow; but finding only a new torture, they cast themselves again into the midst of the flames.

"I contemplated in a stupor these continual vicissitudes of horrible torments, and as far as my sight could extend, I saw nothing but a multitude of souls which suffered without ever having repose. Their very aspect inspired me with fear. I thought at first that I saw Hell; but my guide, who walked before me, turned to me and said, 'No; this is not, as you think, the Hell of the reprobate. Do you know,' he continued, 'what place this is?' 'No,' I answered. 'Know,' he resumed, 'that this valley, where you see so much fire and so much ice, is the place where the souls of those are punished who, during life, have neglected to confess their sins, and who have deferred their conversion to the end. Thanks to a special mercy of God, they have had the happiness of sincerely repenting before death, of confessing and detesting their sins. This is why they are not damned, and on the great day of judgment will enter into the Kingdom of Heaven. Several of them will obtain their deliverance before that time, by the merits of prayers, alms, and fasts, offered in their favour by the living, and especially in virtue of the Holy Sacrifice of the Mass offered for their relief.'"

Such was the recital of Drithelm. When asked why he so rudely treated his body, why he plunged himself into frozen water, he replied that he had seen other torments, and cold of another kind.

If his brethren expressed astonishment that he could endure these extraordinary austerities, "I have seen," said he, "penances still more astonishing." To the day when it pleased God to call him to Himself, he ceased not to afflict his body, and although broken down with age, he would accept no alleviation.

This event produced a deep sensation in England; a great number of sinners, touched by the words of Drithelm, and struck by the austerity of his life, became sincerely converted.

This fact, adds Bellarmine, appears to me of incontestable

truth, since, besides being conformable to the words of Holy Scripture, *Let him pass from the snow waters to excessive heat*,[1] Venerable Bede relates it as a recent and well-known event. More than this, it was followed by the conversion of a great number of sinners, the sign of the work of God, who is accustomed to work prodigies in order to produce fruit in souls.

CHAPTER XII.

Pains of Purgatory—Bellarmine and St. Christine the Admirable.

THE learned and pious Cardinal then proceeds to relate the history of St. Christine the Admirable,[2] who lived in Belgium at the close of the twelfth century, and whose body is preserved to-day in St. Trond, in the church of the Redemptorist Fathers. The Life of this illustrious virgin was, he says, written by Thomas de Cantimpré, a Religious of the Order of St. Dominic, an author worthy of credit and contemporary with the saint. Cardinal James de Vitry, in the preface to the Life of Maria d'Ognies, speaks of a great number of holy women and illustrious virgins; but the one whom he admires above all others is St. Christine, of whom he relates the most wonderful deeds.

This servant of God, having passed the first years of her life in humility and patience, died at the age of thirty-two. When she was about to be buried, and the body was already in the church resting in an open coffin, according to the custom of the time, she arose full of vigour, stupefying with amazement the whole city of St. Trond, which had witnessed this wonder. The astonishment increased when

---

[1] Job xxiv. 19.   [2] July 24.

they learned from her own mouth what had happened to her after her death. Let us hear her own account of it.

"As soon," said she, "as my soul was separated from my body, it was received by angels, who conducted it to a very gloomy place, entirely filled with souls. The torments which they there endured appeared to me so excessive, that it is impossible for me to give any idea of their rigour. I saw among them many of my acquaintances, and, deeply touched by their sad condition, I asked what place it was, for I believed it to be Hell. My guide answered me that it was Purgatory, where sinners were punished who, before death, had repented of their faults, but had not made worthy satisfaction to God. From thence I was conducted into Hell, and there also I recognised among the reprobates some whom I had formerly known.

"The angels then transported me into Heaven, even to the throne of the Divine Majesty. The Lord regarded me with a favourable eye, and I experienced an extreme joy, because I thought to obtain the grace of dwelling eternally with Him. But my Heavenly Father, seeing what passed in my heart, said to me these words: 'Assuredly, my dear daughter, you will one day be with Me. Now, however, I allow you to choose, either to remain with Me henceforth from this time, or to return again to earth to accomplish a mission of charity and suffering. In order to deliver from the flames of Purgatory those souls which have inspired you with so much compassion, you shall suffer for them upon earth; you shall endure great torments, without, however, dying from their effects. And not only will you relieve the departed, but the example which you will give to the living, and your life of continual suffering, will lead sinners to be converted and to expiate their crimes. After having ended this new life, you shall return here laden with merits.'

"At these words, seeing the great advantages offered to me for souls, I replied, without hesitation, that I would return to life, and I arose at that same instant. It is for this sole object, the relief of the departed and the conversion of sinners, that I have returned to this world. Therefore be not astonished at the penances that I shall practise, nor at the life that you will see me lead from henceforward. It will be so extraordinary that nothing like to it has ever been seen."

All this was related by the saint herself; let us now see what the biographer adds in the different chapters of her Life. "Christine immediately commenced the work for which she had been sent by God. Renouncing all the comforts of life, and reduced to extreme destitution, she lived without house or fire, more miserable than the birds of the air, which have a nest to shelter them. Not content with these privations, she eagerly sought all that could cause her suffering. She threw herself into burning furnaces, and there suffering so great torture that she could no longer bear it, she uttered the most frightful cries. She remained for a long time in the fire, and yet, on coming forth, no sign of burning was found upon her body. In winter, when the Meuse was frozen, she plunged herself into it, staying in that cold river not only hours and days, but for entire weeks, all the while praying to God and imploring His mercy. Sometimes, whilst praying in the icy waters, she allowed herself to be carried by the current down to a mill, the wheel of which whirled her round in a manner frightful to behold, yet without breaking or dislocating one of her bones. On other occasions, followed by dogs, which bit and tore her flesh, she ran, enticing them into the thickets and among the thorns, until she was covered with blood; nevertheless, on her return, no wound or scar was to be seen."

Such are the works of admirable penance described by the author of the Life of St. Christine. This writer was a Bishop, a suffragan of the Archbishop of Cambray; "and we have," says Bellarmine, "reason for believing his testimony, since he has for guarantee another grave author,

James de Vitry, Bishop and Cardinal, and because he relates what happened in his own time, and even in the province where he lived. Besides, the sufferings of this admirable virgin were not hidden. Every one could see that she was in the midst of the flames without being consumed, and covered with wounds, every trace of which disappeared a few moments afterwards. But more than this was the marvellous life she led for forty-two years after she was raised from the dead, God clearly showing that the wonders wrought in her by virtue from on high. The striking conversions which she effected, and the evident miracles which occurred after her death, manifestly proved the finger of God, and the truth of that which, after her resurrection, she had revealed concerning the other life."

Thus, argues Bellarmine, "God willed to silence those libertines who make open profession of believing in nothing, and who have the audacity to ask in scorn, 'Who has returned from the other world? Who has ever seen the torments of Hell or Purgatory?' Behold two witnesses. They assure us that they have seen them, and that they are dreadful. What follows, then, if not that the incredulous are inexcusable, and that those who believe and nevertheless neglect to do penance are still more to be condemned?"

CHAPTER XIII.

Pains of Purgatory—Brother Antony Pereyra—The Venerable Angela Tholomei.

To the two preceding facts we shall add a third, taken from the Annals of the Company of Jesus. We speak of a prodigy which was wrought in the person of Antony Pereyra, Brother Coadjutor of that Company, who died in the odour of sanctity at the College of Evora, in Portugal, August 1, 1645. Forty-six years previous, in 1599, five years after his entrance into the noviciate, this brother was attacked by a mortal malady in the island of St. Michael, one of the Azores. A few moments after he had received the last sacraments, in presence of the whole community, who assisted him in his agony, he appeared to breathe forth his soul, and soon became as cold as a corpse. The appearance, though almost imperceptible, of a slight beating of the heart, alone prevented them from interring him immediately. He was therefore left for three entire days upon his bed, and his body already gave evident signs of decomposition, when suddenly, on the fourth day, he opened his eyes, breathed, and spoke.

He was then obliged by obedience to relate to his superior, Father Louis Pinheyro, all that had passed within him since the last terrible moments of his agony. We here give an abridged account of it, as written by his own hand.

"I saw first," he says, "from my deathbed my Father, St. Ignatius, accompanied by several of our Fathers from Heaven, who came to visit his sick children, seeking those whom he thought worthy to be offered by him and his companions to our Lord. When he drew near to me I believed for a moment that he would take me, and my heart thrilled with joy; but soon he pointed out to me that of which I must correct myself before obtaining so great a happiness."

Then, nevertheless, by a mysterious disposition of Divine Providence, the soul of Brother Pereyra separated itself momentarily from his body, and immediately a hideous troup of demons rushing towards him filled him with terror. At the same moment his guardian-angel and St. Antony of Padua, his countryman and patron, descended from Heaven, put to flight his enemies, and invited him to accompany them to take a glimpse of, and taste for a moment, the joys and sufferings of eternity. "They led me then by turns," he adds, "towards a place of delights, where they showed me a crown of incomparable glory, but which I had not as yet merited; then to the brink of an abyss, where I saw the reprobate souls fall into the eternal fire, crushed like the grains of wheat cast upon a millstone that turns without intermission. The infernal gulf was like one of those limekilns, where, at times, the flames are, as it were, stifled by the mass of materials thrown into them, but which feeds the fire that it may burst forth with more terrible violence." Led from thence to the tribunal of the Sovereign Judge, Antony Pereyra heard himself condemned to the fire of Purgatory; and nothing, he assures us, can give an idea of what is suffered there, nor of the state of agony to which the souls are reduced by the desire and the delay of the enjoyment of God and of His sacred presence.

When, by the command of God, his soul had been reunited with his body, the renewed tortures of his malady for six entire months, with the additional torture of fire and iron, caused the flesh (already incurably tainted with the corruption of his first death) to fall in pieces; yet not this, nor the frightful penances to which he unceasingly delivered himself, so far as obedience permitted, during the forty-six years of his new life, could appease his thirst for suffering and expiation. "All this," he said, "is nothing in comparison with what the justice and infinite mercy of God has caused me not only to witness, but also to endure."

In fine, as an authentic seal upon so many marvels, Brother Pereyra discovered to his superior in detail the secret designs of Providence regarding the future restoration of the kingdom of Portugal, more than half a century before it happened. But we may add without fear, that the highest guarantee of all these prodigies was the astonishing degree of sanctity to which Brother Pereyra ceased not to elevate himself from day to day.

Let us relate a similar instance which confirms in every point that which we have just read. We find it in the Life of the venerable servant of God, Angela Tholomei, a

Dominican nun.[1] She was raised from the dead by her own brother, and gave a testimony of the rigour of God's judgments exactly conformable to the precedent.

Blessed John Baptist Tholomei,[2] whose rare virtues and the gift of miracles has placed him on our altars, had a sister, Angela Tholomei, the heroism of whose virtue has also been recognised by the Church. She fell dangerously sick, and her holy brother by earnest prayer besought her cure. Our Lord replied, as He did formerly to the sister of Lazarus, that He would not cure Angela, but that He would do more; He would raise her from the dead, for the glory of God and the good of souls. She died, recommending herself to the prayers of her holy brother.

Whilst she was being carried to the tomb, Blessed John Baptist, in obedience, no doubt, to an inspiration of the Holy Spirit, approached the coffin, and, in the name of our Lord Jesus Christ, commanded his sister to come forth. Immediately she awoke as from a profound slumber, and returned to life.

That holy soul seemed struck with terror, and related such things concerning the severity of God's judgments as make us shudder. She commenced, at the same time, to lead a life which proved the truth of her words. Her penance was frightful. Not content with the ordinary practices of the saints, such as fasting, watching, hair-shirts, and bloody disciplines, she went so far as to cast herself into flames, and to roll herself therein until her flesh was entirely burnt. Her macerated body became an object of pity and of horror. She was censured and accused of destroying, by her excess, the idea of true Christian penance. She continued, nevertheless, and contented herself with replying, "If you knew the rigours of the judgments of God, you would not speak thus. What are my trifling

---

[1] Cf. Rossignoli, *Merveilles*, 7.

[2] July 24 and Novemb. 9. Cf. Marchese, *Sagro Diario Dominicano*, Napoli, 1672, tom. iii. p. 483, et tom. i. p. 22.

penances compared with the torments reserved in the other life for those infidelities which we so easily permit ourselves in this world? What are they? What are they? Would that I could do a hundred times more!"

There is no question here, as we see, of the tortures to which great sinners converted before death are subjected, but of the chastisements which God inflicts upon a fervent Religious for the slightest faults.

CHAPTER XIV.

Pains of Purgatory—Apparition of Foligno—The Dominican Religious of Zamora.

THE same rigour reveals itself in a more recent apparition, where a Religious who died after an exemplary life makes known her sufferings in a manner calculated to inspire all souls with terror. The event took place on November 16, 1859, at Foligno, near Assisi, in Italy. It made a great noise in the country, and besides the visible mark which was seen, an inquiry made in due form by competent authority establishes it as an incontestable fact.

There was at the convent of Franciscan Tertiaries in Foligno, a sister named Teresa Gesta, who had been for many years mistress of novices, and who at the same time had charge of the sacristy of the community. She was born at Bastia, in Corsica, in 1797, and entered the monastery in the year 1826.

Sister Teresa was a model of fervour and charity. We need not be astonished, said her director, if God glorifies her by some prodigy after her death.

She died suddenly, November 4, 1859, of a stroke of apoplexy.

Twelve days later, on November 16, a sister named

Anna Félicia, who succeeded her in office, went to the sacristy and was about to enter, when she heard moans which appeared to come from the interior of the room. Somewhat afraid, she hastened to open the door; there was no one. Again she heard moans, and so distinctly that, notwithstanding her ordinary courage, she felt herself overpowered by fear. "Jesus! Mary!" she cried, "what can that be?" She had not finished speaking when she heard a plaintive voice, accompanied with a painful sigh, "Oh! my God, how I suffer! *Oh! Dio, che peno tanto!*" The sister, stupefied, immediately recognised the voice of poor Sister Teresa. Then the room was filled with a thick smoke, and the spirit of Sister Teresa appeared, moving towards the door, and gliding along by the wall. Having reached the door, she cried aloud, "*Behold a proof of the mercy of God.*" Saying these words, she struck the upper panel of the door, and there left the print of her right hand, burnt in the wood as with a red-hot iron. She then disappeared.

Sister Anna Félicia was left half dead with fright. She burst forth into loud cries for help. One of her companions ran, then a second, and finally the whole community. They pressed around her, astonished to find a strong odour of burnt wood. Sister Anna Félicia told what had occurred, and showed them the terrible impression on the door. They instantly recognised the hand of Sister Teresa, which had been remarkably small. Terrified, they took to flight and ran to the choir, where they passed the night in prayer and penance for the departed, and the following morning all received Holy Communion for the repose of her soul. The news spread outside the convent walls, and many communities in the city united their prayers with those of the Franciscans. On the third day, November 18, Sister Anna Félicia, on going in the evening to her cell, heard herself called by her name, and recognised perfectly the voice of Sister Teresa. At the same instant a globe of brilliant light appeared before her, illuminating her cell with the brightness of daylight. She then heard Sister Teresa pronounce these words in a joyful and triumphant voice: "*I died on a Friday, the day of the Passion, and behold, on a Friday, I enter into eternal glory!* Be strong to bear the cross, be courageous to suffer, love poverty." Then adding, affectionately, " Adieu, adieu, adieu!" she became transfigured, and like a light, white, and dazzling cloud, rose towards Heaven and disappeared.

During the investigation which was held immediately, November 23, in the presence of a large number of witnesses, the tomb of Sister Teresa was opened, and the impression upon the door was found to correspond exactly with the hand of the deceased. "The door, with the burnt print of the hand," adds Mgr. Ségur, "is preserved with great veneration in the convent. The Mother Abbess, witness of the fact, was pleased to show it to me herself."

Wishing to assure myself of the perfect exactitude of these details related by Mgr. Ségur, I wrote to the Bishop of Foligno. He replied by giving me a circumstantial account, perfectly according with the above, and accompanied by a facsimile of the miraculous mark. This narrative explains the cause of the terrible expiation to which Sister Teresa was subjected. After saying, " Ah! how much I suffer! *Oh! Dio, che peno tanto!*" she added that it was for having, in the exercise of her office of Sacristan, transgressed in some points the strict poverty prescribed by the Rule.

Thus we see Divine Justice punishes most severely the slightest faults. It may here be asked why the apparition, when making the mysterious mark on the door, called it a proof of the mercy of God. It is because, in giving us a warning of this kind, God shows us a great mercy. He urges us, in the most efficacious manner, to assist the poor suffering souls, and to be vigilant in our own regard.

Whilst speaking of this subject, we may relate a similar

instance which happened in Spain, and which caused great rumours in that country. Ferdinand of Castile thus relates it in his "History of Saint Dominic."[1] A Dominican Religious led a holy life in his convent at Zamora, a city of the kingdom of Léon. He was united in the bonds of a pious friendship with a Franciscan brother like himself, a man of great virtue. One day, when conversing together on the subject of eternity, they mutually promised that, if it pleased God, the first who died should appear to the other to give him some salutary advice. The Friar Minor died first; and one day, whilst his friend, the son of St. Dominic, was preparing the refectory, he appeared to him. After saluting him with respect and affection, he told him that he was among the elect, but that before he could be admitted to the enjoyment of eternal happiness, there remained much to be suffered for an infinity of small faults of which he had not sufficiently repented during his life. "Nothing on earth," he added, "can give an idea of the torments which I endure, and of which God permits me to give you a visible proof." Saying these words, he placed his right hand upon the table of the refectory, and the mark remained impressed upon the charred wood as though it had been applied with a red-hot iron.

Such was the lesson which the fervent deceased Franciscan gave to his living friend. It was of profit not only to him, but to all those who came to see the burnt mark, so profoundly significant; for this table became an object of piety which people came from all parts to look upon. "*It is still to be seen at Zamora,*" says Father Rossignoli,[2] "*at the time at which I write;*[3] *to protect it* the spot has been covered with *a sheet of copper.*" It was preserved until the end of the last century. Since then it has been destroyed, during the revolutions, like so many other religious memorials.

[1] Malvenda, *Annal. Ord. Prædic.*
[2] *Merveilles,* 28.   [3] Towards the middle of the last century.

CHAPTER XV.

Pains of Purgatory—The Brother of St. Magdalen de Pazzi — Stanislaus Chocosca — Blessed Catherine de Racconigi.

ST. MAGDALEN DE PAZZI, in her celebrated vision, where the different prisons of Purgatory were shown to her, saw the soul of her brother, who had died after having led a most fervent Christian life. Nevertheless, this soul was detained in suffering for certain faults, which it had not sufficiently expiated upon earth. These, says the saint, are the most intolerable sufferings, and yet they are endured with joy. Ah! why are they not understood by those who lack the courage to bear their cross here below? Struck with this frightful spectacle which she had just contemplated, she ran to her Prioress, and casting herself upon her knees, she cried out, "O my dear Mother, how terrible are the pangs of Purgatory! Never could I have believed it, had not God manifested it to me. . . . And, nevertheless, I cannot call them cruel; rather are they advantageous, since they lead to the ineffable bliss of Paradise." To impress this more and more upon our minds, it has pleased God to give certain holy persons a small share in the pains of expiation, like a drop of the bitter cup which the poor souls have to drink, a spark of the fire which consumes them.

The historian Bzovius, in his History of Poland, under the date 1598, relates a miraculous event which happened to the Venerable Stanislaus Chocosca, one of the luminaries of the Order of St. Dominic in Poland.[1] One day, whilst this Religious, full of charity for the departed, recited the rosary, he saw appear near him a soul all enveloped in flames. As she besought him to have pity on her, and to

[1] Cf. Rossign., *Merv.*, 67.

alleviate the intolerable sufferings which the fire of Divine Justice caused her to endure, the holy man asked her if this fire was more painful than that of earth? "Ah!" she cried, "all the fires of earth compared to that of Purgatory are like a refreshing breeze" (*Ignes alii levis auræ locum tenent si cum ardore meo comparentur*). Stanislaus could scarcely believe it. "I wish," he said, "to have a proof. If God will permit, for your relief, and for the good of my soul, I consent to suffer a part of your pains." "Alas! you could not do this. Know that no human being could endure such torment and live. However, God will permit you to feel it in a light degree. Stretch forth your hand." Chocosca extended his hand, and the departed let fall a drop of sweat, or at least of a liquid which resembled it. At the same instant the Religious uttered a piercing cry and fell fainting to the ground, so frightfully intense was the pain. His brethren ran to the spot and hastened to give him the assistance which his condition required. When restored to consciousness, he related the terrible event which had occurred, and of which they had a visible proof. "Ah! my dear Fathers," he continued, "if we knew the severity of the Divine chastisements, we should never commit sin, nor should we cease to do penance in this life, in order to avoid expiation in the next."

Stanislaus was confined to his bed from that moment. He lived one year longer in the most cruel suffering caused by his terrible wound; then, for the last time, exhorting his brethren to remember the rigours of Divine Justice, he peacefully slept in the Lord. The historian adds that this example reanimated fervour in all the monasteries of that province.

We read of a similar fact in the Life of B. Catherine de Racconigi.[1] One day, when suffering so intensely as to need the assistance of her sisters in religion, she thought of the souls in Purgatory, and, to temper the heat of their flames, she

---

[1] *Diario Dominicano*, Septemb. 4; cf. Rossig., *Merv.*, 63.

offered to God the burning heat of her fever. At that moment, being rapt in ecstasy, she was conducted in spirit into the place of expiation, where she saw the flames and braziers in which the souls are purified in great torture. Whilst contemplating, full of compassion, this piteous spectacle, she heard a voice which said to her, " Catherine, in order that you may procure most efficaciously the deliverance of these souls, you shall participate, in some manner, in their torments." At that same moment a spark detached itself from the fire and settled upon her left cheek. The sisters present saw the spark distinctly, and saw also with horror that the face of the sick person was frightfully swollen. She lived several days in this state, and, as B. Catherine told her sisters, the suffering caused by that simple spark far surpassed all that she had previously endured in the most painful maladies. Until that time Catherine had always devoted herself with charity to the relief of the souls in Purgatory, but from thenceforward she redoubled her fervour and austerities to hasten their deliverance, because she knew by experience the great need in which they stood of her assistance.

CHAPTER XVI.

Pains of Purgatory—St. Antoninus and the Religious—Father Rossignoli on a Quarter of an Hour in Purgatory—Brother Angelicus.

THAT which shows still more the rigour of Purgatory is that the shortest period of time there appears to be of very long duration. Every one knows that days of enjoyment pass quickly and appear short, whilst the time passed in suffering we find very long. Oh, how slowly pass the hours of the night for the poor sick, who spend them in sleeplessness and pain. We may say that the more intense the pain the longer appears the shortest duration of time. This rule furnishes us with a new means of estimating the sufferings of Purgatory.

We find in the Annals of the Friar Minors, under the year 1285, a fact which is also related by St. Antoninus in his *Summa*.[1] A religious man suffering for a long time from a painful malady, allowed himself to be overcome by discouragement, and entreated God to permit him to die, that he might be released from his pains. He did not think that the prolongation of his sickness was a mercy of God, who wished to spare him more severe suffering. In answer to his prayer, God charged His angel-guardian to offer him his choice, either to die immediately and submit to the pains of Purgatory for three days, or to bear his sickness for another year and then go directly to Heaven. The sick man, having to choose between three days in Purgatory and one year of suffering upon earth, did not hesitate, but took the three days in Purgatory. After the lapse of an hour, his angel went to visit him in his sufferings. On seeing him, the poor patient complained that he had been left so long in those torments. "And yet," he added, "you promised that I should remain here but three days." "How long," asked the angel, "do you think you have already suffered?" "At least for several years," he replied, "and I had to suffer but three days." "Know," said the angel, "that you have been here only one hour. The intensity of the pain deceives you as to the time; it makes an instant appear a day, and an hour years." "Alas! then," said he with a sigh, "I have been very blind and inconsiderate in the choice I have made. Pray God, my good angel, to pardon me, and permit me to return to earth. I am ready to submit to the most cruel maladies, not only for two years, but as long as it shall please Him. Rather six years of horrible suffering than one single hour in this abyss of unutterable agonies."

[1] Part iv. § 4.

The following is taken from a pious author quoted by Father Rossignoli.[1] Two Religious, of eminent virtue, vied with each other in leading a holy life. One of them fell sick, and learned in a vision that he should soon die, that he should be saved, and that he should remain in Purgatory only until the first Mass should be celebrated for the repose of his soul. Full of joy at these tidings, he hastened to impart them to his friend, and entreated him not to delay the celebration of the Mass which was to open Heaven to him.

He died the following morning, and his holy companion lost no time in celebrating the Holy Sacrifice. After Mass, whilst he was making his thanksgiving, and still continuing to pray for his departed friend, the latter appeared to him radiant with glory, but in a tone sweetly plaintive he asked why that one Mass of which he stood in need had been so long delayed. "My blessed brother," replied the Religious, "I delayed so long, you say? I do not understand you." "What! did you not leave me to suffer for more than a year before offering Mass for the repose of my soul." " Indeed, my dear brother, I commenced Mass immediately after your death; not a quarter of an hour had elapsed." Then, regarding him with emotion, the blessed soul cried out, " How terrible are those expiatory pains, since they have caused me to mistake minutes for a year. Serve God, my dear brother, with an exact fidelity, in order that you may avoid those chastisements. Farewell! I fly to heaven, where you will soon join me."

This severity of Divine Justice in regard to the most fervent souls is explained by the infinite Sanctity of God, who discovers stains in that which appears to us most pure. The Annals of the Order of St. Francis [2] speak of a Religious whose eminent sanctity had caused him to be surnamed Angelicus. He died in odour of sanctity at the monastery

---

[1] *Merv.*, 17.
[2] *Chronique des Frères Min.*, p. 2, 1, 4. c. 8; cf. Rossign.

of the Friars Minors in Paris, and one of his brethren in religion, a doctor in theology, persuaded that, after a life so perfect, he had gone directly to Heaven, and that he stood in no need of prayers, omitted to celebrate for him the three Masses of obligation which, according to the custom of the Institute, were offered for each departed member.

After a few days, whilst he was walking and meditating in a retired spot, the deceased appeared before him enveloped in flames, and said to him, in a mournful voice, "Dear master, I beg of you have pity upon me!" "What! Brother Angelicus, do you need my assistance?" "I am detained in the fires of Purgatory, awaiting the fruit of the Holy Sacrifice which you should have offered three times for me." "Beloved brother, I thought you were already in possession of eternal glory. After a life so fervent and exemplary as yours had been, I could not imagine that there remained any pain to be suffered." "Alas! alas!" replied the departed, "no one can believe with what severity God judges and punishes His creatures. His infinite Sanctity discovers in our best actions defective spots, imperfections which displease Him. He requires us to give an account even to the last farthing. *Usque ad novissimum quadrantem.*"

CHAPTER XVII.

Pains of Purgatory—Blessed Quinziani— The Emperor Maurice.

IN the Life of Blessed Stephana Quinziani,[1] a Dominican nun, mention is made of a sister named Paula, who died at the convent of Mantua, after a long life of eminent

[1] Auctore Franc. Seghizzo; cf. *Mort.*, 42; Marchese, 2 Jan.

virtue. The body was carried to the church and placed uncovered in the choir among the Religious. During the recitation of the Office, Blessed Quinziani knelt near the bier, recommending to God the deceased Religious, who had been very dear to her. Suddenly the latter let fall the crucifix, which had been placed between her hands, extended the left arm, seized the right hand of Blessed Quinziani, and pressed it tightly, as a poor patient in the burning heat of fever would ask the assistance of a friend. She held it for a considerable time, and then, withdrawing her arm, sank back lifeless into the coffin. The Religious, astonished at this prodigy, asked an explanation of the Blessed Sister. She replied that, whilst the deceased pressed her hand, an inarticulate voice had spoken in the depths of her heart, saying, "Help me, dear sister, succour me in the frightful torture which I endure. Oh! if you knew the severity of the Judge who desires all our love, what atonement He demands for the least faults before admitting us to the reward! If you knew how pure we must be to see the face of God! Pray! pray, and do penance for me, who can no longer help myself."

Blessed Quinziani, touched by the prayer of her friend, imposed upon herself all kinds of penances and good works, until she learned, by a new revelation, that Sister Paula was delivered from her sufferings, and had entered into eternal glory.

The natural conclusion which follows from these terrible manifestations of Divine Justice is that we must hasten to make satisfaction for our sins in this life. Surely a criminal condemned to be burned alive would not refuse a lighter pain, if the choice were left to him. Suppose it should be said to him, You can deliver yourself from that terrible punishment on condition that for three days you fast on bread and water; should he refuse it? He who should prefer the torture of fire to that of a light penance, would he not be regarded as one who had lost his reason?

Now, to prefer the fire of Purgatory to Christian penance is an infinitely greater folly. The Emperor Maurice understood this and acted wisely. History relates [1] that this prince, notwithstanding his good qualities, which had endeared him to St. Gregory the Great, towards the close of his reign committed a grave fault, and atoned for it by an exemplary repentance.

Having lost a battle against the Khan or King of the Avari, he refused to pay the ransom of the prisoners, although he was asked but the sixth part of a gold coin, which is less than a dollar of our money. This mean refusal put the barbarous conqueror into such a violent rage, that he ordered the immediate massacre of all the Roman soldiers, to the number of twelve thousand. Then the Emperor acknowledged his fault, and felt it so keenly, that he sent money and candles to the principal churches and monasteries, to beg that God would be pleased to punish him in this life rather than in the next. These prayers were heard. In the year 602, wishing to oblige his troops to pass the winter on the opposite bank of the Danube, a mutiny arose among them; they drove away their general, and proclaimed as Emperor, Phocas, a simple centurion. The imperial city followed the example of the army. Maurice was obliged to fly in the night, after having divested himself of all marks of royalty, which now served but to increase his fears. Nevertheless, he was recognised. He was taken, together with his wife, five of his sons, and three daughters—that is to say, his entire family with the exception of his eldest son, whom he had already caused to be crowned Emperor, and who, thus far, had escaped the tyrant. Maurice and his five sons were unmercifully slaughtered near Chalcedon. The carnage began with the youngest of the princes, who was put to death before the eyes of the unfortunate father, without uttering a word of complaint. Remembering the pains of

---

[1] Berault, *Histoire Eccles.*, année 602.

the other world, he esteemed himself happy to suffer in the present life, and throughout the massacre he spoke no other words than those of the Psalmist, *Thou art just, O Lord, and Thy judgment is right* (Ps. cxviii.).

CHAPTER XVIII.

Pains of Purgatory—St. Perpetua—St. Gertrude— St. Catherine of Genoa—Brother John de Via.

As we have already said, the pain of sense has different degrees of intensity. It is less terrible for those souls that have no grievous sins to atone for, or who, having already completed the most rigorous part of their expiation, approach the moment of their deliverance. Many of those souls suffer then no more than the pain of loss, and even begin to perceive the first rays of heavenly glory, and to have a foretaste of beatitude.

When St. Perpetua[1] saw her young brother Dinocrates in Purgatory, the child did not seem to be subjected to any cruel torture. The illustrious martyr herself writes the account of this vision in her prison at Carthage, where she was confined for the faith of Christ during the persecution under Septimus Severus in the year 205. Purgatory appeared to her under the figure of an arid desert, where she saw her brother Dinocrates who had died at the age of seven years. The child had an ulcer on his face, and, tormented by thirst, he tried in vain to drink from the waters of a fountain which was before him, but the brim of which was too high for him to reach. The holy martyr understood that her brother was in the place of expiation, and that he besought the assistance of her prayers. She

[1] Cf. Mar., ch. 7.

then prayed for him, and three days later, in another vision, she saw the same Dinocrates in the midst of lovely gardens. His face was beautiful, like that of an angel; he was clad in a shining robe; the brink of the fountain was beneath him, and he drank copiously of those refreshing waters from a golden cup. The saint then knew that the soul of her young brother now enjoyed the bliss of Paradise.

We read in the Revelations of St. Gertrude [1] that a young Religious of her convent, for whom she had a special love on account of her great virtues, died in the most beautiful sentiments of piety. Whilst she was fervently recommending this dear soul to God, she was rapt in ecstasy and had a vision. The deceased sister was shown to her standing before the throne of God, surrounded by a brilliant halo and in rich garments. Nevertheless, she appeared sad and troubled; her eyes were cast down, as though she were ashamed to appear before the face of God; it seemed as though she would hide herself and retire. Gertrude, much surprised, asked of the Divine Spouse of Virgins the cause of this sadness and embarrassment on the part of so holy a soul. "Most sweet Jesus," she cried, "why does not your infinite goodness invite your spouse to approach you, and to enter into the joy of her Lord? Why do you leave her aside, sad and timid?" Then our Lord, with a loving smile, made a sign to that holy soul to draw near; but she, more and more troubled, after some hesitation, all trembling, withdrew.

At this sight the saint addressed herself directly to the soul. "What! my daughter," she said to her, "do you retire when our Lord calls you? You, that have desired Jesus during your whole life, withdraw now that He opens His arms to receive you!" "Ah! my dear Mother," replied the soul, "I am not worthy to appear before the Immaculate Lamb. I have still some stains which I

---

[1] 15 Nov., *Revelationes Gertrudianæ ac Mechtildianæ.* Henri Oudin, Poitiers, 1875.

contracted upon earth. To approach the Sun of Justice, one must be as pure as a ray of light. I have not yet that degree of purity which He requires of His saints. Know, that if the door of Heaven were to be opened to me, I should not dare to cross the threshold before being entirely purified from all stain. It seems to me that the choir of virgins who follow the Lamb would repulse me with horror." "And yet," continued the Abbess, "I see you surrounded with light and glory!" "What you see," replied the soul, "is but the border of the garment of glory. To wear this celestial robe we must not retain even the shadow of sin."

This vision shows a soul very near to the glory of Heaven; but her enlightenment concerning the infinite Sanctity of God was of a different order from that which has been given to us. This clear knowledge causes her to seek, as a blessing, the expiation which her condition requires to render her worthy of the vision of the thrice holy God. This is precisely the exact teaching of St. Catherine of Genoa. We know that this saint received particular light from God concerning the state of the souls in Purgatory. She wrote a work entitled "A Treatise on Purgatory," which has an authority equal to that of St. Teresa. In chapter viii. she thus expresses herself:—"The Lord is all-merciful. He stands before us, His arms extended in order to receive us into His glory. But I see also that the Divine Essence is of such purity that the soul, unless she be absolutely immaculate, cannot bear the sight. If she finds in herself the least atom of imperfection, rather than dwell with a stain in the presence of the Divine Majesty, she would plunge herself into the depths of Hell. Finding in Purgatory a means to blot out her stains, she casts herself into it. She esteems herself happy that, by the effect of a great mercy, a place is given to her where she can free herself from the obstacles to supreme happiness."

The "History of the Seraphic Order"[1] makes mention of a holy Religious named Brother John de Via, who died piously in a monastery on the Canary Islands. His infirmarian, Brother Ascension, was in his cell praying and recommending to God the soul of the departed, when suddenly he saw before him a Religious of his Order, but who appeared to be transfigured. So radiant was he, that the cell was filled with a beautiful light. The brother, almost beside himself with astonishment, did not recognise him, but ventured to ask who he was and what was the object of his visit. "I am," answered the apparition, "the spirit of Brother John de Via. I thank you for the prayers which you have poured forth to Heaven in my behalf, and I come to ask of you one more act of charity. Know that, thanks to the Divine mercy, I am in the place of salvation, among those predestined for Heaven—the light which surrounds me is a proof of this. Yet I am not worthy to see the face of God on account of an omission which remains to be expiated. During my mortal life I omitted, through my own fault, and that several times, to recite the Office for the Dead, when it was prescribed by the Rule. I beseech you, my dear brother, for the love you bear Jesus Christ, to say those offices in such a manner that my debt may be paid, and I may go to enjoy the vision of my God."

Brother Ascension ran to the Father Guardian, related what had happened, and hastened to say the offices required. Then the soul of Blessed Brother John de Via appeared again, but this time more brilliant than before. He was in possession of eternal happiness.

[1] Part iv. n. 7 ; cf. *Merv.*, 83.

CHAPTER XIX.

Pains of Purgatory—St. Magdalene de Pazzi and Sister Benedicta—St. Gertrude—Blessed Margaret Mary and Mother de Montoux.

WE read in the Life of St. Magdalene de Pazzi that one of her sisters, named Maria-Benedicta, a Religious of eminent virtue, died in her arms. During her agony she saw a multitude of angels, which surrounded her with a joyful air, waiting until she should breathe forth her soul, that they might bear it to the Heavenly Jerusalem; and at the moment she expired, the saint saw them receive the soul under the form of a dove, the head of which was of a golden hue, and disappear with her. Three hours later, watching and praying near the remains, Magdalene knew that the soul of the deceased was neither in Paradise nor Purgatory, but in a particular place where, without suffering any sensible pain, she was deprived of the sight of God.

The following day, whilst Mass was being celebrated for the soul of Maria-Benedicta, at the *Sanctus* Magdalene was again rapt in ecstasy, and God showed her that blessed soul in the glory to which she had been just admitted. Magdalene ventured to ask our Saviour why He had not allowed this dear soul to enter sooner into His holy presence. She received for answer that in her last sickness Sister Benedicta had shown herself too sensitive to the cares bestowed upon her, which interrupted her habitual union with God and her perfect conformity to His Divine Will.

Let us return to the Revelations of St. Gertrude, to which we have just alluded. There we shall find another instance which shows how, for certain souls at least, the sun of glory is preceded by a dawn which breaks by degrees. A Religious died in the flower of her age in the embrace of the

Lord. She had been remarkable for her tender devotion to the Blessed Sacrament. After her death St. Gertrude saw her, brilliant with a celestial light, kneeling before the Divine Master, whose glorified wounds appeared like lighted torches, from whence issued five flaming rays that pierced the five senses of the deceased. The countenance of the latter, however, was clouded by an expression of deep sadness. "Lord Jesus," cried the saint, "how comes it that whilst you thus illumine your servant, why does she not experience perfect joy?"

"Until now," replied the good Master, "this sister has been worthy to contemplate my glorified humanity only, and to enjoy the sight of my five wounds, in recompense for her tender devotion to the mystery of the Holy Eucharist; but unless numerous suffrages are offered in her favour, she cannot yet be admitted to the beatific vision, on account of some slight defects in the observation of her holy rules."

Let us conclude what we have said concerning the nature of these pains by some details which we find in the Life of Blessed Margaret Mary of the Visitation. They are taken in part from the Memoir of Mother Greffier, who, wisely diffident on the subject of the extraordinary graces granted to Blessed Sister Margaret, recognised the truth only after a thousand trials. Mother Philiberte Emmanuel de Montoux, Superior at Annecy, died February 2, 1683, after a life which had edified the whole Order. Mother Greffier recommended her specially to the prayers of Sister Margaret. After some time the latter told her superior that our Lord had made known to her that this soul was most dear to Him on account of her love and fidelity in His service, and that an ample recompense awaited her in Heaven when she should have accomplished her purification in Purgatory.

The Blessed Sister saw the departed in the place of expiation. Our Lord showed her the sufferings which she endured, and how greatly she was relieved by the suffrages and good works which were daily offered for her throughout the whole Order of the Visitation. During the night from Holy Thursday to Good Friday, whilst Sister Margaret was still praying for her, He showed her the soul of the departed as placed under the chalice which contained the Sacred Host on the altar of repose. There she participated in the merits of His agony in the Garden of Olives. On Easter Sunday, which that year fell on April 18, Sister Margaret saw the soul enjoying the commencement, as it were, of eternal felicity, desiring and hoping soon to be admitted to the vision and possession of God.

Finally, a fortnight after, on May 2, Sunday, Feast of the Good Shepherd, she saw the soul of the departed as rising sweetly into eternal glory, chanting melodiously the canticle of Divine Love.

Let us see how Blessed Margaret herself gives the account of this last apparition in a letter addressed on the same day, May 2, 1623, to Mother de Saumaise at Dijon:—"Jesus for ever! My soul is filled with so great a joy that I can scarcely restrain myself. Permit me, dear Mother, to communicate it to your heart, which is one with mine in that of our Lord. This morning, Sunday of the Good Shepherd, on my awaking, two of my good suffering friends came to bid me adieu. To-day the Supreme Pastor receives them into His eternal fold with a million other souls. Both joined this multitude of blessed souls, and departed singing canticles of joy. One is the good Mother Philiberte Emmanuel de Montoux, the other Sister Jeanne Catherine Gâcon. One repeated unceasingly these words: *Love triumphs, love rejoices in God;* the other, *Blessed are the dead who die in the Lord, and the Religious who live and die in the exact observance of their rules.* Both desired that I should say to you on their part that death may separate souls, but can never disunite them. If you knew how my soul was transported with joy! For whilst I was speaking to them, I saw them sink by degrees into glory like a person who plunges into the vast ocean. They ask of you in thanksgiving to the Holy Trinity one *Laudate* and three times *Gloria Patri*. As I desired them to remember us, their last words were that *ingratitude is unknown in Heaven.*"

CHAPTER XX.

Diversity of the Pains—King Sancho and Queen Guda— St. Lidwina and the Soul Transpierced—Blessed Margaret Mary and the Bed of Fire.

According to the saints, there is great diversity in the corporal pains of Purgatory. Although fire is the principal instrument of torture, there is also the torment of cold, the torture of the members, and the torture applied to the different senses of the human body. This diversity of suffering seems to correspond to the nature of the sins, each one of which demands its own punishment, according to these words: *Quia per quæ peccat quis, per hæc et torquetur*—" By what things a man sinneth, by the same also is he tormented."[1] It is just that it should be so with regard to the chastisement, since the same diversity exists in the distribution of the reward. In Heaven each one receives according to his works, and, as Venerable Bede says, each one receives his crown, his robe of glory. For the martyr this robe is of a rich purple colour, whilst that of the confessor has the brilliancy of a dazzling whiteness.

The historian John Vasquez, in his chronicle of the year 940, relates how Sancho, king of Leon, appeared to Queen Guda, and by the piety of this princess was delivered from Purgatory. Sancho, who had led a truly Christian life, was

[1] Wisdom xi. 17.

poisoned by one of his subjects. After his death, Queen Guda passed her time in praying and causing prayers to be offered for the repose of his soul. Not content with having a great number of Masses offered for his release, in order that she might weep and pray near the dear remains, she took the veil in the convent of Castile, where the body of her husband had been deposited. One Saturday, whilst praying at the feet of the Blessed Virgin, and recommending to her the soul of her departed husband, Sancho appeared to her; but in what a condition! Great God! he was clad in garments of mourning and wore a double row of red-hot chains around his waist. Having thanked his pious widow for her suffrages, he conjured her to continue her work of charity. "Ah! if you knew, Guda, what I suffer," said he to her, "you would do still more. By the bowels of Divine Mercy, I conjure you help me, dear Guda; help me, for I am devoured by these flames."

The Queen redoubled her prayers and good works; she distributed alms among the poor, caused Masses to be celebrated in all parts of the country, and gave to the convent a magnificent ornament for use of the altar.

At the end of forty days the King again appeared. He had been relieved of the burning cincture and of all his other sufferings. In place of his robes of mourning, he wore a mantle of dazzling whiteness, like the sacred ornament which Guda had given to the convent. "Behold me, dear Guda," said he, "thanks to your prayers, delivered from all my sufferings. May you be for ever blessed. Persevere in your holy exercises; often meditate upon the severity of the pains of the other life, and upon the joys of Paradise, whither I go to await you." With these words he disappeared, leaving the pious Guda overflowing with consolation.

One day a woman, quite disconsolate, went to tell St. Lidwina that she had lost her brother. "My brother has just died," she said, "and I come to recommend his poor soul to your charity. Offer to God for him some prayers and a part of the sufferings occasioned by your malady." The holy patient promised her to do so, and some time after, in one of her frequent ecstasies, she was conducted by her angel-guardian into the subterranean dungeons, where she saw with extreme compassion the torments of the poor souls plunged in flames. One of them in particular attracted her attention. She saw her transpierced by iron pins. Her angel told her that it was the deceased brother of that woman who had asked her prayers. "If you wish," he added, "to ask any grace in his favour, it will not be refused to you." "I ask, then," she replied, "that he may be delivered from those horrible irons that transpierce him." Immediately she saw them drawn from the poor sufferer, who was then taken from this special prison and placed in the one occupied by those souls that had not incurred any particular torment. The sister of the deceased returning shortly after to St. Lidwina, the latter made known to her the condition of her brother, and advised her to assist him by multiplying her prayers and alms for the repose of his soul. She herself offered to God her supplications and sufferings, until finally he was delivered.[1]

We read in the Life of Blessed Margaret Mary that a soul was tortured in a bed of torments on account of her indolence during life; at the same time she was subjected to a particular torture in her heart, on account of certain wicked sentiments, and in her tongue, in punishment of her uncharitable words. Moreover, she had to endure a frightful pain of an entirely different nature, caused neither by fire nor iron, but by the sight of a condemned soul. Let us see how the Blessed Margaret describes it in her writings.

"I saw in a dream," she says, "one of our sisters who had died some time previous. She told me that she suffered much in Purgatory, but that God had inflicted upon her a

[1] *Vie de Sainte Lidvine.*

suffering which surpassed all other pains, by showing her one of her near relatives precipitated into Hell.

"At these words I awoke, and felt as though my body was bruised from head to foot, so that it was with difficulty I could move. As we should not believe in dreams, I paid little attention to this one, but the Religious obliged me to do so in spite of myself. From that moment she gave me no rest, and said to me incessantly, 'Pray to God for me; offer to Him your sufferings united to those of Jesus Christ, to alleviate mine; and give me all you shall do until the first Friday in May, when you will please communicate for me.' This I did, with permission of my superior.

"Meanwhile the pain which this suffering soul caused me increased to such a degree that I could find neither comfort nor repose. Obedience obliged me to seek a little rest upon my bed; but scarcely had I retired when she seemed to approach me, saying, 'You recline at your ease upon your bed; look at the one upon which I lie, and where I endure intolerable sufferings.' I saw that bed, and the very thought of it makes me shudder. The top and bottom was of sharp flaming points, which pierced the flesh. She told me then, that this was on account of her sloth and negligence in the observance of the rules. 'My heart is torn,' she continued, 'and causes me the most terrible suffering for my thoughts of disapproval and criticism of my superiors. My tongue is devoured by vermin, and, as it were, torn from my mouth continually, for the words I spoke against charity and my little regard for the rule of silence. Ah! would that all souls consecrated to God could see me in these torments. If I could show them what is prepared for those who live negligently in their vocation, their zeal and fervour would be entirely renewed, and they would avoid those faults which now cause me to suffer so much.'

"At this sight I melted into tears. 'Alas!' said she,

'one day passed by the whole community in exact observance would heal my parched mouth; another passed in the practice of holy charity would cure my tongue; and a third passed without any murmuring or disapproval of superiors would heal my bruised heart; but no one thinks to relieve me.'

"After I had offered the Communion which she had asked of me, she said that her dreadful torments were much diminished, but she had still to remain a long time in Purgatory, condemned to suffer the pains due to those souls that have been tepid in the service of God. As for myself," adds Blessed Margaret Mary, "I found that I was freed from my sufferings, which I had been told would not diminish until the soul herself should be relieved." [1]

CHAPTER XXI.

Diversity of the Pains—Blasio Raised from the Dead by St. Bernardine—Venerable Frances of Pampeluna and the Pen of Fire—St. Corpreus and King Malachy.

THE celebrated Blasio Masseï, who was raised from the dead by St. Bernardine of Sienna, saw that there was great diversity in the pains of Purgatory. The account of this miracle is given at length in the *Acta Sanctorum* (Appendix, May 20).

A short time after the canonisation of St. Bernardine of Sienna, there died at Cascia, in the kingdom of Naples, a child aged eleven years, named Blasio Masseï. His parents had inspired him with the same devotion which they themselves had towards this new saint, and the latter was not slow to recompense it. The day after his death, when the

[1] Languet, *Vie de la B. Marguerite.*

body was being carried to the grave, Blasio awoke as from a profound slumber, and said that St. Bernardine had restored him to life, in order to relate the wonders which the saint had shown him in the other world.

We can easily understand the curiosity which this event produced. For a whole month young Blasio did nothing but talk of what he had seen, and answer the questions put to him by visitors. He spoke with the simplicity of a child, but at the same time with an accuracy of expression and a knowledge of the things of the other life far above his years.

At the moment of his death, he said, St. Bernardine appeared to him, and taking him by the hand, said, "Be not afraid, but pay great attention to what I am going to show you, so that you may remember, and afterwards be able to relate it."

Now the saint conducted his young protégé successively into the regions of Hell, Purgatory, Limbo, and finally allowed him to see Heaven.

In Hell, Blasio saw indescribable horrors, and the divers tortures by which the proud, the avaricious, the impure, and other sinners are tormented. Amongst them he recognised several whom he had seen during life, and he even witnessed the arrival of two who had just died, Buccerelli and Frascha. The latter was damned for having kept ill-gotten goods in his possession. The son of Frascha, struck by this revelation as by a thunderbolt, and knowing well the truth of the statement, hastened to make complete restitution ; and not content with this act of justice, that he might not expose himself to share one day the sad lot of his father, he distributed the rest of his fortune to the poor and embraced the monastic life.

From thence conducted into Purgatory, Blasio there saw the most dreadful torments, varied according to the sins of which they were the punishment. He recognised a great number of souls, and several begged him to acquaint their parents and relatives with their suffering condition; they even indicated the suffrages and good works of which they stood in need. When interrogated as to the state of a departed soul, he answered without hesitation, and gave the most precise details, "Your father," said he to one of his visitors, "has been in Purgatory since such a day; he charged you to pay such a sum in alms, and you have neglected to do so." "Your brother," he said to another, "asked you to have so many Masses celebrated; you agreed to do so, and you have not fulfilled your engagement; so many Masses remain to be said."

Blasio also spoke of Heaven, the last place into which he had been taken; but he spoke almost like St. Paul, who, having been ravished to the third Heaven, whether with his body or without his body he knew not, there heard mysterious words which no mortal tongue could repeat. What most attracted the attention of the child was the immense multitude of angels that surrounded the throne of God, and the incomparable beauty of the blessed Virgin Mary, elevated above all the choirs of angels.

The life of Venerable Mother Frances of the Blessed Sacrament, a Religious of Pampeluna,[1] presents several facts which show that the pains of Purgatory are suited to the faults to be expiated. This venerable servant of God had the most intimate communication with the souls in Purgatory, so that they came in great numbers and filled her cell, humbly awaiting each one in turn to be assisted by her prayers. Frequently, the more easily to excite her compassion, they appeared with the instruments of their sins, now become the instruments of their torture. One day she saw a Religious surrounded by costly pieces of furniture, such as pictures, arm-chairs, &c., all in flames. She had collected these things in her cell contrary to her vow of religious poverty, and after her death they became her torment.

[1] *La Vie* par le F. Joachim; cf. *Merv.*, 26.

A notary appeared to her one day with all the insignia of his profession. Being heaped around him, the flames which issued therefrom caused him the most intense suffering. "I have used this pen, this ink, this paper," said he, "to draw up illegal deeds. I also had a passion for gambling, and these cards which I am forced to hold continually in my hands now constitute my punishment. This flaming purse contains my unlawful gains, and causes me to expiate them."

From all this we should draw great and salutary instruction. Creatures are given to man as a means to serve God; they must be the instruments of virtue and good works. If he abuse them, and make them instruments of sin, it is just they should be turned against him, and become the instruments of his chastisement.

The Life of St. Corpreus an Irish Bishop, which we find in the *Bollandists* on March 6, furnishes us with another example of the same kind. One day, whilst this holy prelate was in prayer after the Office, he saw appear before him a horrible spectre, with livid countenance, a collar of fire about his neck, and upon his shoulders a miserable mantle all in tatters. "Who are you?" asked the saint, not in the least disturbed. "I am a soul from the other life." "What has brought you to the sad condition in which I see you?" "My faults have drawn this chastisement upon me. Notwithstanding the misery to which I now see myself reduced, I am Malachy, formerly king of Ireland. In that high position I could have done much good, and it was my duty to do so. I neglected this, and therefore I am punished." "Did you not do penance for your faults?" "I did not do sufficient penance, and this is due to the culpable weakness of my confessor, whom I bent to my caprices by offering him a gold ring. It is on this account that I now wear a collar of fire about my neck." "I should like to know," continued the Bishop, "why you are covered with these rags?" "It is another chastisement. I did not clothe the naked. I did not assist the poor with the charity, respect, and liberality which became my dignity of king and my title of Christian. This is why you see me clothed like the poor and covered with a garment of confusion." The biography adds that St. Corpreus with his Chapter united in prayer, and at the end of six months obtained a mitigation of the suffering, and somewhat later the entire deliverance of King Malachy.

CHAPTER XXII.

Duration of Purgatory—Opinions of the Doctors—Bellarmine —Calculations of Father Mumford.

FAITH does not teach us the precise duration of the pains of Purgatory. We know in general that they are measured by Divine Justice, and that for each one they are proportioned to the number and gravity of the faults which he has not yet expiated. God may, however, without prejudice to His Justice, abridge these sufferings by augmenting their intensity; the Church Militant also may obtain their remission by the Holy Sacrifice of the Mass and other suffrages offered for the departed.

According to the common opinion of the doctors, the expiatory pains are of long duration. "There is no doubt," says Bellarmine,[1] "that the pains of Purgatory are not limited to ten or twenty years, and that they last in some cases entire centuries. But allowing it to be true that their duration did not exceed ten or twenty years, can we account it as nothing to have to endure for ten or twenty years the most excruciating sufferings without the least alleviation? If a man was assured that he should suffer some violent

---

[1] *De Gemitu*, lib. ii. c. 9.

pain in his feet, or his head, or teeth for the space of twenty years, and that without ever sleeping or taking the least repose, would he not a thousand times rather die than live in such a state? And if the choice were given to him between a life thus miserable and the loss of all his temporal goods, would he hesitate to make the sacrifice of his fortune to be delivered from such a torment? Shall we then find any difficulty in embracing labour and penance to free ourselves from the sufferings of Purgatory? Shall we fear to practise the most painful exercises: vigils, fasts, almsgiving, long prayers, and especially contrition, accompanied with sighs and tears?"

These words comprise the whole doctrine of the saints and theologians.

Father Mumford, of the Company of Jesus, in his "Treatise on Charity towards the Departed," bases the long duration of Purgatory on a calculation of probability, which we shall give in substance. He goes out on the principle that, according to the words of the Holy Ghost, *The just man falls seven times a day*,[1] that is to say, that even those who apply themselves most perfectly to the service of God, notwithstanding their good-will, commit a great number of faults in the infinitely pure eyes of God. We have but to enter into our own conscience, and there analyse before God our thoughts, our words, and works, to be convinced of this sad effect of human misery. Oh! how easy it is to lack respect in prayer, to prefer our ease to the accomplishment of duty, to sin by vanity, by impatience, by sensuality, by uncharitable thoughts and words, by want of conformity to the will of God! The day is long; is it very difficult for even a virtuous person to commit, I do not say seven, but twenty or thirty of this kind of faults and imperfections?

Let us take a moderate estimate, and suppose that you commit about ten faults a day; at the end of 365 days you

[1] Prov. xxiv. 16.

will have a sum of 3650 faults. Let us diminish, and, to facilitate the calculation, place it at 3000 per year. At the end of ten years this will amount to 30,000, and at the end of twenty years to 60,000. Suppose that of these 60,000 faults you have expiated one half by penance and good works, there will still remain 30,000 to be atoned for.

Let us continue our hypothesis: You die after these twenty years of virtuous life, and appear before God with a debt of 30,000 faults, which you must discharge in Purgatory. How much time will you need to accomplish this expiation? Suppose, on an average, each fault requires one hour of Purgatory. This measure is very moderate, if we judge by the revelations of the saints; but at any rate this will give you a Purgatory of 30,000 hours. Now, do you know how many years these 30,000 hours represent? Three years, three months, and fifteen days. Thus a good Christian who watches over himself, who applies himself to penance and good works, finds himself liable to thrĕe years, three months, and fifteen days of Purgatory.

The preceding calculation is based on an estimate which is lenient in the extreme. Now, if you extend the duration of the pain, and, instead of an hour, you take a day for the expiation of a fault, if, instead of having nothing but venial sins, you bring before God a debt resulting from mortal sins, more or less numerous, which you formerly committed, if you assign, on the average, as St. Frances of Rome says, seven years for the expiation of one mortal sin, remitted as to the guilt, who does not see that we arrive at an appalling duration, and that the expiation may easily be prolonged for many years, and even for centuries?

Years and centuries in torments! Oh! if we only thought of it, with what care should we not avoid the least faults! with what fervour should we not practise penance to make satisfaction in this world!

CHAPTER XXIII.

Duration of Purgatory—The Cistercian Abbot and Pope Innocent III.—John de Lierre.

IN the Life of St. Lutgarda,[1] written by her contemporary, Thomas de Cantempré, mention is made of a Religious who was otherwise fervent, but who for an excess of zeal was condemned to forty years of Purgatory. This was an Abbot of the Cistercian Order, named Simon, who held St. Lutgarda in great veneration. The saint, on her part, willingly followed his advice, and in consequence a sort of spiritual friendship was formed between them. But the Abbot was not as mild towards his subordinates as he was towards the saint. Severe with himself, he was also severe in his administration, and carried his exactions in matters of discipline even to harshness, forgetting the lesson of the Divine Master, who teaches us to be meek and humble of heart. Having died, and whilst St. Lutgarde was fervently praying and imposing penances upon herself for the repose of his soul, he appeared to her, and declared that he was condemned to forty years of Purgatory. Fortunately he had in Lutgarda a generous and powerful friend. She redoubled her prayers and austerities, and having received from God the assurance that the departed soul should soon be delivered, the charitable saint replied, "I will not cease to weep; *I will not cease to importune your Mercy until I see him freed from his pains.*"

Since I am mentioning St. Lutgarda, ought I to speak of the celebrated apparition of Pope Innocent III.? I acknowledge the perusal of this incident shocked me, and I would fain pass it over in silence. I was reluctant to think that a Pope, and such a Pope, had been condemned

[1] June 16.

to so long and terrible a Purgatory. We know that Innocent III., who presided at the celebrated Council of Lateran in 1215, was one of the greatest Pontiffs who ever filled the chair of St. Peter. His piety and zeal led him to accomplish great things for the Church of God and holy discipline. How, then, admit that such a man was judged with so great severity at the Supreme Tribunal? How reconcile this revelation of St. Lutgarda with Divine Mercy? I wished, therefore, to treat it as an illusion, and sought for reasons in support of this idea. But I found, on the contrary, that the reality of this apparition is admitted by the gravest authors, and that it is not rejected by any single one. Moreover, the biographer, Thomas de Cantimpré, is very explicit, and at the same time very reserved. "Remark, reader," he writes at the end of his narrative, "that it was from the mouth of the pious Lutgarda herself that I heard of the faults revealed by the defunct, and which I omit here through respect for so great a Pope."

Aside from this, considering the event in itself, can we find any good reason for calling it into question? Do we not know that God makes no exception of persons—that the Popes appear before His tribunal like the humblest of the faithful—that all the great and the lowly are equal before Him, and that each one receives according to his works? Do we not know that those who govern others have a great responsibility, and will have to render a severe account? *Judicium durissimum his qui præsunt fiet*—"A most severe judgment shall be for them that bear rule."[1] It is the Holy Ghost that declares it. Now, Innocent III. reigned for eighteen years, and during most turbulent times; and, add the Bollandists, is it not written that the judgments of God are inscrutable, and often very different from the judgments of men? *Judicia tua abyssus multa.*[2]

The reality of this apparition cannot, then, be reason-

---

[1] Wisdom vi. 6.   [2] Ps. xxxv. 7.

ably called in question. I see no reason for omitting it, since God does not reveal mysteries of this nature for any other purpose than that they should be made known for the edification of His Church.

Pope Innocent III. died July 16, 1216. The same day he appeared to St. Lutgarda in her monastery at Aywieres, in Brabant. Surprised to see a spectre enveloped in flames, she asked who he was and what he wanted. "I am Pope Innocent," he replied. "Is it possible that you, our common Father, should be in such a state?" "It is but too true. I am expiating three faults which might have caused my eternal perdition. Thanks to the Blessed Virgin Mary, I have obtained pardon for them, but I have to make atonement. Alas! it is terrible; and it will last for centuries if you do not come to my assistance. In the name of Mary, who has obtained for me the favour of appealing to you, help me." With these words he disappeared. Lutgarda announced the Pope's death to her sisters, and together they betook themselves to prayer and penitential works in behalf of the august and venerated Pontiff, whose demise was communicated to them some weeks later from another source.

Let us add here a more consoling fact, which we find in the life of the same saint. A celebrated preacher, named John de Lierre, was a man of great piety and well known to our saint. He had made a contract with her, by which they mutually promised that the one who should die first, with the permission of God, should appear to the other. John was the first to depart this life. Having undertaken a journey to Rome for the arrangement of certain affairs in the interest of the Religious, he met his death among the Alps. Faithful to his promise, he appeared to Lutgarda in the celebrated cloister of Aywieres. On seeing him, the saint had not the slightest idea that he was dead, and invited him, according to the Rule, to enter the parlour that she might converse with him. "I am no more of this world," he replied, "and I come here only in fulfilment of my promise." At these words Lutgarda fell on her knees and remained for some time quite confounded. Then, raising her eyes to her blessed friend, "Why," said she, "are you clothed in such splendour? What does this triple robe signify with which I see you adorned?" "The white garment," he replied, "signifies virginal purity, which I have always preserved; the red tunic implies the labours and sufferings which have prematurely exhausted my strength; and the blue mantle, which covers all, denotes the perfection of the spiritual life." Having said these words, he suddenly left Lutgarda, who remained divided between regret for having lost so good a Father, and the joy she experienced on account of his happiness.

St. Vincent Ferrer, the celebrated wonder-worker of the Order of St. Dominic, who preached with so much eloquence the great truth of the Judgment of God, had a sister who remained unmoved either by the words or example of her saintly brother. She was full of the spirit of the world, intoxicated with its pleasures, and walked with rapid strides towards her eternal ruin. Meanwhile, the saint prayed for her conversion, and his prayer was finally answered. The unfortunate sinner fell mortally sick; and, at the moment of death, entering into herself, she made her confession with sincere repentance.

Some days after her death, whilst her brother was celebrating the Holy Sacrifice, she appeared to him in the midst of flames and a prey to the most intolerable torments. "Alas! my dear brother," said she, "I am condemned to undergo these torments until the day of the last judgment. Nevertheless, you can assist me. The efficacy of the Holy Sacrifice is so great: offer for me about thirty Masses, and I may hope the happiest result." The saint hastened to accede to her request. He celebrated the thirty Masses, and on the thirtieth day his sister again appeared to him surrounded by angels and soaring to Heaven. Thanks to

PURGATORY, THE MYSTERY OF JUSTICE. 75

the virtue of the Divine Sacrifice, an expiation of several centuries was reduced to thirty days.

This example shows us at once the duration of the pains which a soul may incur, and the powerful effect of the Holy Sacrifice of the Mass, when God is pleased to apply it to a soul. But this application, like all other suffrages, does not always take place, at least not always in the same plenitude.

CHAPTER XXIV.

Duration of Purgatory—The Duellist—Father Schoofs and the Apparition at Antwerp.

THE following example shows not only the long duration of the punishment inflicted for certain faults, but also the difficulty of inclining Divine Justice in favour of those who have committed faults of this nature.

The history of the Order of the Visitation mentions, among the first Religious of that Institute, Sister Marie Denise, called in the world Mdlle. Marie Martignat. She was most charitably devoted to the souls in Purgatory, and felt herself particularly drawn to recommend to God in a special manner those who had held high positions in the world, for she knew by experience the dangers to which their positions exposed them. A certain prince, whose name is not given, but who it is believed belonged to the House of France, was killed in a duel, and God permitted him to appear to Sister Denise to ask of her the assistance of which he stood so greatly in need. He told her that he was not damned, although his crime merited damnation. Thanks to an act of perfect contrition which he had made at the moment of death, he had been saved; but, in punishment for his guilty life and death, he was condemned to the most rigorous chastisement in Purgatory until the Day of Judgment.

The charitable sister, deeply touched by the state of this soul, generous offered herself as a victim for him. But it is impossible to say what she had to suffer for many years in consequence of that heroic act. The poor prince left her no repose, and made her partake of his torments. She completed her sacrifice by death; but before expiring she confided to her Superior that, in return for so much expiation, she had obtained for her protégé the remission of but a few hours of pain. When the Superior expressed her astonishment at this result, which seemed to her entirely disproportionate with what the sister had suffered, Sister Denise replied, "Ah! my dear Mother, the hours of Purgatory are not computed like those of earth; years of grief, weariness, poverty, or sickness in this world are nothing compared to one hour of the suffering of Purgatory. It is already much that Divine Mercy permits us to exercise any influence whatever over His Justice. I am less moved by the lamentable state in which I have seen this soul languish, than by the extraordinary return of grace which has consummated the work of his salvation. The act in which the prince died merited Hell; a million others might have found their eternal perdition in the same act in which he found his salvation. He recovered consciousness but for one instant, just time sufficient to co-operate with that precious movement of grace which disposed him to make an act of perfect contrition. That blessed moment seems to me to be an excess of the goodness, clemency, and infinite love of God."

Thus spoke Sister Denise; she admired at once the severity of God's Justice, and His infinite Mercy. Both one and the other shone forth in this example in the most striking manner.

Continuing the subject of the long duration of Purgatory, we will here relate an instance of more recent occurrence.

Father Philip Schoofs, of the Company of Jesus, who died in Louvain in 1878, related the following fact, which happened in Antwerp during the first years of his ministry in that city. He had just preached a mission, and had returned to the College of Notre Dame, then situated in the Rue l'Empereur, when he was told some one asked for him in the parlour. Descending immediately, he found there two young men in the flower of their age, with a pale and sickly child of about ten years. " Father," said they, "here is a poor child that we have adopted, and who deserves our protection because he is good and pious. We feed and educate him and, for more than a year that he has formed part of our family, he has been happy and enjoyed good health. It is only for the last few weeks that he has commenced to grow thin and pine away, as you now see him." " What is the cause of this change ? " asked the Father. " It is fright," they replied; "the child is awaked every night by apparitions. A man, he assures us, presents himself before him, and he sees him as distinctly as he sees us in full daylight. This is the cause of his continual fear and uneasiness. We come, Father, to ask of you some remedy." " My friends," replied Father Schoofs, " with God there is a remedy for all things. Begin, both of you, by making a good confession and Communion, beg God to deliver you from all evil, and fear nothing. As for you, my child, say your prayers well, then sleep so soundly that no ghost can awake you." He then dismissed them, telling them to return in case anything more should happen. Two weeks passed, and they again returned. " Father," said they, " we have followed your orders, and yet the apparitions continue as before. The child always sees the same man appear." " From this evening," said Father Schoofs, "watch at the door of the child's room, provided with paper and ink with which to write the answers. When he warns you of the presence of that man, ask in the name of God who he is, the time of his death, where he lived, and why he returns."

The following day they returned, carrying the paper on which was written the answers which they had received." "We saw," they said, "the man that appears to the child." They described him as an old man, of whom they could but see the bust, and he wore a costume of the olden times. He told them his name, and the house in which he had dwelt in Antwerp. He had died in 1636, had followed the profession of banker in that same house, which in his time comprised the two houses which to-day may be seen situated to the right and left of it. Let us remark here that certain documents which prove the accuracy of these indications have since been discovered in the archives of the city of Antwerp. He added that he was in Purgatory, and that few prayers had been said for him. He then begged the persons of the house to offer Holy Communion for him, and finally asked that a pilgrimage might be made for him to Notre Dame des Fièvres, and another to Notre Dame de la Chapelle in Brussels. "You will do well to comply with all these requests," said Father Schoofs, "and if the spirit returns, before speaking to him, require him to say the *Pater, Ave,* and *Credo.*"

They accomplished the good works indicated with all possible piety, and many conversions were effected. When all was finished, the young men returned. "Father, he prayed," they said to Father Schoofs, "but in a tone of indescribable faith and piety. We never heard any one pray thus. What reverence in the Our Father! What love in the Hail Mary! What fervour in the I Believe! Now we know what it is to pray. Then he thanked us for our prayers; he was greatly relieved, and would have been entirely delivered had not an assistant in our shop made a sacrilegious Communion. We have," they continued, "reported these words to the person. She turned pale, acknowledged her guilt, then running to her confessor, hastened to repair her crime."

"Since that day," adds Father Schoofs, "that house has never been troubled. The family that inhabit it have prospered rapidly, and to-day they are rich. The two brothers continue to conduct themselves in an exemplary manner, and their sister became a Religious in a convent, of which she is at the present time Superior."

Everything leads us to believe that the prosperity of that family was the result of the succour given to the departed soul. After two centuries of punishment there remained to the latter but a small part of the expiation, and the performance of some good works which he asked. When these were accomplished, he was delivered, and wished to show his gratitude by obtaining the blessings of God upon his benefactors.

CHAPTER XXV.

Duration of Purgatory—The Abbey of Latrobe—A Hundred Years of Suffering for Delay in the Reception of the Last Sacraments.

THE following incident is related with authentic proof by the journal, *The Monde*, in the number of April 1860. It took place in America, in the Abbey of the Benedictines, situated in the village of Latrobe. A series of apparitions occurred during the course of the year 1859. The American press took up the matter, and treated those grave questions with its usual levity. In order to put a stop to scandal, the Abbot Wimmer, superior of the house, addressed the following letter to the newspapers.

" The following is a true statement of the case :—In our

Abbey of St. Vincent, near Latrobe, on September 10, 1859, a novice saw an apparition of a Benedictine in full choir dress. This apparition was repeated every day from September 18 until November 19, either at eleven o'clock at noon, or at two o'clock in the morning. It was only on the 19th November that the novice interrogated the spirit, in presence of another member of the community, and asked the motive of these apparitions. He replied that he had suffered for seventy-seven years for having neglected to celebrate seven Masses of obligation; that he had already appeared at different times to seven other Benedictines, but that he had not been heard, and that he would be obliged to appear again after eleven years if the novice did not come to his assistance. Finally, the spirit asked that these seven Masses might be celebrated for him; moreover, the novice must remain in retreat for seven days, keep strict silence, and during thirty days recite three times a day the psalm *Miserere*, his feet bare, and his arms extended in the form of a cross. All the conditions were fulfilled between November 20 and December 25, and on that day, after the celebration of the last Mass, the apparition disappeared.

"During that period the spirit showed itself several times, exhorting the novice in the most urgent manner to pray for the souls in Purgatory; for, said he, they suffer frightfully, and are extremely grateful to those who co-operate in their deliverance. He added, sad to relate, that of the five priests who had died in our Abbey, not one had yet entered Heaven, all were suffering in Purgatory. I do not draw any conclusion, but this is correct."

This account, signed by the hand of the Abbot, is an incontestable historical document.

As regards the conclusion which the venerable prelate leaves us to draw, it is evident.

Seeing that a Religious is condemned to Purgatory for seventy-seven years, let it suffice for us to learn the necessity of reflecting on the duration of future punishment, as well for priests and Religious as for the ordinary faithful living in the midst of the corruption of the world.

A too frequent cause of the long continuance of Purgatory is that many deprive themselves of a great means established by Jesus Christ for shortening it, by delaying, when dangerously sick, to receive the last Sacraments. These Sacraments, destined to prepare souls for their last journey, to purify them from the remains of sin, and to spare them the pains of the other life, require, in order to produce their effects, that the sick person receive them with the requisite dispositions. Now, the longer they are deferred, and the faculties of the sick person allowed to become weak, the more defective do those dispositions become. What do I say? Very often it happens, in consequence of this imprudent delay, that the sick person dies deprived of this absolutely necessary help. The result is, that if the deceased is not damned, he is plunged into the deepest abysses of Purgatory, loaded with all the weight of his debts.

Michael Alix[1] speaks of an ecclesiastic who, instead of promptly receiving the Extreme Unction, and therein giving a good example to the faithful, was guilty of negligence in this respect, and was punished by a hundred years of Purgatory. Knowing that he was seriously ill and in danger of death, this poor priest should have made known his condition, and immediately had recourse to the succours which the Mother Church reserves for her children in that supreme hour. He omitted to do so; and, whether through an illusion common among sick people, he would not declare the gravity of his situation, or whether he was under the influence of that fatal prejudice which causes weak Christians to defer the reception of the last Sacraments, he neither asked for nor thought of receiving them. But we know how death comes by stealth; the unfortunate man deferred so long that he died without having had the time to receive

---

[1] Hort. Past., Tract. 6. Cf. Rossignoli, *Merveilles*, 86.

either the Viaticum or Extreme Unction. Now, God was pleased to make use of this circumstance to give a great warning to others. The deceased himself came to make known to a brother ecclesiastic that he was condemned to Purgatory for a hundred years. "I am thus punished," he said, "for delaying to receive the grace of the last purification. Had I received the Sacraments as I ought to have done, I should have escaped death through the virtue of Extreme Unction, and I should have had time to do penance."

CHAPTER XXVI.

Duration of Purgatory—Venerable Catherine Paluzzi and Sister Bernardine—Brothers Finetti and Rudolfini— St. Peter Claver and the two Poor Women.

LET us cite some other examples which will serve to convince us still more of the long duration of the sufferings of Purgatory. We shall see therein that Divine Justice is relatively severe towards souls called to perfection, and who have received much grace. Does not Jesus Christ say in the Gospel, *Unto whom much is given, of him much shall be required: and to whom they have committed much, of him they will demand the more?*[1]

We read in the Life of Venerable Catherine Paluzzi that a holy Religious, who died in her arms, was not admitted to eternal beatitude until after she had passed an entire year in Purgatory. Catherine Paluzzi led a holy life in the diocese of Nepi, in Italy, where she founded a convent of Dominicans. There lived with her a Religious named Bernardine, who was far advanced in the ways of the spiritual life. These two saints emulated each other in

[1] Luke xii. 48.

fervour, and helped each other to progress more and more in the perfection to which God called them.

The biographer of Venerable Catherine compares them to two live coals that communicate heat to each other; and again, to two harps tuned to harmonise together in one perpetual hymn of love to the greater glory of God.

Bernardine died; a painful malady, which she bore with Christian patience, carried her to the grave. When about to expire, she told Catherine that she would not forget her before God, and, if God so permitted, she would return to converse with her on such spiritual matters as would contribute to her sanctification.

Catherine prayed much for the soul of her friend, and at the same time besought God to allow her to appear to her. An entire year elapsed and the deceased did not return. Finally, on the anniversary of the death of Bernardine, Catherine being in prayer, saw a pit from whence issued volumes of smoke and flames; then she perceived coming out of the pit a form surrounded by dark clouds. By degrees these vapours were dispersed, and the apparition became radiant with an extraordinary brilliancy. In this glorious personage Catherine recognised Bernardine and ran towards her. "Is it you, my dearest sister?" said she. "But whence do you come? What signifies this pit, this fiery smoke? Does your Purgatory end only to-day?" "You are right," replied the soul; "for a year I have been detained in that place of expiation, and to-day, for the first time, shall I enter Heaven. As regards yourself, persevere in your holy exercises: continue to be charitable and merciful, and you will obtain mercy."[1]

The following incident belongs to the history of the Society of Jesus. Two scholastics or young Religious of that Institute, Brothers Finetti and Rudolphini, pursued their studies at the Roman College towards the end of the sixteenth century. Both were models of piety and regu-

[1] *Diario Domenicano.* Cf. Rossign., *Merv.*, part ii. 51.

larity, both also received a warning from Heaven, which they disclosed, according to the Rule, to their spiritual director. God made known to them their approaching death and the suffering that awaited them in Purgatory. One was to remain there for two years; the other, four. They died, in fact, one after the other. Their brethren in religion immediately offered the most fervent prayers and all kinds of penances for the repose of their souls. They knew that if the Sanctity of God imposes long expiations upon His elect, they may be abridged and entirely remitted by the suffrages of the living. If God is severe towards those who have received much knowledge and grace, on the other hand He is very indulgent towards the poor and the simple, provided they serve Him with sincerity and patience.

St. Peter Claver, of the Company of Jesus, Apostle of the Negroes of Carthagena, knew of the Purgatory of two souls, who had led poor and humble lives upon earth; their sufferings were reduced to a few hours. We find the following account of it in the Life of this great servant of God.[1] He had persuaded a virtuous negress, named Angela, to take into her house another negress named Ursula, who had lost the use of her limbs and was covered with sores. One day when he went to visit them, as he did from time to time, to hear their confessions and to carry them some little provisions, the charitable hostess told him with grief that Ursula was at the point of death. *No, no,* replied the Father, consoling her, *she has yet four days to live, and she will not die until Saturday.* When Saturday came, he said Mass for her intention, and went out to prepare her for death. After spending some time in prayer, he said to the hostess with an air of confidence, *Be consoled, God loves Ursula; she will die to-day, but she will be only three hours in Purgatory. Let her remember me when she shall be with God, that she may pray for me, and for the one who until now had been a mother to her.* She

---

[1] *Vie de S. Pierre Claver*, par le P. Fleurian.

died at noon, and the fulfilment of one part of the prophecy gave great reason for belief in the accomplishment of the other.

Another day, having gone to hear the confession of a poor sick person whom he was accustomed to visit, he learned that she was dead. The parents were extremely afflicted, and he himself, who had not believed her to be so near her end, was inconsolable at the thought of not having been able to assist her in her last moments. He knelt down to pray by the corpse, then suddenly rising, with a serene countenance he said, "*Such a death is more worthy of our envy than of our tears ; this soul is condemned to Purgatory, but only for twenty-four hours. Let us endeavour to shorten this time by the fervour of our prayers.*"

Enough has been said on the duration of the pains. We see that they may be prolonged to an appalling degree; even the shortest, if we consider their severity, are long. Let us endeavour to shorten them for others and to mitigate them for ourselves, or better still to prevent them altogether.

Now we prevent them by removing the causes. What are the causes? What is the matter of expiation in Purgatory?

CHAPTER XXVII.

The Cause of Suffering—Matter of the Expiations of Purgatory—Doctrine of Suarez—St. Catherine of Genoa.

WHY must souls thus suffer before being admitted to see the face of God? What is the matter, what is the subject of these expiations? What has the fire of Purgatory to purify, to consume in them? It is, say the doctors, the stains left by their sins.

But what is here understood by *stains*? According to most theologians, it is not the guilt of sin, but the pain or the debt of pain proceeding from sin. To understand this well, we must remember that sin produces a double effect on the soul, which we call the debt (*reatus*) of guilt and the debt of pain; it renders the soul not only guilty, but deserving of pain or chastisement. Now, after the guilt is pardoned, it generally happens that the pain remains to be undergone, either entirely or in part, and this must be endured either in the present life or in the life to come.

The souls in Purgatory retain not the slightest stain of guilt; the venial guilt which they had at the moment of their death has disappeared in the order of pure charity, with which they are inflamed in the other life, but they still bear the debt of suffering which they had not discharged before death.

This debt proceeds from all the faults committed during their life, especially from mortal sins remitted as to the guilt, but which they have neglected to expiate by worthy fruits of exterior penance.

Such is the common teaching of theologians, which Suarez sums up in his "Treatise on the Sacrament of Penance."[1] "We conclude then," he says, "that all venial sins with which a just man dies are remitted as to the guilt, at the moment when the soul is separated from the body, by virtue of an act of love of God, and the perfect contrition which it then excites over all its past faults. In fact, the soul at this moment knows its condition perfectly, and the sins of which it has been guilty before God; at the same time, it is mistress of its faculties, to be able to act. On the other hand, on the part of God, the most efficacious helps are given to her, that she may act according to the measure of sanctifying grace which she possesses. It follows, then, that in this perfect disposition, the soul

[1] Vol. xix. *De Pœnit.*, Disput. xi. sect 4.

acts without the least hesitation. It turns directly towards its God, and finds itself freed from all its venial sins by an act of sovereign loathing of sin. This universal and efficacious act suffices for the remission of their guilt.

All stain of guilt has then disappeared; but the pain remains to be endured, in all its rigour and long duration, at least for those souls that are not assisted by the living. They cannot obtain the least relief for themselves, because the time of merit has passed; they can no longer merit, they can but suffer, and in that way pay to the terrible justice of God all that they owe, even to the last farthing. *Usque ad novissimum quadrantem.*[1]

These debts of pain are *the remains of sin*, and a kind of stain, which intercepts the vision of God, and places an obstacle to the union of the soul with its last end. Since the souls in Purgatory are freed from the guilt of sin, writes St. Catherine of Genoa,[2] there is no other barrier between them and their union with God save the remains of sin, from which they must be purified. This hindrance which they feel within them causes them to suffer the torments of the damned, of which I have spoken elsewhere, and retards the moment when the instinct by which they are drawn towards God as to their Sovereign Beatitude will attain its full perfection. They see clearly how serious before God is even the slightest obstacle raised by the remains of sin, and that it is by necessity of justice that He delays the full gratification of their desire of everlasting bliss.

This sight enkindles within them a burning flame, like that of Hell, yet without the guilt of sin.

---

[1] Matt. v. 26.   [2] *Traité du Purgatoire*, chap. iii.

CHAPTER XXVIII.

Matter of Expiation—The Remains of Mortal Sin—Lord Stourton—Sins of Lust not fully Expiated upon Earth —Saint Lidwina.

WE have said that the total amount of the debt of suffering for Purgatory comes from all the faults not atoned for upon earth, but especially from mortal sins remitted to their guilt. Now men who pass their whole lives in a habitual state of mortal sin, and who delay their conversion until death, supposing that God grants them that rare grace, will have to undergo the most frightful punishment. The example of Lord Stourton gives them good cause for reflection. Lord Stourton, an English nobleman, was at heart a Catholic, although, to retain his position at court, he regularly attended the Protestant service. He kept a Catholic priest concealed in his house, at the risk of great danger, promising himself to make good use of his ministry by being reconciled with God at the hour of his death. But he met with a sudden accident, and, as often happens in such cases, by a just decree of God, he had not the time to realise his desire of tardy conversion. Nevertheless Divine Mercy, taking into consideration what he had done for the persecuted Catholic Church in England, vouchsafed him the grace of perfect contrition, and consequently secured his salvation. But he had to pay dearly for his culpable negligence.

Years passed by. His widow married again and had children. It was one of her daughters, Lady Arundel, who relates this fact as an eye-witness:—

"One day my mother asked F. Cornelius, a Jesuit of much merit, and who, later, died a martyr,[1] to say Mass

[1] He was betrayed by a servant of the Arundel family, and was executed at Dorchester in 1594.

for the repose of the soul of John, Lord Stourton, her first husband. He promised to do so; and whilst at the altar, between the *Consecration* and the *Memento* for the dead, he paused for a long time as if absorbed in prayer. After Mass, in an exhortation which he addressed to those present, he told them of a vision which he had just had during the Holy Sacrifice. He had seen an immense forest stretched out before him, but entirely on fire, forming one vast cauldron. In the midst of it was the deceased nobleman, uttering lamentable cries, bewailing the guilty life he led in the world and at court. Having made a full confession of his faults, the unfortunate man ended with these words, which Holy Scripture places in the mouth of Job: *Have pity on me! Have pity on me, at least you my friends, for the hand of the Lord hath touched me.* He then disappeared.

"Whilst relating this, F. Cornelius shed abundance of tears, and we all, members of the family, to the number of twenty-four persons, wept also. Suddenly, whilst the Father was still speaking, we perceived upon the wall against which the altar stood what seemed to be the reflection of burning coals."

Such is the recital of Dorothy, Lady Arundel, which may be read in the "History of England," by Daniel.[1]

St. Lidwina saw in Purgatory a soul that suffered also for mortal sins not sufficiently expiated on earth. The incident is thus related in the Life of the saint. A man who had been for a long time a slave of the demon of impurity, finally had the happiness of being converted. He confessed his sins with great contrition, but, prevented by death, he had not time to atone by just penance for his numerous sins. Lidwina, who knew him well, prayed much for him. Twelve years after his death she still continued to pray, when, in one of her ecstasies, being taken into Purgatory by her angel-guardian, she heard a mournful voice issuing from a deep pit. "It is the soul of that

[1] Bk. v.; cf. Rossign., *Merv.*, 715.

man," said the angel, "for whom you have prayed with so much fervour and constancy." She was astonished to find him so deep in Purgatory twelve years after his death. The angel, seeing her so greatly affected, asked if she was willing to suffer something for his deliverance. "With all my heart," replied the charitable maiden. From that moment she suffered new pains and frightful torments, which appeared to surpass the strength of human endurance. Nevertheless, she bore them with courage, sustained by a charity stronger than death, until it pleased God to send her relief. She then breathed as one restored to a new life, and, at the same time, she saw that soul for which she had suffered so much come forth from the abyss as white as snow and take its flight to Heaven.

CHAPTER XXIX.

Matter of Expiation—Worldliness—St. Bridget—The Young Person—The Soldier—Blessed Mary Villani and the Worldly Lady.

SOULS that allow themselves to be dazzled by the vanities of the world, even if they have the good fortune to escape damnation, will have to undergo terrible punishment. Let us open the "Revelations of St. Bridget,"[1] which are held in such esteem by the Church. We read there in Book vi. that the saint saw herself transported in spirit into Purgatory, and that, among others, she saw there a young lady of high birth who had formerly abandoned herself to the luxury and vanities of the world. This unfortunate soul related to her the history of her life, and the sad state in which she then was. "Happily,"

[1] Oct. 8.

said she, "before death I confessed my sins in such dispositions as to escape Hell, but now I suffer here to expiate the worldly life that my mother did not prevent me from leading! Alas!" she added, with a sigh, "this head, which loved to be adorned, and which sought to draw the attention of others, is now devoured with flames within and without, and these flames are so violent that every moment it seems to me that I must die. These shoulders, these arms, which I loved to see admired, are cruelly bound in chains of red-hot iron. These feet, formerly trained for the dance, are now surrounded with vipers that tear them with their fangs and soil them with their filthy slime; all these members which I have adorned with jewels, flowers, and divers other ornaments, are now a prey to the most horrible torture. O mother, mother!" she cried, "how culpable have you been in my regard! It was you who, by a fatal indulgence, encouraged my taste for display and extravagant expense; it was you that took me to theatres, parties, and balls, and to those worldly assemblies which are the ruin of souls. . . . If I have not incurred eternal damnation, it was because a special grace of God's mercy touched my heart with sincere repentance. I made a good confession, and thus I have been delivered from Hell, yet only to see myself precipitated into the most horrible torments of Purgatory." We have remarked already that what is said of the tortured members must not be taken literally, because the soul is separated from the body; but God, supplying the want of corporal organs, makes the soul experience such sensations as have been just described. The biographer of the saint tells us that she related this vision to a cousin of the deceased, who was likewise given to the illusions of worldly vanity. The cousin was so struck that she renounced the luxuries and dangerous amusements of the world, and devoted the remainder of her life to penance in an austere religious order.

The same St. Bridget, during another ecstasy, beheld the judgment of a soldier who had just died. He had lived in the vices too common in his profession, and would have been condemned to Hell had not the Blessed Virgin, whom he had always honoured, preserved him from that misfortune by obtaining for him the grace of a sincere repentance. The saint saw him appear before the judgment-seat of God and condemned to a long Purgatory for the sins of all kinds which he had committed. "The punishment of the eyes," said the Judge, "shall be to contemplate the most frightful objects; that of the tongue, to be pierced with pointed needles and tormented with thirst; that of the touch, to be plunged in an ocean of fire." Then the Holy Virgin1 interceded, and obtained some mitigation of the rigour of the sentence.

Let us relate still another example of the chastisements reserved for worldlings in Purgatory, when they have not, like the rich glutton of the Gospel, been buried in Hell.

Blessed Mary Villani, a Dominican Religious,[1] had a lively devotion to the holy souls, and it often happened that they appeared to her, either to thank her or to beg the assistance of her prayers and good works. One day, whilst praying for them with great fervour, she was transported in spirit to their prison of expiation. Among the souls that suffered there she saw one more cruelly tormented than the others, in the midst of flames which entirely enveloped her. Touched with compassion, the servant of God interrogated the soul. "I have been here," she replied, "for a very long time, punished for my vanity and my scandalous extravagance. Thus far I have not received the least alleviation. Whilst I was upon earth, being wholly occupied with my toilet, my pleasures, and worldly amusements, I thought very little of my duties as a Christian, and fulfilled them only with great reluctance, and in a slothful manner. My only serious thought was to further the

[1] *Sa Vie*, par Marchi, i. ii. c. 5; *Merv.*, 41.

worldly interests of my family. See now how I am punished: they bestow not so much as a passing thought upon me: my parents, my children, those friends with whom I was most intimate—all have forgotten me."

Mary Villani begged this soul to allow her to feel something of what she suffered, and immediately it appeared as though a finger of fire touched her forehead, and the pain which she experienced instantly caused her ecstasy to cease. The mark remained, and so deep and painful was it that two months afterwards it was still to be seen, and caused the holy Religious most terrible suffering. She endured this pain in the spirit of penance, for the relief of the soul that had appeared to her, and some time later the same soul came to announce her deliverance.

CHAPTER XXX.

Matter of Expiation—Sins of Youth—St. Catherine of Sweden and the Princess Gida.

IT often happens that Christians do not sufficiently reflect on the necessity of doing penance for the sins of their youth: they must one day be atoned for by the most rigorous penance of Purgatory. Such was the case with the Princess Gida, daughter-in-law of St. Bridget, as we read in the "Lives of the Saints," March 24, Life of St. Catherine.[1] St. Bridget was in Rome with her daughter, Catherine, when the latter had an apparition of the soul of her sister-in-law, Gida, of whose death she was ignorant. Being one day in prayer in the ancient basilica of St. Peter, Catherine saw before her a woman dressed in a white robe and black mantle, and who came to ask her

[1] Cf. *Merv.*, 823.

prayers for a person who was dead. "It is one of your countrywomen," she added, "who needs your assistance." "Her name?" asked the saint. "It is the Princess Gida of Sweden, the wife of your brother Charles." Catherine then begged the stranger to accompany her to her mother Bridget, to impart to her the sad tidings. "I am charged with a message for you alone," said the stranger, "and I am not allowed to make any other visits, for I must depart immediately. You have no reason to doubt the truth of this fact; in a few days another messenger will arrive from Sweden, bringing the gold crown of Princess Gida. She has bequeathed it to you by testament, in order to secure the assistance of your prayers; but extend to her from this very moment your charitable aid, for she stands in most urgent need of your suffrages." With these words she withdrew.

Catherine would have followed her; but although her costume would have easily distinguished her, she was nowhere to be seen.

Struck and surprised with this strange adventure, she hastened to return to her mother, and related all that had happened. St. Bridget replied with a smile, "It was your sister-in-law Gida herself that appeared to you. Our Lord has been pleased to reveal this to me. The dear departed died in the most consoling sentiments of piety; that is why she attained the favour of appearing to you asking your prayers. She has still to expiate the numerous faults of her youth. Let us both do all in our power to give her relief. The gold crown which she sends you imposes this obligation upon you."

A few weeks later an officer from the court of Prince Charles arrived in Rome, carrying the crown, and believing himself to be the first to convey the tidings of the death of Princess Gida. The beautiful crown was sold, and the money used for Masses and good works for the repose of the soul of the deceased Princess.

CHAPTER XXXI.

*Matter of Expiation—Scandal given—Immodest Paintings—
Father Zucci and the Novice.*

THOSE who have had the misfortune to give bad example, and to wound or cause the perdition of souls by scandal, must take care to repair all in this world, if they would not be subjected to the most terrible expiation in the other. It was not in vain that Jesus Christ cried out, *Woe to the world because of scandals! Woe to that man by whom the scandal cometh!*[1]

Hear what Father Rossignoli relates in his *Merveilles du Purgatoire.*[2] A painter of great skill and otherwise exemplary life had once made a painting not at all conformable to the strict rules of Christian modesty. It was one of those paintings which, under the pretext of being works of art, are found in the best families, and the sight of which causes the loss of so many souls.

True art is an inspiration from Heaven, which elevates the soul to God; profane art, which appeals to the senses only, which presents to the eye nothing but the beauties of flesh and blood, is but an inspiration of the evil spirit; his works, brilliant though they may be, are not works of art, and the name is falsely attributed to them. They are the infamous productions of a corrupt imagination.

The artist of whom we speak had allowed himself to be misled in this point by bad example. Soon, however, renouncing this pernicious style, he confined himself to the production of religious pictures, or at least of those which were perfectly irreproachable. Finally, he was painting a large picture in the convent of the discalced Carmelites, when he was attacked by a mortal malady.

[1] Matt. xviii. 7. [2] *Merv.*, 24.

Feeling that he was about to die, he asked the Prior to allow him to be interred in the church of the monastery, and bequeathed to the community his earnings, which amounted to a considerable sum of money, charging them to have Masses said for the repose of his soul. He died in pious sentiments, and a few days passed, when a Religious who had stayed in the choir after Matins saw him appear in the midst of flames and sighing piteously.

"What!" said the Religious, "have you to endure such pain, after leading so good a life and dying so holy a death?" "Alas!" replied he, "it is on account of the immodest picture that I painted some years ago. When I appeared before the tribunal of the Sovereign Judge, a crowd of accusers came to give evidence against me. They declared that they had been excited to improper thoughts and evil desires by a picture, the work of my hand. In consequence of those bad thoughts some were in Purgatory, others in Hell. The latter cried for vengeance, saying that, having been the cause of their eternal perdition, I deserved, at least, the same punishment. Then the Blessed Virgin and the saints whom I had glorified by my pictures took up my defence. They represented to the Judge that that unfortunate painting had been the work of youth, and of which I had repented; that I had repaired it afterwards by religious objects which had been a source of edification to souls.

"In consideration of these and other reasons, the Sovereign Judge declared that, on account of my repentance and my good works, I should be exempt from damnation; but at the same time, He condemned me to these flames until that picture should be burned, so that it could no longer scandalise any one."

Then the poor sufferer implored the Religious to take measures to have the painting destroyed. "I beg of you," he added, "go in my name to such a person, proprietor of the picture; tell him in what a condition I am for having yielded to his entreaties to paint it, and conjure him to make a sacrifice of it. If he refuses, woe to him! To prove that this is not an illusion, and to punish him for his own fault, tell him that before long he will lose his two children. Should he refuse to obey Him who has created us both, he will pay for it by a premature death."

The Religious delayed not to do what the poor soul asked of him, and went to the owner of the picture. The latter, on hearing these things, seized the painting and cast it into the fire. Nevertheless, according to the words of the deceased, he lost his two children in less than a month. The remainder of his days he passed in penance, for having ordered and kept that immodest picture in his house.

If such are the consequences of an immodest picture, what, then, will be the punishment of the still more disastrous scandals resulting from bad books, bad papers, bad schools, and bad conversations? *Væ mundo a scandalis! Væ homini illi per quem scandalum venit!*—" Woe to the world because of scandals! Woe to that man by whom the scandal cometh!"[1]

Scandal makes great ravages in souls by the seduction of innocence. Ah! those accursed seducers! They shall render to God a terrible account of the blood of their victims. We read the following in the Life of Father Nicholas Zucchi,[2] written by Fr. Daniel Bartoli, of the Company of Jesus.

The holy and zealous Father Zucchi, who died in Rome, May 21, 1670, had drawn to a life of perfection three young ladies, who consecrated themselves to God in the cloister. One of them, before leaving the world, had been sought in marriage by a young nobleman. After she had entered the noviciate, this gentleman, instead of respecting her holy vocation, continued to address letters to her whom he wished to call his betrothed, urging her to quit, as he said, the dull service of God, to embrace again the joys of

[1] Matt. xviii. 7.   [2] Cf. *Merv.*, 841.

life. The Father, meeting him one day in the streets, begged him to give up such conduct. "I assure you," he said, "that before long you will appear before the tribunal of God, and it is high time for you to prepare yourself by sincere penance."

In fact, a fortnight afterwards, this young man died, carried away by a rapid death, that left him little time to put the affairs of his conscience in order, so that there was everything to fear for his salvation.

One evening, whilst the three novices were engaged together in holy conversation, the youngest was called away to the parlour. There she found a man wrapped in a heavy cloak, and with measured steps pacing the room. "Sir," she said, "who are you? and why did you send for me?" The stranger, without answering, drew near and threw aside the mysterious mantle which covered him. The Religious then recognised the unfortunate deceased, and saw with horror that he was entirely surrounded by chains of fire that clasped his neck, wrists, knees, and ankles. "*Pray for me!*" he cried, and disappeared. This miraculous manifestation showed that God had had mercy upon him at the last moment; that he had not been damned, but that he paid his attempt at seduction by a terrible Purgatory.

CHAPTER XXXII.

Matter of Expiation—The Life of Pleasure—The Pursuit of Comfort—Venerable Frances of Pampeluna and the Man of the World—St. Elizabeth and the Queen, her Mother.

IN our days there are Christians who are total strangers to the Cross and the mortification of Jesus Christ. Their effeminate and sensual life is but one chain of pleasures; they fear everything that is a sacrifice; scarcely do they observe the strict laws of fasting and abstinence prescribed by the Church. Since they will not submit to any penance in this world, let them reflect on what will be inflicted upon them in the next. It is certain that in this worldly life they do nothing but accumulate debts. Since they omit to do penance, no part of the debt is paid, and a total is reached that affrights the imagination. The venerable servant of God, Frances of Pampeluna, who was favoured with several visions of Purgatory, saw one day a man of the world, who, although he had otherwise been a tolerably good Christian, passed fifty-nine years in Purgatory on account of seeking his ease and comfort. Another passed thirty-five years there for the same reason; a third, who had too strong a passion for gambling, was detained there for sixty-four years. Alas! these injudicious Christians have allowed their debts to remain before God, and those which they might so easily have acquitted by works of penance they have had to pay afterwards by years of torture.

If God is severe towards the rich and the pleasure-seekers of the world, He will not be less so towards princes, magistrates, parents, and in general towards all those who have the charge of souls and authority over others.

A severe judgment, says He Himself, *shall be for them that bear rule.*[1]

Laurence Surius relates[2] how an illustrious queen, after her death, bore witness to this truth. In the Life of St. Elizabeth, Duchess of Thuringia, it is said that the servant of God lost her mother, Gertrude, Queen of Hungary, about the year 1220. In the spirit of a holy Christian daughter, she gave abundant alms, redoubled her prayers and mortifications, exhausted the resources of her charity for the relief of that dear soul. God revealed to her that she had not done too much. One night the deceased appeared to her

---

[1] Sap. vi. 6.   [2] *Merv.*, 93.

with a sad and emaciated countenance; she placed herself on her knees next to the bed, and said to her, weeping, "My daughter, you see at your feet your mother overwhelmed with suffering. I come to implore you to multiply your suffrages, that Divine Mercy may deliver me from the frightful torments I endure. Oh! how much are those to be pitied who exercise authority over others? I expiate now the faults that I committed upon the throne. Oh! my daughter, I pray you by the pangs I endured when bringing you into the world, by the cares and anxieties which your education cost me, I conjure you to deliver me from my torments." Elizabeth, deeply touched, arose immediately, took the discipline to blood, and implored God, with tears, to have mercy on her mother, Gertrude, declaring that she would not cease to pray until she had obtained her deliverance. Her prayers were heard.

Let us here remark that, in the preceding example, there is spoken of a queen only; how much more severely will kings, magistrates, and all superiors be treated whose responsibility and influence are much greater!

CHAPTER XXXIII.

Matter of Expiation—Tepidity—St. Bernard and the Religious of Citeaux—Venerable Mother Agnes and Sister de Haut Villars—Father Surin and the Religious of Loudun.

GOOD Christians, Priests, and Religious, who wish to serve God with their whole hearts, must avoid the rock of tepidity and negligence. God will be served with fervour; those who are tepid and careless excite His disgust; He even goes so far as to threaten with His malediction those who perform holy actions in a careless manner—that is to say, He will severely punish in Purgatory all negligence in His service.

Among the disciples of St. Bernard, who perfumed the celebrated valley of Clairvaux with the odour of their sanctity, there was one whose negligence sadly contrasted with the fervour of his brethren. Notwithstanding his double character of Priest and of Religious, he allowed himself to sink into a deplorable state of tepidity. The moment of death arrived, and he was summoned before God without having given any token of amendment.

Whilst the Mass of Requiem was being celebrated, a venerable Religious of uncommon virtue learned by an interior light, that though the deceased was not eternally lost, his soul was in a most miserable condition. The following night the soul appeared to him in a sad and wretched condition. "Yesterday," he said, "you learned my deplorable fate; behold now the tortures to which I am condemned in punishment for my culpable tepidity." He then conducted the old man to the edge of a large, deep pit, filled with smoke and flames. "Behold the place," said he, "where the ministers of Divine Justice have orders to torment me; they cease not to plunge me into this abyss, and draw me out only to precipitate me into it again, without giving me one moment's respite."

The next morning the Religious went to St. Bernard to make known to him his vision. The holy Abbot, who had had a similar apparition, received it as a warning from Heaven to his community. He convened a Chapter, and with tearful eyes related the double vision, exhorting his Religious to succour their poor departed brother by their charitable suffrages, and to profit by this sad example to preserve their fervour, and to avoid the least negligence in the service of God.[1]

The following instance is related by M. de Lantages in

[1] Rossign., *Merv.*, 47.

the Life of Venerable Mother Agnes of Langeac, a Dominican Religious.[1] Whilst this Religious was one day praying in choir, a Religious whom she did not know suddenly appeared before her, miserably clad and with a countenance expressive of the deepest grief. She looked at her with astonishment, asking herself who it might be; when she heard a voice saying distinctly, "*It is Sister de Haut Villars.*"

Sister de Haut Villars had been a Religious in the monastery at Puy, and had died about ten years previous to this vision. The apparition said not a word, but showed sufficiently by her sad countenance how greatly she stood in need of assistance.

Mother Agnes understood this perfectly, and began from that day to offer most fervent prayers for the relief of this soul. The deceased was not content with the first visit; she continued to appear for the space of three weeks, almost everywhere and at all times, especially after Holy Communion and prayer, manifesting her sufferings by the doleful expression of her countenance.

Agnes, by the advice of her confessor, without speaking of the apparition, asked her Prioress to allow the community to offer extra prayers for the dead, for her intention. Since, notwithstanding, these prayers, the apparitions continued, she greatly feared some delusion. God, however, deigned to remove this fear. He clearly made known to His charitable servant, by the voice of her angel-guardian, *that it was really a soul from Purgatory, and that she thus suffered for her negligence in the service of God.* From the moment these words were uttered, the apparitions ceased, and it is not known how long that unfortunate soul may have had to remain in Purgatory. Let us cite another example, qualified to stimulate the fervour of the faithful. A holy Religious named Mary of the Incarnation, of the convent of the Ursulines, in Loudun, appeared some time

[1] Oct. 19.

after her death to her Superior, a women of intelligence and merit, who wrote the details of the apparition to Father Surin of the Company of Jesus. "On November 6th," she wrote, "between three and four o'clock in the morning, Mother of the Incarnation stood before me, with an expression of sweetness on her countenance that appeared more like that of humility than of suffering; yet I saw that she suffered much. When I first perceived her near me, I was seized with great fright, but as there was nothing about her that inspired fear, I soon felt reassured. I asked her in what state she was, and if we could render her any service. She replied, 'I satisfy Divine Justice in Purgatory.' I begged her to tell me why she was detained there. Then with a deep sigh she answered, 'It is for being negligent in several common exercises; a certain weakness by which I allowed myself to be led by the example of imperfect Religious; finally, and especially, the habit which I had of retaining in my possession things of which I had no permission to dispose, and of making use of them to suit my needs and natural inclinations. Ah! if Religious knew,' continued the good Mother, 'the wrong they do their souls by not applying themselves to perfection, and how dearly they shall one day expiate the satisfactions which they give themselves contrary to the light of their consciences, their efforts to do violence to themselves during life would be very different. Ah! God's point of view is different from ours, His judgments are different.'

"I asked her again if we could do anything to relieve her sufferings. She replied, 'I desire to see and possess God, but I am content to satisfy His Justice as long as it shall please Him.' I asked her to tell me whether she suffered much. 'My pains,' she replied, 'are incomprehensible to those who do not feel them.' Saying these words, she drew near my face to take leave of me. It seemed as though I was burned by a coal of fire, although her face did not touch mine; and my arm, which had barely grazed her mantle, was burned and caused me considerable pain."

A month later she appeared to the same Superior to announce her deliverance.

CHAPTER XXXIV.

Matter of Expiation—Negligence in Holy Communion—Louis of Blois—St. Magdalen de Pazzi and the Departed Soul in Adoration.

To tepidity is allied negligence in the preparation for the Eucharistic Banquet. If the Church unceasingly calls her children to the Holy Table, if she desires that they communicate frequently, she always intends that they should do so with that fervour and piety which so great a mystery demands. All voluntary neglect in so holy an action is an offence to the Sanctity of Jesus Christ, an offence which must be repaired by a just expiation. Venerable Louis of Blois, in his *Miroir Spirituel*, speaks of a great servant of God who learned in a supernatural manner how severely these faults are punished in the other life. He received a visit from a soul in Purgatory imploring his aid in name of the friendship by which they had formerly been united. She endured, she said, horrible torments, for the negligence with which she had prepared for Holy Communion during the days of her earthly pilgrimage. She could not be delivered but by a fervent Communion which would compensate for her former tepidity.

Her friend hastened to gratify her desire, received Holy Communion with great purity of conscience, with all the faith and devotion possible; and then she saw the holy soul appear, brilliant with an incomparable splendour, and rise towards heaven.[1]

[1] *Merv.*, 44.

In the year 1589, in the monastery of St. Mary of the Angels, in Florence, died a Religious who was much esteemed by her sisters in religion, but who soon appeared to St. Magdalen de Pazzi to implore her assistance in the rigorous Purgatory to which she was condemned. The saint was in prayer before the Blessed Sacrament when she perceived the deceased kneeling in the middle of the church in an attitude of profound adoration. She had around her a mantle of flames that seemed to consume her, but a white robe that covered her body protected her in part from the action of the fire. Greatly astonished, Magdalen desired to know what this signified, and she was answered that this soul suffered thus for having had little devotion toward the August Sacrament of the Altar. Notwithstanding the rules and holy customs of her Order, she had communicated but rarely, and then with indifference. It was for this reason Divine Justice had condemned her to come every day to adore the Blessed Sacrament, and to submit to the torture of fire at the feet of Jesus Christ. Nevertheless, in reward for her virginal purity, represented by the white robe, her Divine Spouse had greatly mitigated her sufferings.

Such was the revelation which God made to His servant. She was deeply touched, and made every effort to assist the poor soul by all the suffrages in her power. She often related this apparition, and made use of it to exhort her spiritual daughters to zeal for Holy Communion.

CHAPTER XXXV.

Matter of Expiation—Want of Respect in Prayer—Mother Agnes of Jesus and Sr. Angelique—St. Severin of Cologne—Venerable Frances of Pampeluna and the Priests—Father Streit, S.J.

We should treat holy things in a holy manner. All irreverence in religious exercises is extremely displeasing to God. When the Venerable Agnes of Langeac, of whom we have already spoken, was Prioress of her convent, she very much recommended to her Religious respect and fervour in their relations with God, reminding them of these words of Holy Scripture, *Accursed be he that doth the work of God with negligence.* A sister of the community named Angelique died. The pious Superior was praying near her tomb, when she suddenly saw the deceased sister before her, dressed in the religious habit; she felt at the same time as though a flame of fire touched her face. Sister Angelique thanked her for having stimulated her to fervour, and particularly for having frequently made her repeat during life these words, *Accursed be he that doth the work of God with negligence.* "Continue, Mother," she added, "to urge the sisters to fervour; let them serve God with the utmost diligence, love Him with their whole heart, and with all the power of their soul. If they could but understand how rigorous are the torments of Purgatory, they would never be guilty of the least neglect."

The foregoing warning regards in a special manner priests, whose relations with God are continual and more sublime. Let them, therefore, remember it always, and never forget it, whether they offer to God the incense of prayer, whether they dispense the Divine Treasures of the Sacraments, or whether at the altar they celebrate the mysteries of the Body and Blood of Jesus Christ. See what St. Peter Damian relates in his XIVth Letter to Desiderius.[1]

St. Severin, Archbishop of Cologne,[2] edified his church by an example of all virtues. His apostolic life, his great labours for the extension of God's kingdom in souls, have merited for him the honours of canonisation. Nevertheless, after his death he appeared to one of the canons of his cathedral to ask for prayers. This worthy priest not being able to understand that a holy prelate, such as he had known Severin to be, could stand in need of prayers in the other life, the deceased Bishop replied, "It is true God gave me grace to serve Him with all my heart and to labour in His vineyard, but I often offended Him by the haste with which I recited the Holy Office. The occupations of each day so absorbed my attention, that when the hour of prayer came, I acquitted myself of that great duty without recollection, and sometimes at another hour than that appointed by the Church. At this moment I am expiating those infidelities, and God permits me to come and ask your prayers." The biography adds that Severin was six months in Purgatory for that one fault.

Venerable Sister Frances of Pampeluna, whom we have before mentioned, one day saw in Purgatory a poor priest whose fingers were eaten away by frightful ulcers. He was thus punished for having at the altar made the sign of the cross with too much levity, and without the necessary gravity. She said that in general priests remain in Purgatory longer than laymen, and that the intensity of their torments is in proportion to their dignity. God revealed to her the fate of several deceased priests. One of them had to undergo forty years of suffering for having by his neglect allowed a person to die without the Sacraments; another remained there for forty-five years for having performed the sublime functions of his ministry with a certain

[1] Cf. *Merv.*, 37.   [2] Oct. 23.

levity. A Bishop, whose liberality had caused him to be named almoner, was detained there for five years for having sought that dignity; another, not so charitable, was condemned for forty years for the same reason.[1]

God wills that we should serve Him with our whole heart, and that we should avoid, in so far as the frailty of human nature will permit, even the slightest imperfections; but the care to please Him and the fear of displeasing Him must be accompanied by a humble confidence in His mercy.

Jesus Christ has admonished us to hear those whom He has appointed in His place to be our spiritual guides as we should Himself, and to follow the advice of our superior or confessor with perfect confidence. Thus an excessive fear is an offence against His Mercy.

On November 12, 1643, Father Philip Streit, of the Society of Jesus, a Religious of great sanctity, died at the Noviciate of Brünn in Bohemia. Every day he made his examination of conscience with the greatest care, and acquired by this means great purity of soul. Some hours after his death, he appeared all radiant to one of the Fathers of his Order, Venerable Martin Strzeda. " One single fault," he said, " prevents me from going to Heaven, and detains me eight hours in Purgatory; it is that of not having sufficiently confided in the words of my Superior, who, in the last moments of my life, strove to calm some little trouble of conscience. I ought to have regarded his words as the voice of God Himself."

[1] *Vie de la Vénér. Mère Franc.* Cf. *Merv.*, 25.

CHAPTER XXXVI.

Matter of Expiation and Chastisement—Unmortification of the Senses—Father Francis of Aix—Unmortification of the Tongue—Durand.

CHRISTIANS who wish to escape the rigours of Purgatory must love the mortification of their Divine Master, and beware of being delicate members under a Head crowned with thorns. On February 10, 1656, in the province of Lyons, Father Francis of Aix, of the Society of Jesus, passed away to a better life. He carried all the virtues of a Religious to a high degree of perfection. Penetrated with a profound veneration towards the Most Blessed Trinity, he had for particular intention in all his prayers and mortifications to honour this August Mystery; to embrace by preference those works for which others showed less inclination, had a particular charm for him. He often visited the Blessed Sacrament, even during the night, and never left the door of his room without going to say a prayer at the foot of the altar. His penances, which were in a manner excessive, gave him the name of the *man of suffering*. He replied to one who advised him to moderate them, "*The day which I should allow to pass without shedding some drops of my blood to offer to my God would be for me the most painful and the severest mortification. Since I cannot hope to suffer martyrdom for the love of Jesus Christ, I will at least have some part in His sufferings.*"

Another Religious, Brother Coadjutor of the same Order, did not imitate the example of this good Father. He had little love for mortification, but, on the contrary, sought his ease and comfort, and all that could gratify the senses.

This brother, some days after his death, appeared to Father d'Aix, clothed in frightful haircloth, and suffering great torments, in punishment for the faults of sensuality which he had committed during life. He implored the assistance of his prayers, and immediately disappeared.

Another fault against which we must guard, because we so easily fall into it, is the unmortification of the tongue. Oh! how easy it is to err in words! How rare a thing it is to speak for any length of time without offending against meekness, humility, sincerity, or Christian charity! Even pious persons are often subject to this defect; when they have escaped all the other snares of the demon, they allow themselves to be taken, says St. Jerome, in this last trap—slander. Let us listen to what is related by Vincent de Beauvais.[1]

When the celebrated Durand, who, in the eleventh century, shed lustre on the Order of St. Dominic, was yet a simple Religious, he showed himself a model of regularity and fervour; yet he had one defect. The vivacity of his disposition led him to talk too much; he was excessively found of witty expressions, often at the expense of charity. Hugh, his Abbot, brought this under his notice, even predicting that, if he did not correct himself of this fault, he would certainly have to expiate it in Purgatory. Durand did not attach sufficient importance to this advice, and continued to give himself, without much restraint, to the disorders of the tongue. After his death, the prediction of the Abbot Hugh was fulfilled. Durand appeared to a Religious, one of his friends, imploring him to assist him by his prayers, because he was frightfully punished for the unmortification of his tongue. In consequence of this apparition, the members of the community unanimously agreed to observe strict silence for eight days, and to practise other good works for the repose of the

[1] *Specul. Historiale*, l. 26, c. 5: cf. *Merv.*, 37.

deceased. These charitable exercises produced their effect; some time after Durand again appeared, but now to announce his deliverance.

CHAPTER XXXVII.

Matter of Expiation—Intemperance of the Tongue—The Dominican Father—Sisters Gertrude and Margaret— St. Hugh of Cluny and the Infringer of the Rule of Silence.

WE have just seen how immoderation in the use of words is expiated in Purgatory. Father P. Rossignoli speaks of a Dominican Religious who incurred the chastisements of Divine Justice for a like defect. This Religious, a preacher full of zeal, a glory to his Order, appeared after his death to one of his brethren at Cologne. He was clad in magnificent robes, wearing a crown of gold upon his head, but his tongue was fearfully tormented. These ornaments represented the recompense of his zeal for souls and his perfect exactitude in all the points of his Rule. Nevertheless, his tongue was tortured because he had not been sufficiently guarded in his words, and his language was not always becoming the sacred lips of a priest and a Religious.

The following instance is drawn from Cesarius.[1] In a monastery of the Order of Citeaux, says this author, lived two young Religious, named Gertrude and her sister Margaret. The former, although otherwise virtuous, did not sufficiently watch over her tongue; she frequently allowed herself to transgress the rule of silence prescribed, sometimes even in choir, before and after the chanting of the

[1] *Dial. de Miraculis.*

Office. Instead of recollecting herself with the reverence due to that holy place, she addressed useless words to her sister, who was placed next to her, so that, besides her violation of the rule of silence and her lack of piety, she was a subject of disedification to her companion. She died whilst still young, and a very short time after her death, Sister Margaret, on going to Office, saw her come and place herself in the same stall she had occupied whilst living.

At this sight the sister was almost about to faint. When she had sufficiently recovered from her astonishment, she went and told the Superior what she had just seen. The Superior told her not to be troubled, but, should the deceased appear again, to ask her, in the name of God, why she came.

She reappeared the next day in the same way, and, according to the order of the Prioress, Margaret said to her, "My dear Sister Gertrude, whence do you come, and what do you want?" "I come," she said, "to satisfy the Justice of God in this place where I have sinned. It was here, in this holy sanctuary, that I offended God by words, both useless and contrary to religious respect, by disedification to all, and by the scandal which I have given to you in particular. Oh, if you knew," she added, "what I suffer! I am devoured by flames, my tongue especially is dreadfully tormented." She then disappeared, after having asked for prayers.

When St. Hugh,[1] who succeeded St. Odilo in 1049, governed the fervent monastery of Cluny, one of his Religious, who had been careless in the observance of the rule of silence, having died, appeared to the holy Abbot to beg the assistance of his prayers. His mouth was filled with frightful ulcers, in punishment, he said, for idle words. Hugh imposed seven days of silence upon his community. They were passed in recollection and prayer. Then the

[1] April 29.

deceased reappeared, freed from his ulcers, his countenance radiant, and testifying his gratitude for the charitable succour he had received from his brethren. If such is the chastisement of idle words, what will be that of words more culpable?

CHAPTER XXXVIII.

Matter of Expiation—Failure in matters of Justice—Father d'Espinoza and the Payments—Blessed Margaret of Cortona and the Assassinated Merchants.

A MULTITUDE of revelations show us that God chastises with implacable rigour all sins contrary to Justice and Charity; and in matters of Justice He seems to exact that reparation be made before the penalty is remitted; as in the Church Militant her ministers must exact restitution in order to remit the guilt, according to the axiom, *Without restitution no remission.*

Father P. Rossignoli[1] speaks of a Religious of his Order, named Augustin d'Espinoza, whose saintly life was but one act of devotion to the souls in Purgatory. A rich man who went to him to confession, having died without having sufficiently regulated his affairs, appeared to him, and asked him first if he knew him.

"Certainly," replied the Father; "I administered the Sacrament of Penance to you a few days before your death." "You must know, then," added the soul, "that I come to you by a special grace of God, to conjure you to appease His Justice, and to do for me that which I can no longer do for myself. Follow me."

The Father first went to see his Superior, to tell him

[1] *Merv.*, 92.

what was asked of him, and to obtain permission to follow the strange visitor. The permission obtained, he went out and followed the apparition, who, without uttering a single word, led him to one of the bridges of the city. There it begged the Father to wait a little, disappeared for a moment, then returned with a bag of money, which it begged the Father to carry, and both returned to the cell of the Religious. Then the deceased gave him a written note, and showed him the money. "All this," said he, "is at your disposal. Have the charity to take it, that you may satisfy my creditors, whose names are written upon this paper, with the amount due to each. Be pleased to take what remains and use it for good works at your own discretion, for the repose of my soul." With these words he disappeared, and the Father hastened to carry out his wishes.

Eight days had scarcely elapsed when Father d'Espinoza received another visit from the same soul. He thanked the Father most heartily. "Thanks to the charitable exactitude," he said, "with which you have paid the debts that I left on earth, thanks also to the Holy Masses which you have celebrated for me, I am delivered from all my sufferings, and am admitted into eternal beatitude." We find an example of the same kind in the Life of Blessed Margaret of Cortona.[1] This illustrious penitent also distinguished herself by her charity towards the departed souls. They appeared to her in great numbers, to implore her assistance and suffrages. One day, among others, she saw before her two travellers, who begged her to assist them in repairing the injustices left to their account. "We are two merchants," they told her, "who have been assassinated on the road by brigands. We could not go to confession or receive absolution; but by the mercy of our Divine Saviour and His Holy Mother, we had the time to make an act of perfect contrition, and we have

[1] *Actes des Saints*, Feb. 22.

been saved. But our torments in Purgatory are terrible, because in the exercise of our profession we have committed many acts of injustice. Until these acts are repaired we can have no repose nor alleviation. This is why we beseech you, servant of God, to go and find such and such of our relatives and heirs, to warn them to make restitution as soon as possible of all the money which we have unjustly acquired." They gave the holy penitent the necessary information and disappeared.

CHAPTER XXXIX.

Matter of Expiation—Sins against Charity—Blessed Margaret Mary—Two Persons of Rank in the Pains of Purgatory—Several Souls Punished for Discord.

WE have already said that Divine Justice is extremely severe in regard to sins against Charity. Charity is, in fact, the virtue which is dearest to the Heart of our Divine Master, and which He recommends to His disciples as that which must distinguish them in the eyes of men. By this, He says, *shall all men know that you are My disciples, if you have love one for another.*[1] It is, then, not astonishing that harshness towards our neighbour, and every other fault against Charity, should be severely punished in the other life.

Of this we have several proofs, taken from the Life of Blessed Margaret Mary. "I learned from Sister Margaret," says Mother Greffier in her Memoirs, "that she one day prayed for two persons of high rank in the world who had just died. She saw them both in Purgatory. The one was condemned for several years to those sufferings, not-

[1] John xiii. 35.

withstanding the great number of Masses which were celebrated for her. All those prayers and suffrages were by Divine Justice applied to the souls belonging to some of the families of her subjects, which had been ruined by their injustice and lack of charity. As nothing was left to those poor people to enable them to have prayers offered for them after their death, God compensated these poor people in the manner we have related. The other was in Purgatory for as many days as she had lived years upon earth. Our Lord made known to Sister Margaret that, among the good works which this person had performed, He had taken into special consideration the Charity with which she had borne the faults of her neighbour, and the pains she had taken to overcome the displeasure they had caused her."

On another occasion our Lord showed Blessed Margaret a large number of souls in Purgatory, who, for not having been united with their Superiors during their life, and for having had some misunderstanding with them, had been severely punished and deprived after death of the aid of the Blessed Virgin and the Saints, and also of the visits of their angel-guardians. Several of those souls were destined to remain for a long time in horrible flames. Some even among them had no other token of their predestination than that they did not hate God. Others, who had been in religion, and who during life showed little charity towards their sisters, were deprived of their suffrages, and received no assistance whatsoever.

Let us add one more extract from the Memoirs of Mother Greffier. "It happened whilst Sister Margaret was praying for two deceased Religious, that their souls were shown to her in the prisons of Divine Justice, but one suffered incomparably more than the other. The former regretted greatly that by her faults against mutual Charity, and the holy friendship that ought to remain in religious communities, she had in part deprived herself, among other punishments, of the suffrages which were offered for her by the community. She received relief only from the prayers of three or four persons of the same community for whom she had had less affection and inclination during her life. This suffering soul reproached herself also for the too great facility with which she took dispensations from the rules and exercises of the community. Finally, she deplored the care which she had taken upon earth to procure for her body so many comforts and commodities. She made known at the same time to our dear Sister that, in punishment for three faults, she had to undergo three furious assaults of the demon during her last agony, and that each time believing herself lost, she was on the point of falling into despair, but by the Blessed Virgin, towards whom she had borne great devotion during her life, she had been snatched three times from the claws of the enemy."

CHAPTER XL.

Matter of Expiation—Lack of Charity and of Respect towards our Neighbour—St. Louis Bertrand and the Departed Soul asking Pardon—Father Nieremberg—Blessed Margaret Mary and the Benedictine Religious.

TRUE Charity is humble and indulgent towards others, respecting them as though they were their superiors. Her words are always friendly, and full of consideration for others, having nothing of bitterness nor coldness, nothing savouring of contempt, because she is born of a heart that is meek and humble like that of Jesus. She also carefully avoids all that could disturb unity; she takes every means, makes every sacrifice to effect a reconciliation, according to the words of our Divine Master, *If thou offer thy gift at the altar, and there thou remember that thy brother hath anything against thee, leave there thy offering before the altar, and go first to be reconciled to thy brother, and then coming thou shalt offer thy gift.*[1]

A Religious having wounded Charity in regard to St. Louis Bertrand, received a terrible chastisement after death. He was plunged into the fire of Purgatory, which he had to endure until he had made satisfaction to Divine Justice; nay, more, he could not be admitted into the abode of the elect until he had accomplished an act of exterior reparation, which should serve as an example to the living. The fact is thus related in the Life of the saint:[2]—

When St. Louis Bertrand, of the Order of St. Dominic, resided at the convent of Valencia, there was a young Religious in the community who attached too much importance to profane science. Doubtless letters and erudition have their value, but, as the Holy Ghost declares, they should yield to the fear of God and the science of the saints. *Non super timentem Dominum*—"There is none above him that feareth the Lord."[3] This science of the saints, which Eternal Wisdom came to teach us, consists in Humility and Charity. The young Religious of whom we speak, while but little advanced in Divine science, allowed himself to reproach Father Bertrand with his little knowledge, and said to him, "*One can see, Father, that you are not very learned!*" "*Brother,*" replied the saint with meek firmness, "*Lucifer was very learned, and yet he was damned.*"

The brother who had committed this fault did not think of repairing it. Nevertheless, he was not a bad Religious, and some time after, falling dangerously sick, he received the last Sacrament in very good dispositions, and expired

[1] Matt. v. 23.
[2] *Acta Sanctor.*, Oct. 10.
[3] Eccli. xxv. 13.

peacefully in the Lord. A considerable time elapsed, and meanwhile Louis was nominated Prior. One day, having remained in choir after Matins, the deceased appeared to him enveloped in flames, and prostrating humbly before him, said, "Father, pardon me the offensive words which I formerly addressed to you. God will not permit me to see His face until you shall have pardoned my fault and offered Holy Mass for me." The saint willingly forgave him, and the next morning celebrated Mass for the repose of his soul. The following night, being again in choir, he saw the deceased brother reappear, but radiant with glory and going up to Heaven.

Father Eusebius Nieremberg, Religious of the Company of Jesus, author of the beautiful book, "Difference between Time and Eternity," resided at the College of Madrid, where he died in the odour of sanctity in 1658. This servant of God, who was singularly devout towards the souls in Purgatory, was praying one day in the church of the college for a Father who had recently died. The deceased, who for a long time had been a professor of theology, had proved himself to be as good a Religious as he was a learned theologian; he had been distinguished for his great devotion to the Blessed Virgin, but one vice had crept in among his virtues—he was uncharitable in his words, and frequently spoke of the faults of his neighbour. Now, whilst Father Nieremberg was recommending his soul to God, this Religious appeared, and revealed to him the state of his soul. He was condemned to frightful torments for having frequently spoken against charity. His tongue, the instrument of his fault, was tortured by a devouring fire. The Blessed Virgin, in recompense for the tender devotion which he had cherished towards her, had obtained permission for him to come and ask for prayers; he was, at the same time, to serve as an example to others, that they might learn to be guarded in all their words. Father Nieremberg, having offered many prayers and penances for him, finally obtained his deliverance.[1]

The Religious of whom mention is made in the Life of Blessed Margaret Mary, and for whom that servant of God suffered so terribly for the space of three months, among other faults, was also punished for his sins against Charity. The revelation is thus related :—

Blessed Margaret Mary, we read in her Life, being one day before the Blessed Sacrament, suddenly saw before her a man totally enveloped in fire, the intense heat of which seemed about to consume herself. The wretched state in which she saw this poor soul caused her to shed tears. He was a Benedictine Religious of the monastery of Cluny, to whom she had formerly confessed, and who had done good to her soul by ordering her to receive Holy Communion. In reward for this service, God had permitted him to address himself to her, that he might find some alleviation in his sufferings.

The poor departed asked that all she should do and suffer for the space of three months might be applied to him. This she promised, after having obtained permission. Then he told her that the principal cause of his intense suffering was for having sought his own interests before the glory of God and the good of souls, by attaching too much importance to his reputation. The second was his want of charity towards his brethren. The third, the natural affection for creatures to whom, through weakness, he had yielded, and to which he had given expression in his spiritual intercourse with them, "this being," he added, "very displeasing to God."

It is difficult to say all that the Blessed Sister had to suffer during the three months following. The deceased never left her. On the side where he stood she seemed all on fire, with such excruciating pain, that she could not cease to weep. Her Superior, touched with compassion,

[1] Life of P. Nieremberg.

ordered her penances and disciplines, because pain and suffering greatly relieved her. The torments which the Sanctity of God inflicted upon her were insupportable. It was a specimen of the suffering endured by the poor souls.

CHAPTER XLI.

Matter of Expiation—Abuse of Grace—St. Magdalen de Pazzi and the Dead Religious—Blessed Margaret Mary and the Three Souls in Purgatory.

THERE is another disorder in the soul which God punishes severely in Purgatory, to wit, the abuse of grace. By this is understood the neglect to correspond to the aids which God gives us, and to the invitations which He presses upon us to the practice of virtue for the sanctification of our souls. This grace which He offers us is a precious gift, which we may not throw away; it is the seed of salvation and of merit, which it is not permitted to leave unproductive. Now, this fault is committed when we do not respond with generosity to the Divine invitation. I receive from God the means of giving alms; an interior voice invites me to do so. I close my heart, or I give with a miserly hand; this is an abuse of grace. I can hear Mass, assist at the sermon, frequent the Sacraments; an interior voice urges me to go, but I will not give myself the trouble. This, again, is an abuse of grace.

A young Religious must be obedient, humble, mortified, devoted to her duties; God requires this, and gives her the grace in virtue of her vocation. She does not apply herself thereto; she does not labour to overcome herself, in order to co-operate with the assistance which God gives her; this is an abuse of grace.

Now this sin, as we have said, is severely punished in Purgatory. St. Magdalen de Pazzi tells us that one of her sisters in religion had much to suffer after death for not having on three occasions corresponded to grace. It happened that on a certain feast-day she felt inclined to do some little work; it was only some simple piece of embroidery, but it was not at all necessary, and could be conveniently postponed to some other time. The inspiration of grace told her to abstain from it through respect for the solemnity of the day, but she preferred to satisfy the natural inclination which she had for that work, under pretext that it was but a trifle. Another time, noticing that the observance of a certain point of the Rule had been omitted, and that by making it known to her superiors some good would have resulted to the community, she omitted to speak of it. The inspiration of grace told her to perform this act of charity, but human respect withheld her. A third fault was an ill-regulated attachment to her relatives in the world. As spouse of Jesus Christ, all her affections belonged to the Divine Spouse; but she divided her heart by being too much occupied with the members of her family. Although she knew that her conduct in this respect was defective, she did not obey the impulse of grace, nor did she labour strenuously to correct it. This sister, otherwise most edifying, died some time after, and Magdalen prayed for her with her usual fervour. Sixteen days passed, when she appeared to the saint to announce her deliverance. Magdalen expressing her astonishment that the sister had been so long in suffering, it was revealed to her that this soul had to expiate her abuse of grace in the three cases of which we have just spoken, and that these faults would have detained her longer in her torments had not God taken into consideration the more satisfactory part of her conduct. He had abridged her sufferings on

PURGATORY, THE MYSTERY OF JUSTICE.

account of her faithful observance of the Rule, her purity of intention, and her charity towards her sisters.[1]

Those who in this world have received more grace, and more means of discharging their spiritual debts, will be treated with less consideration than those who have had less opportunity of making satisfaction during life.

Blessed Margaret Mary having learned the death of three persons who had died quite recently, two Religious and one Secular, began immediately to pray for the repose of their souls. It was the first day of the year. Our Lord, touched by her charity, and treating her with an ineffable familiarity, deigned to appear to her; and showing her the three souls in those fiery prisons where they were languishing, said to her, "My daughter, as New Year's gift, I give you the deliverance of one of these three souls, and I leave the choice to you. Which shall I release?" "Who am I, Lord," she replied, "to say who deserves the preference? Deign yourself to make the choice." Then our Lord delivered the Secular, saying that He felt less in seeing Religious suffer, because they had more means of expiating their sins during life.

[1] Cepari, *Vie de Sainte Madeleine de Pazzi*.

Part Second.

PURGATORY, THE MYSTERY OF MERCY.

CHAPTER I.

Fear and Confidence—The Mercy of God—St. Lidwina and the Priest—Venerable Claude de la Colombière.

WE have just considered the rigours of Divine Justice in the other life; they are terrific, and it is impossible to think of them without trembling. That fire, enkindled by Divine Justice, those excruciating pains, compared to which all the penances of the saints, all the sufferings of the martyrs put together, are as nothing, who is there that thinks he will be able to look upon them and not shudder from very fear?

This fear is salutary and conformable to the spirit of Jesus Christ. Our Divine Master desires that we should fear, and that we should fear not only Hell, but also Purgatory, which is a sort of mitigated Hell. It is to inspire us with this holy fear that He shows us the dungeons of the Supreme Judge, whence we shall not depart until we have paid the last farthing.[1] We may say of the fire of Purgatory that which is said of Hell fire: *Fear ye not them that kill the body and are not able to kill the soul, but rather fear him that can cast both soul and body into Hell.*[2] Yet it is not the intention of our Lord that we should have an excessive and

---

[1] Matt. v. 26.   [2] Matt. x. 28.

barren fear, a fear which tortures and discourages, a gloomy fear without confidence. No; He wishes that our fear should be tempered with great trust in His mercy; He desires that we should fear evil in order to prevent and avoid it; He desires that the thought of those avenging flames should stimulate us to fervour in His service, and cause us to expiate our faults in this world rather than in the other. "*Better is it to purge away our sins, and cut off our vices now,*" says the author of the "Imitation," "*than to keep them for purgation hereafter.*"[1] Moreover, if, notwithstanding our endeavours to live well, and to satisfy for our sins in this world, we have well-grounded fears that we shall have to undergo a Purgatory, we must look forward to that contingency with unbounded confidence in God, who never fails to console those whom He purifies by sufferings.

Now, to give our fear this practical character, this counterpoise of confidence, after having contemplated Purgatory in all the rigour of its pains, we must consider it under another aspect and from a different point of view—that of the Mercy of God, which shines forth therein no less than His Justice.

If God reserves terrible chastisements in the other life for the least faults, He does not inflict them without, at the same time, tempering them with clemency; and nothing shows better the admirable harmony of the Divine perfection than Purgatory, because the most severe Justice is there exercised, together with the most ineffable Mercy. If our Lord chastises those souls that are dear to Him, it is in His love, according to the words, *Such as I love I rebuke and chastise.*[2] With one hand He strikes, with the other He heals. He offers mercy and redemption in abundance: *Quoniam apud Dominum misericordia, et copiosa apud eum redemptio.*[3]

This infinite Mercy of our Heavenly Father must be the firm foundation of our confidence; and, after the

[1] Imit. i. 24.   [2] Apoc. iii. 19.   [3] Ps. cxxix.

example of the saints, we must keep it always before our eyes. The saints never lost sight of it; and it was for this reason that the fear of Purgatory never deprived them of their peace and joy of the Holy Ghost.

St. Lidwina, who so well knew the frightful severity of expiatory suffering, was animated with that spirit of confidence, and endeavoured to inspire others with the same. One time she received a visit from a pious priest. Whilst he was seated at her bedside, together with other virtuous persons, the conversation turned on the sufferings of the other life. Seeing in the hands of a woman a vase filled with grains of mustard-seed, the priest took occasion to remark that he trembled when thinking of the fire of Purgatory. "Nevertheless," he added, "I should be satisfied to go there for as many years as there are grains of seed in this vase; then, at least, I should be certain of my salvation." "What do you say, Father?" replied the saint. "Why so little confidence in the Mercy of God. Ah! if you had a better knowledge of what Purgatory is, of what frightful torments are there endured!" "Let Purgatory be what it may," he replied, "I persist in what I say."

Some time after, this priest died, and the same persons who had been present during this conversation with St. Lidwina, questioning the saint as to his condition in the other world, she replied, "The deceased is well off, on account of his virtuous life; but it would be better for him if he had had more confidence in the Passion of Jesus Christ, and if he had taken a milder view of the subject of Purgatory."

In what consisted this lack of confidence which met the disapproval of our saint? In the opinion which this good priest had that it is almost impossible to be saved, and that we shall enter Heaven only after having undergone innumerable years of torture. This idea is erroneous, and contrary to Christian confidence. Our Saviour came to bring peace to men of good-will, and to impose upon us, as a condition of our salvation, a yoke which is sweet and a burden which is not heavy. Therefore, let your *will* be good, and you will find peace, you will see all difficulties and terrors vanish. *Good-will!* that is everything. Be of good-will, submit to the Will of God, place his Holy Law above all else, serve the Lord with all your heart, and He will give you such powerful assistance that you will enter Paradise with an astonishing facility. I could never have believed, you will say, that it was so easy to enter Heaven! Again, I repeat, to effect in us this wonder of Mercy, God asks on our part an upright heart, *a good-will.*

Good-will consists, properly speaking, in submitting and conforming our will to that of God, who is the rule of all good-will; and this good-will attains its highest perfection when we embrace the Divine Will as the sovereign good, even then when it imposes the greatest sacrifices, the most acute suffering. Oh, admirable state! The soul thus disposed seems to lose the sensation of pain, and this because the soul is animated with the spirit of love; and, as St. Augustine says, when we love we suffer not, or, if we suffer, we love the suffering. *Aut si laboratur, labor ipse amatur.*

Venerable Claude de la Colombière, of the Society of Jesus, possessed this loving heart, this perfect will, and in his *Retrait Spirituelle* he thus expresses his sentiments: —"We must not cease to expiate the past disorders of our life by penance; but it must be done without anxiety, because the worst that can befall us, when our will is good and we are submissive and obedient, is to be sent for a long time to Purgatory, and we may say with good reason that this is a great evil. I do not fear Purgatory. Of Hell I will not speak, for I should wrong the Mercy of God by having the least fear of Hell, although I have merited it more than all the demons together. Purgatory I do not fear. I wish I had not deserved it, since I could not do so without displeasing God; but, as I have merited to go there, I am delighted to go and satisfy His Justice in the most rigorous manner it is possible to imagine, and that even to the Day of Judgment. I know that the torments there endured are horrible, but I know that they honour God, and cannot prove an injury to the souls; that there we are certain never to oppose the will of God; that we shall never resent His severity; that we shall even love the rigours of His justice, and await with patience until it shall be entirely appeased. Therefore, I have given with my whole heart all my satisfactions to the souls in Purgatory, and even bequeath to others all the suffrages which shall be offered for me after my death, in order that God may be glorified in Paradise by souls who shall have merited to be raised to a higher degree of glory than myself."

Behold to what an excess of Charity, the love of God and our neighbour transports us when it has once taken possession of the heart; it transforms, transfigures suffering in such a manner, that all its bitterness is changed into sweetness. "*When thou shalt arrive thus far, that tribulation shall be sweet to thee, and thou shalt relish it for the love of Christ: then think that it is well with thee, for thou hast found a Paradise upon earth*" (Imit. ii. 12). Let us therefore have great love for God, great Charity, and we shall have little fear of Purgatory. The Holy Ghost bears testimony in the depths of our hearts that, being children of God, we have no need to dread the chastisements of a Father.

CHAPTER II.

Confidence—Mercy of God towards Souls—He Consoles them —St. Catherine of Genoa—The Brother of St. Magdalen de Pazzi.

IT is true that all have not attained this high degree of Charity, but there is no one that cannot have confidence in the Divine Mercy. This Mercy is infinite, it imparts peace to all souls that keep it constantly before their eyes and confide therein. Now the Mercy of God is exercised with regard to Purgatory in a threefold manner: (1) in consoling the souls; (2) in mitigating their sufferings; (3) in giving to ourselves a thousand means of avoiding those penal fires. In the first place, God consoles the souls in Purgatory; He Himself consoles them; He also consoles them through the Blessed Virgin and through the holy angels. He consoles the souls by inspiring them with a high degree of faith, hope, and Divine love—virtues which produce in them conformity to the Divine will, resignation, and the most perfect patience. ("God," says St. Catherine of Genoa, "inspires the soul in Purgatory with so ardent a movement of devoted love, that it would be sufficient to annihilate her were she not immortal. Illumined and inflamed by that pure charity, the more she loves God, the more she detests the least stain that displeases Him, the least hindrance that prevents her union with Him. Thus, if she could find another Purgatory more terrible than the one to which she is condemned, that soul would plunge herself therein, impelled by the impetuosity of the love which exists between God and herself, in order that she might be the sooner delivered from all that separates her from her Sovereign God."

"These souls," says again the same saint, "are intimately united to the will of God, and so completely transformed into it, that they are always satisfied with its holy ordinances. The souls in Purgatory have no choice of their own; they can no longer will anything than what God wills. They receive with perfect submission all that God gives them; and neither pleasure, nor contentment, nor pain can ever again make them think of themselves."

St. Magdalen de Pazzi, after the death of one of her brothers, having gone to the choir to offer prayers for him, saw his soul a prey to intense suffering. Touched with compassion, she melted into tears, and cried out in a piteous voice, "Brother, miserable and blessed at the same time! O soul afflicted and yet contented! these pains are intolerable and yet they are endured. Why are they not understood by those here below, who have not the courage to carry their cross? Whilst you were in this world, my dear brother, you would not listen to my advice, and now you desire ardently that I should hear you. O God, equally just and merciful, comfort this brother, who has served you from his infancy. Have regard to your clemency, I beseech you, and make use of your great mercy in his behalf. O God most just, if he has not always been attentive to please you, at least he has not despised those who made profession of serving you with fidelity."

The day on which she had that wonderful ecstasy, during which she visited the different prisons of Purgatory, seeing again the soul of her brother, she said to him, "Poor soul, how you suffer! and nevertheless you rejoice. You burn and you are satisfied, because you know well that these sufferings must lead you to a great and unspeakable felicity. How happy shall I be, should I never have to endure greater suffering! Remain here, my dear brother, and complete your purification in peace."

CHAPTER III.

Consolations of the Souls—St. Stanislaus of Cracow and the Resuscitated Peter Miles.

THIS contentment in the midst of the most intense suffering cannot be explained otherwise than by the Divine consolations which the Holy Ghost infuses into the souls in Purgatory. This Divine Spirit, by means of faith, hope, and charity, puts them in the disposition of a sick person who has to submit to very painful treatment, but the effect of which is to restore him to perfect health. This sick person suffers, but he loves his salutary suffering. The Holy Ghost, the Comforter, gives a similar contentment to the holy souls. Of this we have a striking example in Peter Miles, raised from the dead by St. Stanislaus of Cracow, who preferred to return to Purgatory rather than to live again upon earth.

The celebrated miracle of this resurrection happened in 1070. It is thus related in the *Acta Sanctorum* on May 7. St. Stanislaus was Bishop of Cracow when the Duke Boleslas II. governed Poland. He did not neglect to remind this prince of his duties, who scandalously violated them before all his people.

Boleslas was irritated by the holy liberty of the Prelate, and to revenge himself he excited against him the heirs of a certain Peter Miles, who had died three years previously after having sold a piece of ground to the church of Cracow. The heirs accused the saint of having usurped the ground, without having paid the owner. Stanislaus declared that he had paid for the land, but as the witnesses who should have defended him had been either bribed or intimidated, he was denounced as a usurper of the property of another, and condemned to make restitution. Then, seeing that he had nothing to expect from human justice, he raised his heart to God, and received a sudden inspiration. He asked for a delay of three days, promising to make Peter Miles appear in person, that he might testify to the legal purchase and payment of the lot.

They were granted to him in scorn. The saint fasted, watched, and prayed God to take up the defence of his cause. The third day, after having celebrated Holy Mass, he went out accompanied by his clergy and many of the faithful, to the place where Peter had been interred. By his orders the grave was opened; it contained nothing but bones. He touched them with his crosier, and in the name of Him who is the Resurrection and the Life, he commanded the dead man to arise.

Suddenly the bones became reunited, were covered with flesh, and, in sight of the stupefied people, the dead man was seen to take the Bishop by the hand and walk towards the tribunal. Boleslas, with his court and an immense crowd of people, were awaiting the result with the most lively expectation. "Behold Peter," said the saint to Boleslas; "he comes, prince, to give testimony before you. Interrogate him; he will answer you."

It is impossible to depict the stupefaction of the Duke, of his councillors, and of the whole concourse of people. Peter affirmed that he had been paid for the ground; then turning towards his heirs, he reproached them for having accused the pious prelate against all rights of justice; then he exhorted them to do penance for so grievous a sin.

It was thus that iniquity, which believed itself already sure of success, was confounded. Now comes the circumstance which concerns our subject, and to which we wished to refer. Wishing to complete this great miracle for the glory of God, Stanislaus proposed to the deceased that, if he desired to live a few years longer, he would obtain for him this favour from God. Peter replied that he had no such desire. He was in Purgatory, but he would rather return thither immediately and endure its pains, than expose himself to damnation in this terrestrial life. He entreated the saint only to beg of God to shorten the time of his sufferings, that he might the sooner enter the abode of the blessed. After that, accompanied by the Bishop and a vast multitude, Peter returned to his grave, laid himself down, his body fell to pieces, and his bones resumed the same state in which they had first been found. We have reason to believe that the saint soon obtained the deliverance of his soul.

That which is the most remarkable in this example, and which should most attract our attention, is that a soul from Purgatory, after having experienced the most excruciating torments, prefers that state of suffering to the life of this world; and the reason which he gives for this preference is, that in this mortal life we are exposed to the danger of being lost and incurring eternal damnation.

CHAPTER IV.

Consolations of Souls—St. Catherine de Ricci and the Soul of a Prince.

LET us relate another example of the interior consolations and mysterious contentment which the souls experience in the midst of the most excruciating sufferings: we find it in the Life of St. Catherine de Ricci,[1] a Religious of the Order of St. Dominic, who died in the convent of Prato, February 2, 1590. This servant of God cherished so great a devotion towards the souls in Purgatory that she suffered

[1] Feb. 13.

in their place on earth that which they had to endure in the other world. Among others, she delivered from the expiatory flames the soul of a prince, and suffered the most frightful torments in his place for forty days.

This prince, whose name is not mentioned in history, in consideration, no doubt, of his family, had led a worldly life, and the saint offered many prayers, fasts, and penances that God would enlighten him as to the condition of his soul, and that he might not be condemned. God vouchsafed to hear her, and the unfortunate prince before his death gave evident proofs of a sincere conversion. He died in good sentiments and went to Purgatory. Catherine learned this by Divine revelation in prayer, and offered herself to satisfy Divine Justice for that soul. Our Lord accepted the charitable exchange, received the soul of the prince into glory, and subjected Catherine to pains entirely strange to her for the space of forty days. She was seized with a malady which, according to the judgment of the physicians, was not natural, and could neither be cured nor relieved. According to the testimony of eye-witnesses, the body of the saint was covered with blisters filled with humour and inflammation, like water boiling upon the fire. This occasioned such heat that her cell was like an oven, and seemed filled with fire; it was impossible to remain there for a few moments without going outside to breathe.

It was evident that the flesh of the patient was boiling, and her tongue resembled a piece of red-hot metal. At intervals the inflammation ceased, then the flesh appeared roasted; but soon the blisters arose again and sent forth the same heat.

Nevertheless, in the midst of this torture the saint did not lose the serenity of her countenance nor the peace of her soul; she seemed to rejoice in her torments. Her sufferings sometimes increased to such a degree that she lost her speech for ten or twelve minutes. When her sister Religious told her that she seemed to be on fire, she replied simply, "Yes," without adding anything more. When they represented to her that she carried her zeal too far, and that she ought not to ask of God such excessive suffering, "Pardon me, my dear sisters," she said to them, "if I answer you. Jesus has so much love for souls, that all we do for their salvation is infinitely agreeable to Him; that is why I gladly endure any pain, whatsoever it may be, as well for the conversion of sinners as for the deliverance of the souls detained in Purgatory."

The forty days having expired, Catherine returned to her ordinary state. The relations of the prince asked where his soul was. "Have no fear," she replied; "his soul is in the enjoyment of eternal glory." It was thus known that it was for his soul that she had suffered so much.

This example teaches us many things, but we have cited it to show that the greatest sufferings are not incompatible with interior peace. Our saint, whilst visibly enduring the pains of Purgatory, enjoyed an admirable peace and a superhuman contentment.

CHAPTER V.

Consolations of Souls—The Blessed Virgin—Revelations of St. Bridget—Father Jerome Carvalho—Blessed Renier of Citeaux.

THE souls in Purgatory receive also great consolation from the Blessed Virgin. Is she not the *Consolation of the Afflicted?* and what affliction can be compared to that of the poor souls? Is she not the *Mother of Mercy?* is it not towards these holy suffering souls that she show all the mercy of her heart? We must not, therefore, be astonished that in the "Revelations of St. Bridget" the Queen of Heaven gives herself the beautiful name of Mother of the Souls in Purgatory. "I am," she said to that saint, "the Mother of all those who are in the place of expiation; my prayers mitigate the chastisements which are inflicted upon them for their faults."[1]

On October 25, 1604, in the College of the Society of Jesus at Coimbra, Father Jerome Carvalho died in the odour of sanctity, at the age of fifty years. This admirable and humble servant of God felt a lively apprehension of the sufferings of Purgatory. Neither the cruel macerations which he inflicted upon himself several times every day, not counting those prompted each week by the remembrance of the Passion, nor the six hours which he devoted morning and evening to the meditation of holy subjects, seemed sufficient, in his estimation, to shield him from the chastisement which he imagined awaited him after death. But one day the Queen of Heaven, to whom he had a tender devotion, condescended herself to console her servant by the simple assurance that *she was a Mother of Mercy* to her dear children in Purgatory as well as to those upon earth. Seeking, later, to spread this consoling doctrine, the holy man accidentally let fall, in the ardour of his discourse, these words: "*She told me this herself.*"

It is related that a great servant of Mary, Blessed Renier of Citeaux, trembled at the thought of his sins and the terrible Justice of God after death. In his fear, addressing himself to his great Protectress, who calls herself Mother of Mercy, he was rapt in spirit, and saw the Mother of God supplicating her Son in his favour. "My Son," she said, "deal mercifully with him in Purgatory, because he humbly repents of his sins." "My Mother," replied Jesus, "I place his suffi. in your hands," which meant to say, be it done lost

[1] *Revel. S. Brig.*, lib. iv. c. 50.

to your client according to your desire. Blessed Renier understood with unutterable joy that Mary had obtained his exemption from Purgatory.

CHAPTER VI.

Consolations of Purgatory—The Blessed Virgin Mary—Privilege of Saturday— Venerable Paula of St. Teresa— St. Peter Damian and the Deceased Marozi.

IT is especially on certain days that the Queen of Heaven exercises her mercy in Purgatory. These privileged days are, first, all Saturdays, then the different feast-days of the Blessed Virgin, which thus become as festivals in Purgatory. We see in the revelations of the saints that on Saturday, the day specially consecrated to the Blessed Virgin, the sweet Mother of Mercy descends into the dungeons of Purgatory to visit and console her devoted servants. Then, according to the pious belief of the faithful, she delivers those souls who, having worn the holy scapular, enjoy this Sabbatine privilege, and afterwards gives relief and consolation to other souls who had been particularly devout to her. A witness to this was the Venerable Sister Paula of St. Teresa, a Dominican Religious of the Convent of St. Catherine in Naples.[1]

Being rapt in ecstasy one Saturday, and transported in spirit into Purgatory, she was quite surprised to find it transformed into a Paradise of delights, illuminated by a bright light, instead of the darkness which at other times prevailed. Whilst she was wondering what could be the

[1] Rossign., *Merv.*, 50 ; Marchese, tom. i. p. 56.

cause of this change, she perceived the Queen of Heaven surrounded by a multitude of angels, to whom she gave orders to liberate those souls who had honoured her in a special manner, and conduct them to Heaven.

If such takes place on an ordinary Saturday, we can scarcely doubt that the same occurs on feast-days consecrated to the Mother of God. Among all her festivals, that of the glorious Assumption of Mary seems to be the chief day of deliverance. St. Peter Damian[1] tells us that each year, on the day of the Assumption, the Blessed Virgin delivers several thousands of souls.

The following account of a miraculous vision illustrates this subject:—"It is a pious custom," he says, "which exists among the people of Rome to visit the churches, carrying a candle in the hand, during the night preceding the Feast of the Assumption of Our Lady." Now it happened that a person of rank, being on her knees in the basilica of the Ara-Cœli in the Capitol, saw before her, prostrate in prayer, another lady, her god-mother, who had died several months previous. Surprised, and not being able to believe her eyes, she wished to solve the mystery, and for this purpose placed herself near the door of the church. As soon as she saw the lady go out, she took her by the hand and drew her aside. "Are you not," she said to her, "my god-mother, who held me at the baptismal font?" "Yes," replied the apparition immediately, "it is I." "And how comes it that I find you among the living, since you have been dead more than a year?" "Until this day I have been plunged in a dreadful fire, on account of the many sins of vanity which I committed in my youth, but during this great solemnity the Queen of Heaven descended into the midst of the Purgatorial flames and delivered me, together with a large number of other souls, that we might enter Heaven on the Feast of her Assumption. She exercises this great act of clemency each year;

---
[1] Opusc. xxxiv. c. 3, p. 2.

and, on this occasion alone, the number of those whom she has delivered equals the population of Rome."

Seeing that her god-daughter remained stupefied and seemed still to doubt the evidence of her sense, the apparition added, "In proof of the truth of my words, know that you yourself will die a year hence, on the feast of the Assumption; if you outlive that period, believe that this was an illusion."

St. Peter Damian concluded this recital by saying that the young lady passed the year in the exercise of good works, in order to prepare herself to appear before God. The year following, on the Vigil of the Assumption, she fell sick, and died on the day of the feast itself, as had been predicted.

The feast of the Assumption is, then, the great day of Mary's mercy towards the poor souls; she delights to introduce her children into the glory of Heaven on the anniversary of the day on which she herself first entered its blessed portals. This pious belief, adds Father Louvet, is founded on a great number of particular revelations; it is for this reason that in Rome the Church of St. Mary in Montorio, which is the centre of the arch-confraternity of *suffrages for the dead*, is dedicated under the title of the Assumption.

CHAPTER VII.

Consolations of Purgatory—The Angels—St. Bridget—Venerable Paula of St. Teresa—Brother Peter of Basto.

BESIDES the consolations which the souls receive from the Blessed Virgin, they are also assisted and consoled by the holy angels, and especially by their guardian-angels. The doctors of the Church teach that the tutelary mission of the guardian-angel terminates only on the entrance of their clients into Paradise. If, at the moment of death, a soul in the state of grace is not yet worthy to see the face of the Most High, the angel-guardian conducts it to the place of expiation, and remains there with her to procure for her all the assistance and consolations in his power.

It is an opinion common among the holy doctors, says Father Rossignoli, that God, who will one day send forth His angels to assemble the elect, also sends them from time to time into Purgatory, there to visit and console the suffering souls. No doubt there cannot be any relief more precious than the sight of the inhabitants of Heaven, that blessed abode whither they will one day go to enjoy its glorious and eternal felicity. The Revelations of St. Bridget are filled with examples of this nature, and the Lives of several saints also furnish a great number. Venerable Sister Paula of St. Teresa, of whom we have spoken above, had an extraordinary devotion towards the Church suffering, for which she was rewarded here below with miraculous visions. One day, whilst saying a fervent prayer for this intention, she was transported in spirit into Purgatory, where she saw a great number of souls plunged in flames. Close to them she saw our Saviour, attended by His angels, who pointed out, one after the other, several souls which He desired to take to Heaven, whither they ascended in transports of unutterable joy. At this sight the servant of God, addressing herself to her Divine Spouse, said to Him, "O Jesus, why this choice among such a vast multitude?" "I have released," He deigned to reply, "those who during life performed great acts of charity and mercy, and who have merited that I should fulfil my promise in their regard, *Blessed are the merciful, for they shall obtain mercy.*"[1]

[1] *Merv.*, 50.

In the Life of the servant of God, Peter de Basto, we find an example which shows how the holy angels, even whilst they are watching over us upon earth, interest themselves in behalf of the souls in Purgatory. And since we have mentioned the name of Brother de Basto, we cannot resist the desire to make known this admirable Religious to our readers; his history is as interesting as it is edifying.

Peter de Basto, brother coadjutor of the Society of Jesus, and whom his biographer calls the Alphonsus Rodriguez of Malabar, died in the odour of sanctity at Cochin, March 1, 1645. He was born in Portugal, of the illustrious family of Machado, united by blood to all the nobility of the whole province between the Douro and the Minho. The Dukes of Pastrano and Hixar were among the number of his relatives, and the world held out to him a career of the most brilliant prospects. But God had reserved him for Himself, and had endowed him with the most marvellous spiritual gifts. Whilst still a very little child, when taken to the church, he prayed before the Blessed Sacrament with the fervour of an angel. He believed that all the people saw as he did, with the eyes of the body, the legions of celestial spirits in adoration near the altar and the tabernacle, and from that time forward the Saviour, hidden under the Eucharistic veil, became by excellence the centre of all his affections and the innumerable prodigies which characterised his long and holy life.

It was there that, later, as in a divine sun, he discovered without veils the future and its most unforeseen details. It was there also that God showed him the mysterious symbols of a ladder of gold which united heaven and earth, supported by the tabernacle, and of the lily of purity shooting forth its roots and drawing its nourishment from the flour of the wheat of the elect and the wine which alone can bring forth virgins.

Towards his seventeenth year, thanks to that purity of

heart and that strength of which the Sacrament of the Eucharist was for him the inexhaustible source, Peter made at Lisbon a vow of perpetual chastity at the feet of Our Lady of Perpetual Succour. He did not yet, however, think of quitting the world, and some days later embarked for the Indies, and for two years followed the military profession.

But at the end of that time, on the point of perishing by shipwreck, being tossed about at the mercy of the waves for five entire days, supported and saved by the Queen of Heaven and her Divine Son, who appeared to him, he promised to consecrate himself entirely to their service in the religious state for the remainder of his life. As soon as he returned to Goa, being then but nineteen years of age, he went and offered himself in the quality of lay brother to the Superiors of the Society of Jesus. Fearing that his name might procure for him some mark of distinction or esteem, he adopted henceforward that of the humble village where he had received baptism, and was called simply Peter de Basto.

It was a short time afterwards, during one of the trials of his novitiate, that this wonderful incident occurred which is recorded in the Annals of the Society, and which is so consoling for all the children of St. Ignatius. Brother Peter's novice-master sent him on a pilgrimage with two young companions in the island of Salsette, ordering them not to accept hospitality from any of the missionaries, but to beg from village to village for their daily bread and their night's lodging. One day, fatigued with their long journey, they met a humble family, consisting of an old man, a woman, and a little child, who received them with the greatest charity, and pressed them to partake of a frugal repast. But at the moment of the departure, after having returned them a thousand thanks, when Peter de Basto begged his hosts to tell him their names, wishing, no doubt, to recommend them to God, "We are," replied the mother, "the three founders of the Society of Jesus," and all three disappeared at the same instant.

The whole religious life of this holy man until his death —that is to say, almost fifty-six years—was but a tissue of wonders and extraordinary graces; but we must add that he merited them, and purchased them, so to say, at the price of virtue, labours, and the most heroic sacrifices. Charged by turns with care of the laundry, the kitchen, or the door, in the colleges of Goa, of Tuticurin, of Coulao, and of Cochin, Peter never sought to withdraw himself from the hardest labours, nor to reserve a little leisure time at the expense of his different offices that he might enjoy the delights of prayer. Serious infirmities, the sole cause of which was excessive labour, were, he said smilingly, his most pleasant distractions. Moreover, abandoned, so to speak, to the fury of the demon, the servant of God enjoyed scarcely any repose. These spirits of darkness appeared to him under the most hideous forms. They often beat him severely, especially at that hour each night when, as was his custom, he interrupted his sleep to go and pray before the Blessed Sacrament.

One day whilst travelling, his companions fled at the sound of a troop of formidable-looking men, horses, and elephants, who appeared to approach them with furious gestures. He alone remained calm; and when his companions expressed their astonishment that he had not manifested the least sign of fear, he replied, "If God does not permit the demons to exercise their rage against us, what have we to fear? and if He gives them the permission, why then should I endeavour to escape their blows?" He had only to invoke the Queen of Heaven, when she appeared immediately and put the infernal troop to flight.

Often it seemed as though all was confusion, even to the very depths of his soul, and he found calm, peace, and victory only near his ordinary refuge, Jesus present in the Holy Eucharist. Loaded one day with outrages, which caused him some little disturbance, he prostrated himself at the foot of the altar and asked of our Divine Saviour the gift of patience. Then our Lord appeared to him covered with wounds, a purple mantle about His shoulders, a rope around His neck, a reed in His hands, and a crown of thorns upon His head; then addressing Himself to Peter, He said, "See what the true Son of God has suffered to teach men how to suffer."

But we have not touched the point we wished to illustrate by this holy life—I mean to say, the devotion of Peter de Basto towards the souls in Purgatory, a devotion encouraged and seconded by his good angel-guardian. Notwithstanding his numerous labours, he daily recited the rosary for the dead. One day having forgotten it, he retired without having recited it, but scarcely had he fallen asleep when he was awakened by his angel. "My son," said this heavenly spirit, "the souls in Purgatory await the benefit of your daily alms." Peter arose instantly to fulfil that duty of piety."[1]

CHAPTER VIII.

Consolations of Purgatory—The Angels—Blessed Emilia of Vercelli—The Saints in Heaven.

IF the holy angels interest themselves in behalf of the souls of Purgatory in general, it is easy to understand that they have particular zeal for those of their clients. In the convent of Vercelli, where Blessed Emilia,[2] a Dominican Religious, was Prioress, it was a point of the Rule never to drink between meals, unless with express permission of the Superior. This permission the Blessed Prioress was not

[1] *Menol. de la Comp. de Jésus.*   [2] Aug. 17.

accustomed to accord; she advised her sisters to make that little sacrifice cheerfully, in memory of the burning thirst which our Saviour had endured for our salvation upon the cross; and to encourage them to do this, she suggested to them to confide those few drops of water to their guardian-angels, that he might preserve them until the other life, to temper the heat of Purgatory. The following incident shows how agreeable this pious practice was to God.

A sister named Cecilia Avogadra came one day to ask permission to refresh herself with a little water, for she was parched with thirst. "My daughter," said the Prioress, "make this little sacrifice for the love of God and in consideration of Purgatory." "Mother, this sacrifice is not little; I am dying with thirst," replied the good sister; nevertheless, although somewhat grieved, she obeyed the advice of her Superior. This double act of obedience and mortification was precious in the sight of God, and Sister Cecilia soon received its reward. A few weeks later she died, and after three days she appeared, resplendent in glory, to Mother Emilia. "O Mother!" she said, "how grateful I am to you! I was condemned to a long Purgatory for having had too great affection for my family, and behold, after two days, I saw my angel-guardian enter my prison, holding in his hand the glass of water which you caused me to offer as a sacrifice to my Divine Spouse; he poured that water upon the flames which devoured me, they were extinguished immediately, and I am delivered. I take my flight to Heaven, where my gratitude will never forget you."

It is thus that the angels of God console the souls in Purgatory. It may be here asked how the saints and blessed already crowned in Heaven can assist them? It is certain, says Father Rossignoli, and such is the teaching of all masters in theology, St. Augustine and St. Thomas, that the saints are very powerful in this respect by way of

K

supplication, or, as we say, by *impetration*, but not by *satisfaction*. In other words, the saints in Heaven may pray for the souls, and thus *obtain* from Divine Mercy a diminution of their suffering; but they cannot *satisfy* for them, nor pay their debts to Divine Justice; that is a privilege which God reserves to the Church Militant.

CHAPTER IX.

Assistance given the Holy Souls—Suffrages—Meritorious, Impetratory, and Satisfactory Works—God's Mercy— St. Gertrude—Judas Machabeus.

If God consoles the souls with so much goodness, His mercy shines forth still more clearly in the power which He gives to His Church to shorten the duration of their sufferings. Desiring to execute with clemency the severe sentence of His Justice, He accords abatement and mitigation of the pain; but He does so in an indirect manner through the intervention of the living. To us He gives all power to succour our afflicted brethren by way of *suffrage*, that is to say, by means of *impetration* and *satisfaction*.

The word *suffrage* in ecclesiastical language is a synonym of *prayer;* yet, when the Council of Trent declares that the souls in Purgatory are assisted by *the suffrages of the faithful*, the sense of the word is more comprehensive; it includes in general all that we can offer to God in behalf of the departed. Now, we can thus offer to God, not only our prayers, but all our good works, in so far as they are *impetratory* or *satisfactory*.

To understand these terms, let us recall to mind that

each of our good works, performed in the state of grace, ordinarily possesses a triple value in the sight of God.

1. The work is *meritorious*, that is to say, it increases our merit; it gives us right to a new degree of glory in Heaven.

2. It is *impetratory* (impetrate, obtain), that is to say, that, like a prayer, it has the virtue of obtaining some grace from God.

3. It is *satisfactory*, that is to say, that as having, as it were, a pecuniary value, it can satisfy Divine Justice and pay our debts of temporal punishment before God.

The *merit* is inalienable, and remains the property of the person who performs the action. On the contrary, the impetratory and satisfactory value can benefit others, in virtue of the communion of saints. This understood, let us put this practical question—What are *suffrages* by which, according to the doctrine of the Church, we may aid the souls in Purgatory?

To this question we answer: They consist of prayers, alms, fasts, and penances of any kind, indulgences, and above all the Holy Sacrifice of the Mass. All the works performed in the state of grace Jesus Christ allows us to offer to the Divine Majesty for the relief of our brethren in Purgatory, and God applies them to those souls according to His Justice and Mercy. By this admirable arrangement, whilst protecting the rights of His Justice, our Heavenly Father multiplies the effects of His Mercy, which is thus exercised at the same time in favour of the Church Suffering and of the Church Militant. The merciful assistance which He allows us to give to our suffering brethren is of excellent profit to ourselves. It is a work not only advantageous to the departed, but also holy and salutary for the living. *Sancta et salubris est cogitatio pro defunctis exorare.*

We read in the Revelations of St. Gertrude[1] that a

---

[1] *Legatus Div. Pietatis*, lib. v. c. 5.

humble Religious of her community, having crowned an exemplary life with a very pious death, God deigned to show the saint the state of the deceased in the other life. Gertrude saw her soul adorned with ineffable beauty, and dear to Jesus, who regarded her with love. Nevertheless, on account of some slight negligence not yet atoned for, she could not enter Heaven, but was obliged to descend into the dismal abode of suffering. Scarcely had she disappeared into its depths, when the saint saw her come forth and rise towards Heaven, transported thither by the suffrages of the Church. *Ecclesiæ precibus sursum ferri.*

Even in the Old Law prayers and sacrifices were offered for the dead. Holy Scripture relates as praiseworthy the pious action of Judas Machabeus after his victory over Gorgias, general of King Antiochus. The soldiers had committed a fault by taking from among the spoils some objects offered to the idols, which by law they were forbidden to do. Then Judas, chief of the army of Israel, ordered prayers and sacrifices for the remission of their sin, and for the repose of their souls. Let us see how this fact is related in Scripture (2 Machab. xii. 39).

"After the Sabbath, Judas went with his company to take away the bodies of them that were slain, and to bury them with their kinsmen in the sepulchres of their fathers.

"And they found under the coats of the slain some of the donaries of the idols of Jamnia, which the law forbiddeth to the Jews; so that all plainly saw that for this cause they were slain.

"Then they all blessed the just judgment of the Lord, who had discovered the things that were hidden.

"And so betaking themselves to prayers, they besought Him that the sin which had been committed might be forgotten. But the most valiant Judas exhorted the people to keep themselves from sin, for so much as they saw before their eyes what had happened, because of the sin of those that were slain.

"And making a gathering, he sent twelve thousand drachms of silver to Jerusalem for sacrifice to be offered for the sins of the dead, thinking well and religiously concerning the resurrection.

"(For if he had not hoped that they that were slain should rise again, it would have seemed superfluous and vain to pray for the dead. And because he considered that they who had fallen asleep with godliness had great grace laid up for them.)

"It is therefore a holy and wholesome thought to pray for the dead, that they may be loosed from sins."

CHAPTER X.

Assistance given to the Holy Souls—Holy Mass— St. Augustine and St. Monica.

IN the New Law we have the Holy Sacrifice of the Mass, of which the divers sacrifices of the Mosaic Law were but feeble figures. The Son of God instituted it, not only as a worthy homage given by the creature to the Divine Majesty, but also as *a propitiation* for the living and the dead; that is to say, as an efficacious means of appeasing the Justice of God, provoked by our sins.

The Holy Sacrifice of the Mass was celebrated for the departed, even from the time of the foundation of the Church. "We celebrate the anniversary of the triumph of the martyrs," writes Tertullian in the third century,[1] "and, according to the tradition of our fathers, we offer the Holy

[1] *De Corona,* c. 5.

Sacrifice for the departed on the anniversary of their death."

"It cannot be doubted," writes St. Augustine,[1] "that the prayers of the Church, the Holy Sacrifice, and alms distributed for the departed, relieve those holy souls, and move God to treat them with more clemency than their sins deserve. It is the universal practice of the Church, a practice which she observes as having received it from her forefathers—that is to say, the holy Apostles."

St. Monica, the worthy mother of St. Augustine, when about to expire, asked but one thing of her son, that he would remember her at the altar of God; and the holy Doctor, when relating that touching circumstance in the Book of his Confessions,[2] entreats all his readers to unite with him in recommending her to God during the Holy Sacrifice of the Mass.

Wishing to return to Africa, St. Monica went with St. Augustine to Ostia, in order to embark; but she fell sick, and soon felt that her end was approaching. "It is here," said she to her son, "that you will give burial to your mother. The one thing I ask of you is that you will be mindful of me at the altar of the Lord." *Ut ad altare Domini memineritis mei.*

"May I be pardoned for the tears I then shed, for that death should not be mourned which was but the entrance to true life. Yet, considering with the eyes of faith the miseries of our fallen nature, I might shed before you, O Lord, other tears than those of the flesh, tears which flow at the thought of the peril to which every soul is exposed that has sinned in Adam.

"It is certain that my mother lived in such manner as to give glory to your Name, by the activity of her faith and the purity of her morals; yet dare I affirm that no word contrary to Thy law has ever escaped her lips? Alas! what will become of the holiest life if Thou dost examine

[1] Serm. 34, *De Verbis Apost.*   [2] Liv. ix. c. 12.

it in all the rigours of Thy justice? For this reason, O God of my heart, I leave aside the good works which my mother has performed to ask of Thee only the pardon of her sins. Hear me, by the wounds of Him who died for us upon the cross, and who, now seated at Thy right hand, is our Mediator.

"I know that my mother always showed mercy, that she pardoned from her heart all offences, and forgave all the debts owing to her. Cancel then her debts, if during the course of her long life there are any owing to Thee. Pardon her, O Lord, pardon her, and enter not into judgment against her; for Thy words are true; Thou hast promised mercy to the merciful.

"This mercy, I believe, Thou hast already shown to her, O my God; but accept the homage of my prayer. Remember that on her passage to the other life Thy servant desired for her body neither pompous funeral nor precious perfumes, she asked not a magnificent tomb, nor that she should be carried to that she had caused to be constructed at Tagaste, her native place; but only that we should remember her at Thy altar, whose mysteries she prized.

"Thou knowest, Lord, all the days of her life she took part in those Divine Mysteries which contain the Holy Victim whose blood has effaced the sentence of our condemnation. Let her repose then in peace with my father, her husband, with the spouse to whom she was faithful during all the days of her union, and in the sorrows of her widowhood with him whose humble servant she made herself, to win him for Thee by her meekness and patience. And Thou, O my God, inspire Thy servants, who are my brethren, inspire all those who read these lines to remember at Thy altar Monica, Thy servant, and Patricius, who was her spouse; that all who still live in the false light of this world may piously remember my parents, that the last prayer of my dying mother may be heard beyond her expectations."

This beautiful passage of St. Augustin shows us the opinion of this great Doctor on the subject of suffrages for the departed, and it makes us see clearly that the greatest of all suffrages is the Holy Sacrifice of the Mass.

CHAPTER XI.

Assistance rendered to the Souls—Holy Mass—Jubilee of Leo XIII.—Solemn Commemoration of the Dead on the Last Sunday in September.

WE have witnessed the holy enthusiasm with which the Church celebrated the Sacerdotal Jubilee of her venerated Head, Pope Leo XIII. The faithful from all parts of the world went to Rome, either in person or in heart, to offer their homage and gifts at the feet of the Vicar of Jesus Christ. The entire Church Militant rejoiced in the midst of her long trials.

The Church Triumphant in Heaven shared in this rejoicing by the canonisation and beatification of a large number of her glorious members. Was it not fitting that the Church Suffering should also participate therein?

Could our dear brethren in Purgatory be forgotten? Should not those souls so dear to the heart of Jesus also experience the happy effects of that glorious feast?

Leo XIII. understood this. Always guided by the Holy Spirit, when acting as Supreme Pastor, the Pope, by an Encyclical Letter, dated April 1, 1888, decreed that, throughout the entire Christian world, there should be a solemn *Commemoration of the Dead* on the last Sunday of the month of September. Calling to mind with what admirable love the Church Militant has manifested her joy, and how the Church Triumphant rejoiced with her. "To crown, in a certain sense," says our Holy Father, "this general exultation, we desire to fulfil, as perfectly as possible, the duty of our apostolic charity by extending the fulness of infinite spiritual treasures to those beloved sons of the Church who, having died the death of the just, have quitted this life of combat with the sign of faith, and have become offshoots of the mystic vine, although they are not permitted to enter into eternal peace until they shall have paid the last farthing of the debt which they owe to the avenging justice of God.

"We are moved thereto both by the pious desires of Catholics, to whom we know our resolution will be particularly dear, and by the agonising intensity of the pains suffered by the departed souls; but we are especially inspired by the custom of the Church, who, in the midst of the most joyful solemnities of the year, forgets not the holy and salutary commemoration of the dead that they may be loosed from their sins.

"For this reason, since it is certain from Catholic doctrine that the souls detained in Purgatory are relieved by the suffrages of the faithful, and especially by the august Sacrifice of the Altar, we think we can give no more useful nor more desirable pledge of our love than by everywhere multiplying, for the mitigation of their pains, the pure oblation of the Holy Sacrifice of our Divine Mediator.

"We therefore appoint, with all necessary dispensations and derogations, *the last Sunday of the month of September next* as a day of ample expiation; on which day there shall be celebrated by us, and likewise by our brethren the Patriarchs, Archbishops, Bishops, and by all other Prelates exercising jurisdiction in a diocese, each in his own patriarchal church, metropolitan or cathedral, a special mass for the dead, with all possible solemnity, and according to the rite indicated by the missal for the *Com-*

memoration of all the Faithful Departed. We approve that the same be done in the parochial and collegiate churches, secular as well as regular, provided the Office proper for the Mass of the day everywhere where such obligation exists be not omitted.

"As regards the faithful, we earnestly exhort them, after having received the Sacrament of Penance, to devoutly nourish themselves with the bread of angels by way of suffrage for the souls in Purgatory.

"By our apostolic authority, to those of the faithful who do so we grant a plenary indulgence, to be applied to the souls departed, and the favour of the privileged altar to all those who, as we have said above, shall celebrate Mass.

"Thus the holy souls who expiate the remains of their faults by those sharp pains will receive special and efficacious relief, thanks to the Saving Host which the Universal Church, united to her visible Head, and animated with the same spirit of charity, will offer to God, that He may admit them into the abode of consolation, of light, and of eternal peace.

"Meanwhile, venerable brethren, we grant you affectionately in the Lord, as a pledge of these heavenly gifts, the apostolic benediction to you, to all the clergy, and to all the people confided to your care.

"Given at Rome, under the seal of the Fisherman, on the solemnity of Easter, in the year 1888, the eleventh of our Pontificate."

CHAPTER XII.

Means of Assisting the Souls in Purgatory—Holy Mass— The Religious of Citeaux delivered by the Sacred Host —Blessed Henry Suzo.

No; of all that we can do in favour of the souls in Purgatory, there is nothing more precious than the immolation of our Divine Saviour upon the altar. Besides being the express doctrine of the Church, manifested in her Councils, many miraculous facts, properly authenticated, leave no room for doubt in regard to this point. We have already spoken of the Religious who was delivered from Purgatory by the prayers of St. Bernard and his community. This Religious, whose regularity was not all that could be desired, had appeared after his death to ask the assistance of St. Bernard. The holy Abbot, with all his fervent disciples, hastened to offer prayers, fasts, and Masses for the poor departed brother. The latter was speedily delivered, and appeared, full of gratitude, to an aged Religious of the community who had specially interested himself in his behalf. Questioned as to the suffrage which had been most profitable to him, instead of replying, he took the old man by the hand, and, conducting him to the church where Mass was being celebrated, "Behold," said he, pointing to the altar, "the great redeeming power which has broken my chains; behold the price of my ransom: it is the Saving Host, which takes away the sins of the world." [1]

Here is another incident, related by the historian Ferdinand of Castile, and quoted by Father Rossignoli. There was at Cologne, among the students in the higher

[1] L'Abbé Postel, *Le Purgatoire,* chap. v.; cf. Rossign., *Merv.*, 47.

classes of the university, two Dominican Religious of distinguished talent, one of whom was Blessed Henry Suzo.[1] The same studies, the same kind of life, and above all the same relish for sanctity, had caused them to contract an intimate friendship, and they mutually imparted the favours which they received from Heaven.

When they had finished their studies, seeing that they were about to be separated, to return each one to his own convent, they agreed and promised one another that the first of the two who should die should be assisted by the other for a whole year by the celebration of two Masses each week—on Monday a Mass of Requiem, as was customary, and on Friday that of the Passion, in so far as the Rubrics would permit. They engaged to do this, gave each other the kiss of peace, and left Cologne.

For several years they both continued to serve God with the most edifying fervour. The brother whose name is not mentioned was the first to be called away, and Suzo received the tidings with the most perfect sentiments of resignation to the Divine will. As to the contract they had made, time had caused him to forget it. He prayed much for his friend, imposing new penances upon himself, and many other good works, but he did not think of offering the Masses which he had promised.

One morning, whilst meditating in retirement in the chapel, he suddenly saw appear before him the soul of his departed friend, who, regarding him with tenderness, reproached him with having been unfaithful to his word, given and accepted, and which he had a perfect right to rely upon with confidence. Blessed Suzo, surprised, excused his forgetfulness by enumerating the prayers and mortifications which he had offered, and still continued to offer, for his friend, whose salvation was as dear to him as his own. "Is it possible, my dear brother," he added, "that so many prayers and good works which I have offered

[1] Jan. 25.

to God do not suffice for you?" "Oh! no," dear brother, replied the suffering soul, "that is not sufficient. It is the Blood of Jesus Christ that is needed to extinguish the flames by which I am consumed; it is the August Sacrifice which will deliver me from these frightful torments. I implore you to keep your word, and refuse me not that which in justice you owe me."

Blessed Suzo hastened to respond to the appeal of the suffering soul; and, to repair his fault, he celebrated, and caused to be celebrated, more Masses than he had promised.

On the following day several priests, at the request of Suzo, united with him in offering the Holy Sacrifice for the deceased, and continued this act of charity for several days.

After some time the friend of Suzo again appeared to him, but now in a very different condition; his countenance was joyful, and surrounded with beautiful light. "Oh! thanks, my faithful friend," said he; "behold, by the Blood of my Saviour I am delivered from my sufferings. I am now going to Heaven to contemplate Him whom we so often adored together under the Eucharistic veil." Suzo prostrated himself to thank the God of all mercy, and understood more than ever the inestimable value of the August Sacrifice of the Altar.[1]

[1] Rossignoli, *Merv.*, 34, and Ferdinand de Castile.

CHAPTER XIII.

Relief of the Souls—Holy Mass—St. Elizabeth and Queen Constance — St. Nicholas of Tolentino and Pellegrino d'Osima.

WE read in the Life of St. Elizabeth of Portugal[1] that after the death of her daughter Constance she learned the pitiful state of the deceased in Purgatory and the price which God exacted for her ransom. The young princess had been married but a short time previous to the King of Castile, when she was snatched away by sudden death from the affection of her family and her subjects. Elizabeth had just received these tidings, and set out with the King, her husband, for the city of Santarem, when a hermit, coming forth from his solitude, ran after the royal cortège, crying that he wished to speak to the Queen. The guards repulsed him, but the saint, seeing that he persisted, gave orders that the servant of God should be brought to her.

As soon as he came into her presence, he related that more than once whilst he was praying in his hermitage Queen Constance had appeared to him, urgently entreating him to make known to her mother that she was languishing in the depths of Purgatory, that she was condemned to long and terrible suffering, but that she would be delivered if for the space of a year the Holy Sacrifice of the Mass was celebrated for her every day. The courtiers who heard this communication ridiculed him aloud, and treated the hermit as a visionary, an impostor, or a fool.

As to Elizabeth, she turned towards the King and asked him what he thought of it? "I believe," replied the

[1] July 8.

Prince, "that it is wise to do that which has been pointed out to you in so extraordinary a manner. After all, to have Masses celebrated for our dear deceased relatives is nothing more than a paternal and Christian duty." A holy priest, Ferdinand Mendez, was appointed to say the Masses.

At the end of the year Constance appeared to St. Elizabeth, clad in a brilliant white robe. "To-day, dear mother," said she, "I am delivered from the pains of Purgatory, and am about to enter Heaven." Filled with consolation and joy, the saint went to the church to return thanks to God. There she found the priest Mendez, who assured her that on the previous day he had finished the celebration of the three hundred and sixty-five Masses with which he had been charged. The Queen then understood that God had kept the promise which He had made to the pious hermit, and she testified her gratitude by distributing abundant alms to the poor.

But thou hast saved us from them that afflict us, and thou hast put them to shame that hate us (Ps. xliii.). Such were the words addressed to the illustrious St. Nicholas of Tolentino by the souls that he had delivered in offering for them the Holy Sacrifice of the Mass. One of the greatest virtues of that admirable servant of God, says Father Rossignoli,[1] was his charity, his devotion to the Church Suffering. For her he frequently fasted on bread and water, inflicted cruel disciplines upon himself, and wore about his loins a chain of sharp-pointed iron. When the sanctuary was thrown open to him, and his superiors wished to confer the priesthood upon him, he hesitated a long time before that sublime dignity, and nothing could make him decide to receive holy orders but the thought that by daily celebrating the Holy Sacrifice he could most efficaciously assist the suffering souls in Purgatory. On their part, the souls whom he relieved by so many suffrages

[1] *Merv.*, 21. *Vie de St. Nic. de Tolentino*, Sept. 10.

appeared to him several times to thank him or to recommend themselves to his charity.

He lived near Pisa, entirely occupied with his spiritual exercises, when one Saturday during the night he saw in a dream a soul in pain, who besought him to celebrate Holy Mass on the following morning for her and several other souls that suffered most terribly in Purgatory. Nicholas recognised the voice, but could distinctly call to mind the person who spoke to him. "I am," said the apparition, "your deceased friend Pellegrino d'Osimo. By the Divine Mercy I have escaped eternal chastisement by repentance; not so the temporal punishment due to my sins. I come in the name of many souls as unfortunate as myself to entreat you to offer Holy Mass for us to-morrow; from it we expect our deliverance, or at least great alleviation." The saint replied, with his usual kindness, "May our Lord deign to relieve you by the merits of His precious Blood! But this Mass for the dead I cannot say to-morrow; I must sing the Conventual Mass in choir." "Ah! at least come with me," cried the departed soul, amid sighs and tears; "I conjure you, for the love of God, come and behold our sufferings, and you will no longer refuse; you are too good to leave us in such frightful agonies."

Then it seemed to him that he was transported into Purgatory. He saw an immense plain, where a vast multitude of souls, of all ages and conditions, were a prey to divers tortures most horrible to behold. By gestures and by words they implored most piteously his assistance. "Behold," said Pellegrino, "the state of those who sent me to you. Since you are agreeable in the sight of God, we have confidence that He will refuse nothing to the oblation of the Sacrifice offered by you, and that His Divine Mercy will deliver us."

At this pitiful sight the saint could not repress his tears. He immediately betook himself to prayer, to console them in their sorrow, and the following morning went to the Prior, relating to him the vision he had had, and the request made by Pellegrino concerning the Mass for that day. The Father Prior, sharing his emotion, dispensed him for that day, and for the rest of the week, from saying the conventual Mass, that he might offer the Holy Sacrifice for the departed, and devote himself entirely to the relief of the suffering souls. Delighted with this permission, Nicholas went to the church and celebrated Holy Mass with extraordinary fervour. During the entire week he continued to celebrate the Holy Sacrifice for the same intention, besides offering day and night prayers, disciplines, and all sorts of good works.

At the end of the week Pellegrino again appeared, but no longer in a state of suffering; he was clad in a white garment and surrounded with a celestial light, in which he pointed out a large number of happy souls. They all thanked him, calling him their liberator; then rising towards heaven, they chanted these words of the Psalmist, *Salvasti nos de affligentibus nos, et odientes nos confudisti*— "Thou hast saved us from them that afflict us, and thou hast put them to shame that hate us" (Ps. xliii.) The enemies here spoken of are sins, and the demons who are their instigators.

CHAPTER XIV.

Relief of the Holy Souls—Holy Mass—Father Gerard— The Thirty Masses of St. Gregory.

LET us now consider the supernatural effects of a different kind, but which prove no less clearly the efficacy of the
L

Holy Sacrifice of the Mass offered for the departed. We find them in the Memoirs of Father Gerard, an English Jesuit and Confessor of the Faith during the persecutions in England in the sixteenth century. After relating how he had received the abjuration of a Protestant gentleman, married to one of his cousins, Father Gerard adds, " This conversion led to another under the most extraordinary circumstances. My new convert went to see one of his friends who was dangerously ill. This was an upright man, detained in heresy more by illusion than by any other motive. The visitor urgently exhorted him to be converted, and to think of his soul ; and obtained from him the promise that he would make his confession. He instructed him in everything, taught him how to excite himself to contrition for his sins, and went to seek for a priest. He had great difficulty in finding one, and in the meantime the sick person died. When about to expire, the poor dying man asked frequently whether his friend had not yet returned with the physician whom he had promised to bring ; it was thus he called the Catholic priest.

"What followed showed that God had accepted the good-will of the deceased. The nights following his death, his wife, a Protestant, saw a light moving in her room, and which came even within the curtains of her bed. Being afraid, she desired one of her servant-maids to sleep in her room; but the latter saw nothing, although the light continued to be visible to the eyes of her mistress. The poor lady sent for the friend whose return her husband had awaited with so much anxiety, related to him what had happened, and asked what was to be done.

" This friend before giving an answer consulted a Catholic priest. The priest told him that the light was, for the wife of the deceased, a supernatural sign by which God invited her to return to the true faith. The lady was deeply impressed by these words ; she opened her heart to grace, and in her turn was converted.

"Once a Catholic, she had Mass celebrated in her chamber for some time; but the light always returned. The priest considering these circumstances before God, thought that the deceased, though saved by his repentance accompanied by the desire of confession, was in Purgatory, and stood in need of prayers. He advised the lady to have Mass said for him during thirty days, according to an ancient custom of English Catholics. The good widow followed this advice, and on the thirtieth day, instead of one light, saw three, two of which seemed to support another. The three lights hovered over her bed, then rose heavenward, never more to return. These three lights appear to have signified the three conversions, and the efficacy of the Holy Sacrifice of the Mass to open Heaven to the departed souls."

The thirty Masses which were said for thirty consecutive days is not an English custom only, as it is called by Father Gerard, it is also widely spread in Italy and other Christian countries. These Masses are called the *Thirty Masses of St. Gregory*, because the pious custom seems to trace its origin back to this great Pope. It is thus related in his "Dialogues" (Book iv. chap. xl.):—A Religious, named Justus, had received and kept for himself three gold pieces. This was a grievous fault against his vow of poverty. He was discovered and excommunicated. This salutary penalty made him enter into himself, and some time afterwards he died in true sentiments of repentance. Nevertheless, St. Gregory, in order to inspire the brethren with a lively horror of the sin of avarice in a Religious, did not withdraw the sentence of excommunication: Justus was buried apart from the other monks, and the three pieces of money were thrown into the grave, whilst the Religious repeated altogether the words of St. Peter to Simon the Magician, *Pecunia tua tecum sit in perditionem* —" Keep thy money to perish with thee."

Some time afterwards, the holy Abbot, judging that the

scandal was sufficiently repaired, and moved with compassion for the soul of Justus, called the Procurator and said to him sorrowfully, "Ever since the moment of his death, our brother has been tortured in the flames of Purgatory; we must through charity make an effort to deliver him. Go, then, and take care that from this time forward the Holy Sacrifice be offered for thirty days; let not one morning pass without the Victim of Salvation being offered up for his release."

The Procurator obeyed punctually. The thirty Masses were celebrated in the course of thirty days. When the thirtieth day arrived and the thirtieth Mass was ended, the deceased appeared to a brother named Copiosus, saying, "Bless God, my dear brother, to-day I am delivered and admitted into the society of the saints."

Since that time the pious custom of celebrating thirty Masses for the dead has been established.

CHAPTER XV.

Relief of the Holy Souls—Eugenie Wybo—Lacordaire and the Polish Prince.

NOTHING is more conformable to the Christian spirit than to have the Holy Sacrifice offered up for the relief of the souls departed, and it would be a great misfortune should the zeal of the faithful cool in this respect. God seems to multiply prodigies in order to prevent us from falling into so fatal a relaxation. The following incident is attested by a worthy priest of the diocese of Bruges, who received it from its primitive source, and whose testimony bears all the certainty of an eye-witness with regard to the fact:—

PURGATORY, THE MYSTERY OF MERCY. 165

On October 13, 1849, there died at the age of fifty-two, in the parish of Ardoye, in Flanders, a woman named Eugenie Van de Kerckove, whose husband, John Wybo, was a farmer. She was a pious and charitable woman, giving alms with a generosity proportionate to her means. She had, to the end of her life, a great devotion to the Blessed Virgin, and abstained in her honour on the Friday and Saturday of each week. Although her conduct was not free from certain domestic faults, she otherwise led a most exemplary and edifying life.

A servant named Barbara Vennecke, aged twenty-eight years, a virtuous and devoted girl, and who had assisted her mistress in her last sickness, continued to serve her master, John Wybo, the widower of Eugenie.

About three weeks after her death, the deceased appeared to her servant under circumstances which we are about to relate. It was in the middle of the night; Barbara slept soundly, when she heard herself called distinctly three times by her name. She awoke with a start, and saw before her her mistress, sitting on the side of her bed, clad in a working dress, consisting of a skirt and short jacket. At this sight, strange to say, although seized with astonishment, Barbara was not at all frightened, and preserved her presence of mind. The apparition spoke to her, "*Barbara,*" she said, simply pronouncing her name. "*What do you desire, Eugenie?*" replied the servant. "*Take,*" said the mistress, "*the little rake which I often told you to put in its place; stir the heap of sand in the little room; you know to which one I refer. You will there find a sum of money; use it to have Masses said, two francs for each, for my intention, for I am still suffering.*" "*I will do so, Eugenie,*" replied Barbara, and at the same moment the apparition vanished. The servant, still quite calm, fell asleep again, and reposed quietly until morning.

On awaking, Barbara believed herself the sport of a dream, but she had been so deeply impressed, so wide awake, she had seen her old mistress in a form so distinct, so full of life, she had received from her lips such precise directions, that she could not help saying, "It is not thus that we dream. I saw my mistress in person; she presented herself to my eyes and spoke to me. It is no dream, but a reality."

She therefore went and took the rake as directed, stirred the sand, and drew out a purse containing the sum of five hundred francs.

In such strange and extraordinary circumstances the good girl thought it her duty to seek the advice of her pastor, and went to relate to him all that had happened. The venerable Abbé R., then parish priest of Ardoye, replied that the Masses asked by the departed soul must be celebrated, but, in order to dispose of the sum of money, the consent of the farmer, John Wybo, was necessary. The latter willingly consented that the money should be employed for so holy a purpose, and the Masses were celebrated, being given two francs for each Mass.

We call attention to the circumstance of the fee, because it corresponded with the pious custom of the deceased. The fee for a Mass fixed by the diocesan tariff was about a franc and a half, but the wife of Wybo, through consideration for the clergy, obliged at that time of scarcity to relieve a great number of the poor, gave two francs for each Mass she had been accustomed to have celebrated.

Two months after the first apparition, Barbara was again awakened during the night. This time her chamber was illuminated with a bright light, and her mistress, beautiful and fresh as in the days of her youth, dressed in a robe of dazzling whiteness, appeared before her, regarding her with an amiable smile. "*Barbara,*" she said in a clear and audible voice, "*I thank you; I am delivered.*" Saying these words, she disappeared, and the chamber became dark as before. The servant, amazed at what she had seen, was transported with joy. This apparition made the most lively impression upon her mind, and she preserves to this day the most consoling remembrance of it. It is from her that we have these details, through the favour of the venerable Abbé L., who was curate at Ardoye when these facts occurred.

The celebrated Father Lacordaire, in the beginning of the conferences on the immortality of the soul, which he addressed a few years before his death to the pupils of Sorèze, related to them the following incident:—

The Polish prince of X., an avowed infidel and materialist, had just composed a work against the immortality of the soul. He was on the point of sending it to press, when one day walking in his park, a woman bathed in tears, threw herself at his feet and in accents of profound grief said to him, "My good Prince, my husband has just died. . . . At this moment his soul is perhaps suffering in Purgatory. . . . I am in such poverty that I have not even the small sum required to have a Mass celebrated for the dead. In your kindness come to my assistance in behalf of my poor husband."

Although the gentleman was convinced that the woman was deceived by her credulity, he had not courage to refuse her. He slipped a gold piece into her hand, and the happy woman hastened to the church, and begged the priest to offer some Masses for the repose of her husband's soul. Five days later, towards evening, the prince, in the seclusion of his study, was reading over his manuscript and retouching some details, when, raising his eyes, he saw, close to him, a man dressed in the costume of the peasants of the country. "Prince," said the unknown visitor, "I come to thank you. I am the husband of that poor woman who besought you the other day to give her an alms, that she might have the Holy Sacrifice of the Mass offered for the repose of my soul. Your charity was pleasing to God: it was He who permitted me to come and thank you."

These words said, the Polish peasant disappeared like a shadow. The emotion of the prince was indescribable, and in consequence he consigned his work to the flames, and yielded himself so entirely to the conviction of truth that his conversion was complete. He persevered until death.

CHAPTER XVI.

Relief of the Holy Souls—Liturgy of the Church—Commemoration of the Dead—St. Odilo.

HOLY CHURCH possesses a special liturgy for the dead: it is composed of vespers, matins, lauds and of the mass commonly called the mass of Requiem. This liturgy, as touching as it is sublime, through mourning and tears unfolds to the eyes of the faithful the consoling light of eternity. This liturgy she reads at the funerals of her children, and particularly on the solemn day of the Commemoration of the Dead. Holy Mass here holds the first place; it is like the divine centre round which all other prayers and ceremonies cluster. The day following All Saints' Day, the great solemnity of All Souls, all priests must offer the Holy Sacrifice for the dead; after which the faithful make it their duty to assist, and even to offer Holy Communion, prayers and alms, for the relief of their brethren in Purgatory. This feast of the departed is not of very ancient origin. From the beginning the Church has always prayed for her departed children: she sang psalms, recited prayers, offered Holy Mass for the repose of their souls. Yet we do not see that there was any particular feast on which to recommend to God all the dead in general. It was not until the tenth century that the

Church, always guided by the Holy Ghost, instituted the *Commemoration of all the faithful departed*, to encourage the faithful to fulfil the great duty of prayer for the dead, prescribed by Christian charity.

The cradle of this touching solemnity was the Abbey of Cluny. St. Odilo,[1] who was Abbot there at the close of the tenth century, edified all France by his charity towards his neighbour. Extending his compassion even to the dead, he ceased not to pray for the souls in Purgatory. It was this tender charity which inspired him to establish in his monastery, as also in its dependencies, the feast of the commemoration of all the souls departed. We believe, says the historian Bérault, that he had received a revelation to that effect, for God manifested in a miraculous manner how pleasing to Him was the devotion of His servant. It is thus related by his biographers. Whilst the holy Abbot governed his monastery in France, a pious hermit lived in a little island off the coast of Sicily. A French pilgrim was cast upon the shore of this little island by a tempest. The hermit, whom he went to visit, asked him if he knew the Abbot Odilo. "Certainly," replied the pilgrim, "I know him, and am proud of his acquaintance; but how do you know him, and why do you ask me this question?" "I often hear," replied the hermit, "the evil spirits complain of pious persons who, by their prayers and alms-deeds, deliver the souls from the pains which they endure in the other life, but they complain principally of Odilo, Abbot of Cluny, and his Religious. When, therefore, you shall have returned to your native country, I beg of you, in the name of God, to exhort the holy Abbot and his monks to redouble their good works in behalf of the poor souls."

The pilgrim betook himself to the monastery and did as he was directed. In consequence, St. Odilo gave orders that in all the monasteries of his Institute, on the day following All Saints, a commemoration of all the faithful

[1] Jan. 1.

departed should be made, by reciting the vespers for the dead on the eve, and on following morning matins; by ringing all the bells and celebrating Mass for repose of the holy souls. This decree, which was drawn up at Cluny, as well for that monastery as for all those dependent upon it, is still preserved. A practice so pious soon passed over to other churches, and in course of time became the universal observance of the whole Catholic world.

CHAPTER XVII.

Relief of the Souls—The Sacrifice of the Mass—Brother John of Alvernia at the Altar—St. Magdalen de Pazzi—St. Malachy and his Sister.

THE annals of the Seraphic Order tell us of a holy Religious named John of Alvernia. He ardently loved our Lord Jesus Christ, and embraced in the same love the souls ransomed by His Blood and so dear to His Heart. Those who suffered in the prisons of Purgatory had a large share in his prayers, his penances, and his sacrifices. One day God was pleased to manifest to him the admirable and consoling effects of the Divine Sacrifice offered on All Souls' Day upon every altar. The Servant of God was celebrating Mass for the departed on that solemnity when he was rapt in ectasy. He saw Purgatory opened, and souls coming forth delivered by virtue of the Sacrifice of Propitiation; they resembled innumerable sparks which escaped from a burning furnace. We shall be less astonished at the powerful effects of holy Mass if we call to mind that it is identically the same as that offered by the Son of God Himself upon the cross. It is *the same*

Priest, says the Council of Trent, *it is the same Victim, the only difference is in the manner of immolation;* on the cross the immolation was bloody, on our altar it is unbloody.

Now, that sacrifice of the cross was of infinite value; that of the altar is, in the eyes of God, of equal value. Let us remark, however, that the efficacy of this Divine Sacrifice is only partially applied to the dead, and in a measure known only to the justice of God. The Passion of Jesus Christ and His Precious Blood shed for our salvation are an inexhaustible ocean of merit and satisfaction. It is by virtue of that Passion that we obtain all gifts and mercies from God. The mere commemoration which we make of it by way of prayer, when we offer to God the Blood of His only-begotten Son, to implore His mercy, this prayer I say, thus strengthened by the Passion of Jesus Christ, has great power with God. St. Magdalen de Pazzi learned from our Lord to offer to the Eternal Father the Blood of His Divine Son. It was a simple commemoration of the Passion. She did it fifty times a day, and in one of her ecstasies she saw a large number of sinners converted, and of souls delivered from Purgatory by this practice. "Each time," He added, "that a creature offers to my Father the Blood by which she has been redeemed, she offers Him a gift of infinite value." If such be the value of an offering commemorative of the Passion, what must be said of the sacrifice of the Mass, which is the actual renewal of that same Passion?

Many Christians do not sufficiently know the greatness of the Divine Mysteries accomplished upon our altars; the feebleness of their faith, together with their lack of knowledge, prevents them from appreciating the treasure which they possess in the Divine Sacrifice, and causes them to look upon it with a sort of indifference. Alas! they will see later on, with bitter regret, how they have deceived themselves. The sister of St. Malachy, Archbishop of

Armagh, in Ireland, affords us a striking example of this.

In his beautiful Life of St. Malachy[1] St. Bernard highly praises that prelate for his devotion towards the souls in Purgatory. When he was as yet deacon, he loved to assist at the funerals of the poor, and at the Mass which was celebrated for them; he even accompanied their remains to the cemetery with as much zeal as he ordinarily saw those unfortunate creatures neglected after their death. But he had a sister, who, filled with the spirit of the world, thought that her brother degraded himself and his whole family by thus associating with the poor. She reproached him, showing by her language that she understood neither Christian Charity nor the excellence of the Holy Sacrifice of the Mass. Malachy, notwithstanding, continued the exercise of his humble Charity, contenting himself with replying to his sister that she had forgotten the teaching of Jesus Christ, and that she would one day repent of her thoughtless words.

In the meantime the imprudent rashness of this woman was not to remain unpunished; she died whilst still young, and went to render an account to the Sovereign Judge of the worldly life she had led.

Malachy had reason to complain of her conduct, but when she was dead he forgot all the wrongs she had done him, and thinking only of the needs of her soul, he offered the Holy Sacrifice and prayed much for her. In the course of time, however, having many others to pray for, he neglected his poor sister. "We may believe," says Father Rossignoli, "that God permitted that she should be forgotten, in punishment for the want of compassion which she showed towards the dead."

However this may be, she appeared to her holy brother during his sleep. Malachy saw her standing in the middle of the area before the church, sad, clad in mourning, and

[1] Nov. 3.

entreating his compassion, complaining that for the last thirty days he had neglected her. He thereupon awoke suddenly, and remembered that in reality it was thirty days since he had celebrated Mass for his sister. On the following day he began anew to offer the Holy Sacrifice for her. Then the deceased appeared to him at the door of the church, kneeling upon the threshold, and lamenting that she was not allowed to enter. He continued his suffrages. Some days later he saw her enter the church and advance as far as the middle of the aisle, without being able, notwithstanding all her efforts, to approach the altar. He saw, therefore, it was necessary to persevere, so he continued to offer the Holy Sacrifice for the repose of her soul. Finally, after a few days he saw her near the altar, clad in magnificent attire, radiant with joy, and free from suffering.

"By this we see," adds St. Bernard, "how great is the efficacy of the Holy Sacrifice to remit sins, to combat the powers of darkness, and to open the gates of Heaven to those souls which have quitted this earth."

CHAPTER XVIII.

Relief of the Souls—Holy Mass—St. Malachy at Clairvaux—Sister Zenaïde—Venerable Joseph Anchieta and the Requiem Mass.

WE must not omit to recount the special grace which the great charity of St. Malachy towards the holy souls procured for him. One day, being in the company of several pious persons, and conversing familiarly on spiritual matters, they came to speak of their last end. "If," said he, "the choice were given to each one of you, at what hour and in what place would you like to die?" At this question one mentioned a certain feast, another such an hour, others, again, at such a place. When it came to the saint's turn to express his thoughts, he said that there was no place where he would more willingly end his life than in the Monastery of Clairvaux, governed by St. Bernard, in order that he might immediately enjoy the benefit of the sacrifices of those fervent Religious; and as to the time, he preferred, he said, the day of All Souls, that he might have part in all the Masses and all the prayers offered throughout the entire Catholic world for the faithful departed.

This, his pious desire, was gratified in every point. He was on his way to Rome to visit Pope Eugenius III., when, arriving at Clairvaux a little before All Saints, he was overtaken by a serious malady, which obliged him to remain in that holy retreat. He soon understood that God had heard his prayers, and cried out with the prophet, *This is my rest for ever and ever; here will I dwell, for I have chosen it.*[1] In fact, the day following, All Saints', whilst the whole Church was praying for the departed, he rendered his soul into the hands of his Creator.

"We have known," says the Abbé Postel, "a holy Religious, Sister Zenaïde, who, afflicted with a frightful malady for several years, asked our Lord the grace to die on the Feast of All Souls, towards whom she had always had great devotion. Her desire was granted. On the morning of November 2, after two years of suffering endured with truly Christian courage, she began to sing a hymn of thanksgiving, and calmly expired a few moments before the celebration of the Masses.

We know that in the Catholic liturgy there is a special Mass for the dead; it is celebrated in black vestments, and is called *Mass of Requiem.* It may be asked whether

---

[1] Ps. cxxxi.

this Mass is more profitable to the souls than any other? The Sacrifice of the Mass, notwithstanding the variety of its ceremonies, is always the same infinitely holy Sacrifice of the Body and Blood of Jesus Christ; but as the Mass for the Dead contains special prayers for the holy souls, it also obtains special assistance for them, at least at those times when the liturgical laws permit the priest to celebrate in black. This opinion, based on the institution and practice of the Church, is confirmed by a fact which we read in the Life of Venerable Father Joseph Anchieta.

This holy Religious, justly surnamed the Wonder-worker of Brazil, had, like all the saints, great charity towards the holy souls in Purgatory. One day during the Octave of Christmas, when the Church forbids the celebration of Requiem Masses, on the 27th of December, Feast of St. John the Evangelist, this man of God, to the great astonishment of all, ascended the altar in black vestments, and offered the Holy Sacrifice for the Dead.

His superior, Father Nobrega, knowing the sanctity of Anchieta, doubted not that he had received a Divine inspiration; nevertheless, to remove from such conduct the character of irregularity which it appeared to have, he reprimanded the holy man in presence of all the brethren. "What, Father," said he to him, "do you not know that the Church forbids the celebration of Mass in black to-day? Have you forgotten the Rubrics?"

The good Father, quite humble and obedient, replied with respectful simplicity that God had revealed to him the death of a Father of the Society. This Father, his fellow-student at the University of Coimbra, and who at that time resided in Italy, in the College of the holy House of Loretto, had died that same night. "God," he continued, "made this known to me, and gave me to understand that I should offer the Holy Sacrifice for him immediately, and do all in my power for the repose of his soul." "But," said the Superior, "do you know that the Mass celebrated as you have done will be of any benefit to him?" "Yes," modestly replied Anchieta, "immediately after the *memento for the dead*, when I said these words: *To Thee, God the Father Almighty, in the unity of the Holy Ghost, all honour and glory!* God showed me the soul of that dear friend, freed from all its sufferings and ascending to Heaven, where his crown awaited him."

CHAPTER XIX.

Relief of the Souls through the Holy Sacrifice of the Mass— Venerable Mother Agnes and Sister Seraphique—Margaret of Austria— The Archduke Charles— Father Mancinelli.

WE have just spoken of the efficacy of the Holy Sacrifice in relieving the poor souls. A lively faith in this consoling mystery inflames the devotion of the true faithful, and smoothes the bitterness of their grief. Does death deprive them of a father, a mother, a friend? They turn their tearful eyes towards the altar, which affords the means of testifying their love and gratitude towards their dear departed ones. Hence the numerous Masses which they cause to be celebrated; hence also that eagerness to assist at the Holy Sacrifice of Propitiation in favour of the dead.

Venerable Mother Agnes de Langeac, a Dominican Religious of whom we have already spoken, assisted at Holy Mass with the greatest devotion, and encouraged her Religious to a like fervour. She told them that this Divine Sacrifice was the holiest act of religion, the work of GOD by excellence, and reminded them of Holy Scripture: "Cursed be he that doth the work of the Lord deceitfully." [1]

[1] Jer. xlviii. 10.

A sister of the community, named Sister Seraphique, died; she had not paid sufficient attention to the salutary advice of her Superior, and was condemned to a severe Purgatory. Mother Agnes knew this by revelation. In an ecstasy she was taken in spirit into the place of expiation, and saw many souls in the midst of flames. Among them she recognised Sister Seraphique, who, in piteous accents, entreated her assistance. Touched with the most lively compassion, the charitable Superior did all in her power for the space of eight days; she fasted, communicated, and assisted at Holy Mass for the dear departed sister. Whilst in prayer, with many tears and sighs, imploring the Divine Mercy through the precious Blood of Jesus, that He would be pleased to deliver her dear daughter from those dreadful flames and admit her to the enjoyment of His presence, she heard a voice which said to her, "*Continue to pray; the hour of her deliverance has not yet come.*" Mother Agnes persevered in prayer, and two days later, whilst assisting at the Holy Sacrifice, at the moment of the elevation, she saw the soul of Sister Seraphique ascend to Heaven in a transport of joy. This consoling sight was the reward of her charity, and inflamed anew the ardour of her devotion towards the Holy Sacrifice of the Mass.

Christian families, which possess a spirit of lively faith, make it their duty, according to their rank and means, to have a large number of Masses celebrated for the dead. In their holy liberality, they exhaust their resources in order to multiply the suffrages of the Church, and thus give relief to the holy souls. It is related in the Life of Queen Margaret of Austria, wife of Philip III., that in one single day, which was that of her obsequies, there was celebrated in the city of Madrid nearly eleven hundred Masses for the repose of her soul. This princess had asked for one thousand Masses in her last will; the King caused twenty thousand to be added to it. When the Archduke Albert died at Brussels, the pious Isabella, his widow, had forty thousand Masses offered for the repose of his soul, and for an entire month she herself assisted with the greatest piety at ten each day.[1]

One of the most perfect models of devotion to the Holy Sacrifice of the Mass, and of charity towards the souls in Purgatory, was Father Julio Mancinelli of the Society of Jesus. The Masses offered by this worthy Religious, says F. Rossignoli,[2] appeared to have a particular efficacy for the relief of the faithful departed. The souls frequently appeared to him to beg the favour of a single Mass.

Cæsar Costa, the uncle of Father Mancinelli, was Archbishop of Capua. One day meeting his holy nephew very poorly clad, notwithstanding the severity of the weather, he with the greatest charity gave him an alms to procure for himself a cloak. A short time afterwards, the Archbishop died; and the Father going out to visit the sick, wrapped in his new cloak, met his deceased uncle coming towards him enveloped in flames, and begging him to lend him his mantle. The Father gave it to him; and no sooner had the Archbishop folded it about him, than the flames were extinguished. Mancinelli understood that this soul was suffering in Purgatory, and that it asked his assistance, in return for the charity exercised in his regard. Then taking back his cloak, he promised to pray for the poor suffering soul with all possible fervour, especially at the altar.

This fact became noised abroad, and produced such a salutary impression, that after the death of the Father, it was represented in a painting, which is preserved at the College in Macerata, his native place. Father Julio Mancinelli is there seen at the altar clad in the sacred vestments, he is elevated a little above the steps of the altar, to signify the raptures with which he was favoured by God. From his mouth issue sparks, the emblem of his burning prayers, and of his fervour during the Holy

[1] Father Mumford, *Charité envers les Défuncts*.   [2] *Merv.*, 23.

Sacrifice. Under the altar is seen Purgatory, and the souls receiving the benefit of the suffrages. Above, two angels pour forth from costly vases a shower of gold, which indicates the blessings, graces, and ransoms granted to the poor souls in virtue of the Holy Sacrifice. We also see the mantle spoken of, and an inscription in verse, which translated reads : "*O miraculous garment, given as a protection against the severity of the cold, and which afterwards served to temper the heat of fire. It is thus that charity gives warmth or refreshment according to the sufferings which it relieves.*"

CHAPTER XX.

Relief of the Souls through the Holy Sacrifice of the Mass— St. Teresa and Bernardino de Mendoza—Multiplicity of Masses—Pomp of the Obsequies.

LET us conclude what we have said relative to the Holy Sacrifice by what St. Teresa relates concerning Bernardino de Mendoza. She gives this fact in the " Book of Foundations," chapter x.

"On the Feast of All Souls, Don Bernardino de Mendoza had given a house and beautiful garden, situated in Madrid, to St. Teresa, that she might found a monastery in honour of the Mother of God." Two months after this, he was suddenly taken ill, and lost the power of speech, so that he could not make a confession, though he gave many signs of contrition. "He died," says St. Teresa, "very shortly afterwards, and far from the place where I then was. But our Lord spoke to me, and told me he was saved, though he had run a great risk; that mercy had been shown to him because of the donation to the convent of His Blessed

Mother; but that his soul would not be freed from suffering until the first Mass was said in the new house. I felt so deeply the pains this soul was enduring, that although I was very desirous of accomplishing the foundation of Toledo, I left it at once for Valladolid on St. Lawrence's Day.

"One day, whilst I was in prayer at Medina del Campo, our Lord told me to make all possible haste, for the soul of De Mendoza was a prey to the most intense suffering.

"I immediately ordered the masons to put up the walls of the convent without delay; but as this would take considerable time, I asked the Bishop for permission to make a temporary chapel for the use of the sisters which I had brought with me. This obtained, I had Mass offered; and at the moment I left my place to approach the Holy Table, I saw our benefactor, who, with hands joined and countenance all radiant, thanked me for having delivered him from Purgatory. Then I saw him enter Heaven. I was the more happy as I did not expect this. For although our Lord had revealed to me that the deliverance of this soul would follow the celebration of the first Mass in the house, I thought that it must mean the first Mass when the Blessed Sacrament should be reserved there."

This beautiful incident shows us not only the efficacy of the Holy Sacrifice of the Mass, but also the tender goodness with which Jesus interests Himself in favour of the holy souls, even condescending to solicit our suffrages in their behalf.

But since the Divine Sacrifice is of such value, it may here be asked if a large number of Masses procures for the souls more relief than a smaller number, whose defect is supplied only by magnificent obsequies and abundant alms? The answer to this question may be inferred from the spirit of the Church, which is the spirit of Jesus Christ Himself, and the expression of His will.

Now the Church advises the faithful to have prayers said

for the dead, to give alms, and perform other good works, to apply indulgences to them, but especially to have Holy Mass celebrated, and to assist thereat. Whilst giving the first place to the Divine Sacrifice, she approves and makes use of various kinds of suffrages, according to the circumstances, devotion, or social condition of the deceased or his heirs.

It is a Catholic custom religiously observed from the remotest antiquity to have Mass celebrated for the dead with solemn ceremonies, and a funeral with as much pomp as their means will allow. The expense of this is an alms given to the Church, an alms which, in the eyes of God, greatly enhances the price of the Holy Sacrifice, and its satisfactory value for the deceased.

It is well, however, so to regulate the funeral expenses, that a sufficient sum be left for a certain number of Masses, and also to give alms to the poor.

That which must be avoided is, to lose sight of the Christian character of funerals, and to look upon the funeral service less as a great act of religion than a display of worldly vanity.

What must be further avoided are the profane mourning emblems which are not conformable to Christian tradition, such as the wreaths of flowers, with which, at a great expense, they load the coffins of the dead. This is an innovation justly disapproved by the Church, to which Jesus Christ has intrusted the care of religious rites and ceremonies, not excepting funeral ceremonies. Those of which she makes use at the death of her children are venerable by their antiquity, full of meaning and consolation. All that presents itself to the eyes of the faithful on such occasions, the cross and the holy water, the lights and the incense, the tears and prayers, breathe compassion for the poor souls, faith in the Divine Mercy, and the hope of immortality.

What is there of all this in the cold wreaths of violet?

They say nothing to the Christian soul; they are but profane emblems of this mortal life, that contrast strangely with the cross, and which are foreign to the rites of the Catholic Church.

CHAPTER XXI.

Relief of the Souls—Prayer—Brother Corrado d'Offida— The Golden Fish-Hook and the Silver Thread.

AFTER the Holy Sacrifice of the Mass, we have a multitude of secondary though most efficacious means of relieving the holy souls, if we employ them with spirit, faith, and fervour.

In the first place comes prayer, prayer in all its forms. The Annals of the Seraphic Order speak with admiration of Brother Corrado d'Offida, one of the first companions of St. Francis. He was distinguished by a spirit of prayer and charity, which contributed greatly to the edification of his brethren. Among the latter there was a young monk whose relaxed and disorderly conduct disturbed the holy community; but, thanks to the prayers and charitable exhortations of Corrado, he entirely corrected himself and became a model of regularity. Soon after this happy conversion, he died, and his brethren gave him the ordinary suffrages. A few days elapsed, when Brother Corrado being in prayer before the altar, heard a voice asking the assistance of his prayers. "Who are you?" said the servant of God. "I am," replied the voice, "the soul of the young Religious whom you reanimated to fervour." "But did you not die a holy death? Are you still in so great need of prayers?" "I died a good death, and am saved, but on account of my former sins, which I had not the time to expiate, I suffer the most terrible chastisement, and I beseech you not to refuse me the assistance of your prayers." Immediately the good brother prostrated himself before the tabernacle, and recited a *Pater*, followed by the *Requiem Æternam*. " Oh, my good Father," cried the apparition, "what refreshment your prayer procures for me! Oh, how it relieves me! I entreat you to continue." Corrado devoutly repeated the same prayers. " Beloved Father," again repeated the soul, "still more! still more! I experience such great relief when you pray." The charitable Religious continued his prayers with renewed fervour, and repeated the *Our Father* a hundred times. Then, in accents of unspeakable joy, the deceased soul said unto him, " I thank you, my dear Father, in the name of God. I am delivered; behold! I am about to enter the Kingdom of Heaven."

We see by the preceding example how efficacious are the smallest prayers, the shortest supplications, to alleviate the sufferings of the poor souls. " I have read," says Father Rossignoli, " that a holy Bishop, rapt in ecstasy, saw a child, who, with a golden fish-hook and a silver thread, drew forth from the bottom of a well a woman who had been drowned therein. After his prayer, and whilst on his way to the church, he saw the same child praying at a grave in the cemetery. 'What are you doing there, my little friend?' he asked. 'I am saying the *Our Father* and *Hail Mary*,' answered the child, 'for the soul of my mother, whose body lies buried here.' The prelate immediately understood that God had wished to show him the efficacy of the most simple prayer; he knew that the soul of that woman had been delivered, that the fish-hook was the *Pater*, and that the *Ave* was the silver thread of that mystic line."

CHAPTER XXII.

Relief of the Holy Souls—The Holy Rosary—Father Nieremberg—Mother Frances of the Blessed Sacrament and the Rosary.

WE know that the Holy Rosary holds the first place among all the prayers which the Church recommends to the faithful. This excellent prayer, the source of so many graces for the living, is also singularly efficacious in relieving the dead. Of this we have a touching proof in the Life of Father Nieremberg, whom we have mentioned elsewhere. This charitable servant of God imposed upon himself frequent mortifications, accompanied by devotions and prayers for the relief of the poor suffering souls. He never omitted to recite the *Rosary* each day for their intention, and gained for them all the indulgences in his power; an offering which he recommended to the faithful in a special work which he published on this subject. The chaplet which he used was ornamented with pious medals and enriched with numerous indulgences. It happened one day that he lost it, and he was inconsolable; not that this holy Religious, whose heart was not fettered by anything upon earth, had any material attachment to these beads, but because he saw himself deprived of the means of procuring the relief he was accustomed to give to the poor souls.

He sought everywhere, tried to recollect where he could have put his precious treasure: all was useless, and when evening came, he found himself obliged to replace his indulgenced chaplet by ordinary prayers.

Whilst thus engaged and alone in his cell, he heard a noise in the ceiling like that of his beads, which was well known to him, and raising his eyes, he saw in reality his chaplet, held by invisible hands, descending towards him and fall at his feet. He did not doubt that the invisible hands were those of the souls who were relieved by this means. We can imagine with what renewed fervour he recited his accustomed five decades, and how much this wonder encouraged him to persevere in a practice so visibly approved by Heaven.

Venerable Mother Frances of the Blessed Sacrament [1] had from her infancy the greatest devotion towards the suffering souls, and persevered therein as long as she lived. She was all heart, all devotion towards those poor and holy souls. To assist them she daily recited her Rosary, which she was accustomed to call her *almoner*, and she ended each decade with the *Requiescant in pace*. On feast-days, when she had more free time, she added the Office of the Dead. To prayer she joined penances. The greater part of the year she fasted on bread and water, and on vigils she practised other austerities. She had to endure much labour and fatigue, pain and persecution. All these works were turned into profit for the holy souls, Frances offering all to God for their relief.

Not content with assisting them herself as far as was in her power, she engaged others to do the same. If priests came to the convent, she begged for Masses for them; if they were laymen, she advised them to distribute abundant alms for the faithful departed. In recompense for her charity, God frequently permitted the souls to visit her, either to solicit her suffrages or to return her thanks. Witnesses have testified that several times they visibly waited for her at the door when she was going to the Office of Matins, that they might recommend themselves to her prayers. At other times they entered her cell in order to present their request to her; they surrounded her bed, waiting until she awoke. These appari-

[1] Sa Vie par le P. Joachim. Vid. Rossignoli, *Merv.*, 26.

tions, to which she was accustomed, caused her no fear, and that she might not think herself the sport of a dream or a dupe of the devil, they said on entering, "Hail, servant of God, spouse of the Lord! may Jesus Christ be ever with you!" Then they testified their veneration for a large cross and the relics of the saints which their benefactress kept in her cell. If they found her reciting the Rosary, add the same witnesses, they took her hands and kissed them lovingly, as the instrument of their deliverance.

CHAPTER XXIII.

Relief of the Holy Souls—Fasts, Penances, and Mortifications, however Trifling — A Glass of Cold Water — Blessed Margaret Mary.

AFTER prayer comes fasting, that is to say, not only fasting properly so called, which consists in abstaining from food, but also all penitential works of what nature soever they may be. It must here be remarked that this is a question not only of the great austerities practised by the saints, but of all the tribulations, all the contradictions of this life, as also of the least mortifications, the smallest sacrifices which we impose upon ourselves or accept for the love of God, and which we offer to His Divine Mercy for the relief of the holy souls.

A glass of water, which we refuse ourselves when thirsty, is a trifling thing, and if we consider this act in itself, we can scarcely see the efficacy it possesses to alleviate the sufferings of Purgatory. But such is the Divine Goodness that it deigns to accept this as a sacrifice of great value. "If I am permitted," says the Abbé Louvet, speaking of this subject, "I will relate an example which came almost under my own personal experience. One of my relations was a Religious in a community which she edified, not by that heroism of virtue which shone forth in the saints, but by an ordinary virtue and great regularity of life. It happened that she lost a friend whom she had formerly known in the world, and from the time she heard of her death, she made it her duty to recommend her to God. One evening, being very thirsty, her first impulse was to refresh herself with a glass of water, this being allowed by her Rule; but she remembered her deceased friend, and, for the benefit of her soul, refused herself this little gratification. Instead, then, of drinking this glass of water which she held in her hand, she poured it out, praying God to show mercy to the departed. This good sister reminds us of King David, who, finding himself with his army in a place without water and oppressed with thirst, refused to drink the refreshing water which was brought to him from the cisterns of Bethlehem. Instead of raising it to his parched lips, he poured it out as a libation to the Lord, and Holy Scripture cites this act of the holy King as one most agreeable to God. Now, this slight mortification which our holy Religious imposed upon herself by denying herself this draught of water was so pleasing to God, that He permitted the departed soul to make it manifest by an apparition. On the following night she appeared to the sister, heartily thanking her for the relief she had received. Those few drops of water, which, in the spirit of mortification she had denied herself, were changed into a refreshing bath, to temper the heat of Purgatorial fires.

We wish to remark that what we here say is not restricted to acts of supererogatory mortification; it must be understood of obligatory mortification; that is to say, of all that we have to undergo in the fulfilment of our duties, and in general to all those good works to which our duties as Christians or those of our particular state of life oblige us.

Thus every Christian is bound by virtue of the law of God to refrain from wanton words, slander, and murmuring; thus every Religious must observe silence, charity, and obedience as prescribed by the Rule. Now, these observances, though of obligation, when practised in the true spirit of a Christian, with a view to please God, in union with the labours and sufferings of Jesus Christ, may become suffrages and serve to relieve the holy souls.

In that famous apparition where Blessed Margaret Mary saw the deceased Religious suffering intensely for her tepidity, the poor soul, after having related in detail the torments which she endured, concluded with these words: "Alas! one hour of exactitude in silence would cure my parched mouth; another passed in the practice of charity would heal my tongue; another passed without murmuring or disapprobation of the actions of the Superior would cure my tortured heart."

By this we see that the soul asked not for works of supererogation, but only the application of those to which the Religious are obliged.

CHAPTER XXIV.

Relief of the Holy Souls—Holy Communion—St. Magdalen de Pazzi delivering her Brother—General Communion in the Church.

IF ordinary good works procure so much relief for the souls, what will not be the effects of the holiest work a Christian can accomplish, I mean Holy Communion? When St. Magdalen de Pazzi saw her brother in the sufferings of Purgatory, touched with compassion, she melted into tears and cried in a lamentable voice, "Oh, afflicted soul, how terrible are your pains! Why are they not understood by those who lack the courage to carry their cross here below? Whilst you were still in this world, my dear brother, you would not listen to me, and now you desire so ardently that I should hear you. Poor victim! what do you require of me?" Here she stopped and was heard to count up to the number one hundred and seven; then she said aloud that this was the number of Communions which he begged in a tone of supplication. "Yes," she said to him, "I can easily do what you ask, but, alas! what a length of time it will take me to pay that debt! Oh, if God permitted, how willingly would I go where you are, to deliver you, or to prevent others from descending into it."

The saint, without omitting her prayers and other suffrages, made with the greatest fervour all the Communions which her brother desired for his deliverance.

It is, says Father Rossignoli, a pious custom established in the churches of the Society of Jesus to offer each month a general Communion for the benefit of the souls in Purgatory, and God has deigned to show by a prodigy how agreeable this practice is to Him.

In the year 1615, when the Fathers in Rome celebrated this monthly Communion in the church of Our Lady in Trastevere, a crowd of persons was present. Amongst the fervent Christians there was one great sinner, who, although taking part in the pious ceremonies of religion, had for a long time led a very wicked life. This man, before entering the church, saw coming out and advancing towards him a man of humble appearance, who asked of him an alms for the love of God. He at first refused, but the poor man, as is customary with beggars, persisted, asking for the third time in a most pitiful tone of supplication. Finally, yielding to a good inspiration, our sinner recalled the mendicant and gave him a piece of money.

Then the poor man changed his entreaties into other language. "Keep your money," said he; "I stand in no need of your liberality; but you yourself greatly need to make a change in your life. Know that it was to give you this salutary warning that I came from Mount Gargano to the ceremony which was to take place in this church to-day. It is now twenty years since you have been leading this deplorable life, provoking the anger of God instead of appeasing it by a sincere confession. Hasten to do penance if you would escape the stroke of Divine Justice ready to fall upon your head."

The sinner was struck by these words: a secret fear took possession of him when he heard the secrets of conscience revealed, which he thought were known to God alone. His emotion increased when he saw the poor man vanish like smoke before his eyes. Opening his heart to grace, he entered the church, cast himself upon his knees and shed a torrent of tears. Then sincerely repenting, he sought a confessor, made an avowal of his crimes and asked pardon. After confession, he related to the priest what had happened to him, begging him to make it known in order that devotion towards the holy souls might be increased; for he had no doubt that it was a soul just delivered that had obtained for him the grace of conversion.

It may here be asked who was that mysterious mendicant that appeared to this sinner in order to convert him? Some have believed that it was none other than the Archangel Michael, because he said that he came from Mount Gargano. We know that this mountain is celebrated throughout Italy for an apparition of St. Michael, in whose honour a magnificent shrine has been erected. However this may be, the conversion of this sinner by such a miracle, and at the same moment when prayers and Holy Communion were being offered for the faithful departed, shows plainly the excellence of this devotion and how pleasing it must be in the sight of God.

Let us therefore conclude in the words of St. Bernard, "*May charity lead you to communicate, for there is nothing more efficacious for the eternal repose of the dead.*"

CHAPTER XXV.

Relief of the Holy Souls.—The Stations of the Cross.— Venerable Mary d'Antigna.

AFTER Holy Communion we shall speak of the Stations of the Cross. This holy exercise may be considered in itself, and in the indulgences with which it is enriched. In itself, it is a solemn and very excellent manner of meditating on the Passion of our Saviour, and consequently the most salutary exercise of our holy religion.

In its literal sense, the Way of the Cross is the distance traversed by the Man-God whilst carrying the weight of His cross from the palace of Pilate, where He was condemned to death, to the summit of Calvary, where He was crucified. After the death of her Divine Son, the Blessed Virgin, either alone or in company with the holy women, frequently visited that dolorous path. After her example, the faithful of Palestine, and in the course of ages numerous pilgrims from the most distant countries, went to visit those holy places, bedewed with the sweat and blood of Jesus Christ; and the Church, to encourage their piety, opened to them her treasures of spiritual blessings. But as every one cannot go to the Holy Land, the Holy See allows to be erected in the churches and chapels in other countries, crosses, paintings, or bas-reliefs representing the touching scenes which took place on the real road to Calvary at Jerusalem.

In permitting the erection of these holy Stations, the Roman Pontiffs, who understood all the excellency and all the efficacy of this devotion, deigned also to enrich it with all the Indulgences which they had granted to a real visit to the Holy Land. And thus, according to the Briefs and Constitutions of the Sovereign Pontiffs Innocent XI., Innocent XII., Benedict XIII., Clement XII., and Benedict XIV., *those who make the Stations of the Cross with proper dispositions gain all the Indulgences granted to the faithful who visit in person the Holy Places of Jerusalem, and these Indulgences are applicable to the dead.*

Now it is certain that numerous Indulgences, whether plenary or partial, were granted to those who visited the Holy Places of Jerusalem, as may be seen in the *Bullarium Terræ Sanctæ,* so that as regards Indulgences we may say that of all practices of piety the Way of the Cross is the most richly endowed.

Thus this devotion, as well on account of the excellence of its object as by reason of the Indulgences, constitutes a suffrage of the greatest value for the Holy Souls.

We find an incident relating to this subject in the Life of Venerable Mary d'Antigna.[1] For a long time she had the pious custom of making the Stations of the Cross each day for the relief of the souls departed; but later, for motives more apparent than solid, she did it but rarely, and finally omitted it altogether. Our Lord, who had great designs in regard to this pious virgin, and who desired to make her a victim of love for the consolation of the poor souls in Purgatory, vouchsafed to give her a lesson which serves as an instruction to us all. A Religious of the same convent, who had died a short time previously, appeared to

---

[1] Louvet, *Le Purgatoire,* p. 332.

her, complaining sorrowfully, "My dear sister," she said, "why do you no longer make the Stations of the Cross for the souls in Purgatory? You were formerly accustomed to relieve us every day by that holy exercise; why do you deprive us of that assistance?"

Whilst the soul was still speaking our Lord Himself appeared to His servant, and reproached her with her negligence. "Know, my daughter," He added, "that the Stations of the Cross are very profitable to the souls in Purgatory, and constitute a suffrage of the greatest value. This is why I have permitted this soul, for her own sake and for the sake of others, to implore this of you. Know also that it was on account of your exactitude in practising this devotion that you have been favoured by frequent communication with the dead. It is for this reason also that those grateful souls never cease to pray for you, and to plead your cause at the tribunal of my Justice. Make known this treasure to your sisters, and tell them to draw from it abundantly for themselves and for the dead."

CHAPTER XXVI.

Relief of the Holy Souls—Indulgences—Blessed Mary of Quito and the Heaps of Gold.

LET us pass to those indulgences applicable to the dead. Here Divine Mercy reveals itself with a sort of prodigality. We know that an indulgence is *the remission of the temporal punishment* due to sin, granted by the power of the Keys, outside of the Sacrament of Penance.

In virtue of the power of *the Keys*, which she has received from Jesus Christ, the Church may free the faithful from every obstacle to their entrance into glory. She exercises this power in the Sacrament of Penance, where she absolves them from their sins; she exercises it also outside of the Sacrament, in remitting the debt of temporal punishment which remains after the absolution; in this second instance it is the indulgence. The remission of temporal punishment by indulgences is granted to the faithful in this life only; but the Church may authorise her children whilst still living to transfer to their departed friends the remission accorded to themselves; this is *the indulgence applicable to the souls in Purgatory*. To apply an indulgence to the dead is to offer it to God in the name of His Holy Church, that He may deign to employ it for the benefit of the suffering souls. The satisfactions thus offered to the Divine Justice in the name of Jesus Christ are always accepted, and God applies it either to some soul in particular or to certain souls which He Himself wishes to benefit, or to all in general. Indulgences are either *plenary* or *partial*. A plenary indulgence is, to such as gain it, a remission of all the temporal punishment which it deserves in the sight of God. Suppose that, in order to acquit ourselves of this debt, we should be obliged to perform a hundred years of canonical penance upon earth, or suffer for a still longer time in Purgatory, by the virtue of a plenary indulgence properly gained all this punishment is remitted, and the soul no longer retains in the sight of God any shadow of sin, which prevents it from seeing His Divine face.

The *partial* indulgence consists in the remission of a certain number of days or years. These days and years in no way represent days and years of suffering in Purgatory; it must be understood of days and years of public canonical penance, consisting principally in fasts, and such as were formerly imposed upon sinners, according to the ancient discipline of the Church. Thus, an indulgence of forty days or seven years is a remission such as was merited before God by forty days or seven years of canonical penance. What proportion exists between those days of penance and the duration of the sufferings of Purgatory? This is a secret which it has not pleased God to reveal to us.

Indulgences are, in the Church, a true spiritual treasure laid open to all the faithful; all are permitted to draw therefrom, to pay their own debts and those of others. It was under this figure that God was one day pleased to show them to Blessed Mary of Quito.[1] One day, rapt in ecstasy, she saw in the midst of a large space an immense table covered with heaps of silver, gold, rubies, pearls, and diamonds, and at the same time she heard a voice saying, "These riches are public property; each one may approach and take as much as he pleases." God made known to her that this was a symbol of indulgences.[2] We may say with the pious author of the *Merveilles* how culpable we are if in such abundance we remain poor and destitute ourselves and neglect to assist others. Alas! the souls in Purgatory are in such extreme necessity, they supplicate us with tears in the midst of their torments; we have the means of paying their debts by indulgences, and we make no endeavour to do so.

Does access to this treasury demand painful efforts on our parts, such as fastings, journeys, and privations insupportable to nature? "Even though such were the case," says with reason the eloquent Father Segneri, "we should submit to them." Do we not see how men for love of gold, in order to preserve a work of art, to save a part of their fortune or a precious fabric, expose themselves to the flames of a fire? Ought we not then to do at least as much to save from expiatory flames those souls ransomed by the Blood of Jesus Christ? But Divine goodness asks nothing so painful: it requires only such works as are ordinary and easy—a Rosary, a Communion, a visit to the Blessed Sacrament, an alms

---

[1] May 26.   [2] Rossignoli, *Merv.*, 29.

or the teaching of the elements of the Catechism to abandoned children. And we neglect to acquire the most precious treasures by such easy means, and have no desire to apply them to our poor relatives languishing in the flames of Purgatory.

CHAPTER XXVII.

Relief of the Holy Souls—Indulgences—Mother Frances of Pampeluna and the Bishop de Ribera—St. Magdalen de Pazzi—St. Teresa.

VENERABLE MOTHER FRANCES, of the Blessed Sacrament, of whose charity towards the holy souls we have already spoken, was also most zealous in relieving them by indulgences. One day God showed her the souls of three prelates who had previously occupied the See of Pampeluna, and who still languished in the sufferings of Purgatory. The servant of God understood that she must employ every means to effect their deliverance. As the Holy See had then granted to Spain the Bulls *of the Crusade*, which permitted the gaining of a plenary indulgence under certain conditions, she believed that the best means of assisting those poor souls would be to procure for each of them the advantage of a plenary indulgence.

She spoke to her Bishop, Christopher de Ribera, acquainting him with the fact that three of his predecessors were still in Purgatory, and urging him to procure for her three indulgences of the Crusade. She fulfilled all the conditions required, and applied a plenary indulgence to each of the three Bishops. The following night they all appeared to Mother Frances, delivered from all their sufferings. They thanked her, and begged her to thank also the Bishop Ribera for the indulgences which had opened Heaven to them.[1]

The following is related by Father Cepari in his Life of St. Magdalen de Pazzi. A professed Religious, who, during her last sickness, had been most tenderly cared for by St. Magdalen, died, and as it was the custom to expose the body in the church, Magdalen felt herself inspired to go and look upon it once more. She went, therefore, to the grid of the chapter-room, whence she could see it; but scarcely had she done so, than she was ravished in ecstasy, and saw the soul of the departed sister take its flight to Heaven. Transported with joy, she was heard to say, "Adieu, dear sister; adieu, blessed soul! Like a pure dove, you fly to your celestial home, and leave us in this abode of misery. Oh, how beautiful and glorious you are! Who can describe the glory with which God has crowned your virtues? What a short time you have passed in Purgatory! Your body has not yet been consigned to the tomb, and behold! your soul is already received into the sacred mansions. You now know the truth of those words I so lately addressed to you, 'That all the sufferings of this life are nothing in comparison with the reward which God has reserved for His friends.'" In the same vision, our Lord revealed to her that this soul had passed but fifteen hours in Purgatory, because she had suffered much during life, and because she had been careful to gain the indulgences granted by the Church to her children, in virtue of the merits of Jesus Christ.

St. Teresa in her works speaks of a Religious who set the highest value on the smallest indulgence granted by the Church, and endeavoured to gain all in her power. She led otherwise a very ordinary life, and her virtue was of a very common order. She died, and the saint, to her

[1] *Vie de Françoise du Sacrem., Merv.*, 26.

great surprise, saw her soul ascend to Heaven almost immediately after her death, so that she had, so to say, no Purgatory. When St. Teresa expressed her astonishment at this, our Lord made known to her that it was due to the great care she had taken to gain all the indulgences possible during life. "It was by that means," He added, "that she had discharged almost the whole of her debt, which was quite considerable, before her death; and had therefore appeared with great purity before the tribunal of God."

CHAPTER XXVIII.

Relief of the Holy Souls—Indulgences—Indulgenced Prayers.

THERE are certain indulgences which are easy to be gained, and are applicable to the dead. We hope to afford pleasure to the reader by indicating the principal ones.

1. The prayer: *Oh, good and most sweet Jesus.* — A plenary indulgence for those who, having confessed and communicated, recite this prayer before an image of Christ crucified, and adding some other prayer for the intention of the Sovereign Pontiff.

2. *Indulgenced Rosary Beads.*—Great indulgences are attached to the recitation of the Holy Rosary, if we make use of beads indulgenced either by our Holy Father, the Pope, or by a priest who has received the faculties.

3. *The Stations of the Cross.*—As we have said elsewhere,[1] several plenary indulgences, and a great number of partial indulgences, are attached to the Stations of the Cross. These indulgences do not require Confession and Communion; it suffices to be in the state of grace, and to

[1] Chap. xxv.

have a sincere sorrow for all our sins. As to the exercise itself of the Stations of the Cross, it requires but two conditions—1st, to visit the fourteen Stations, passing from one to the other, as much as circumstances will permit; 2nd, to meditate at the same time on the Passion of Jesus Christ. Persons who do not know how to make connected meditation may content themselves with thinking affectionately of some circumstance of the Passion suited to their capacity. We exhort them, without, however, imposing it as an obligation, to recite a *Pater* and *Ave* before each cross, and to make an act of contrition for their sins.

4. *The Acts of Faith, Hope, and Charity.*—An indulgence of seven years and seven quarantines each time they are recited.

5. *The Litany of the Blessed Virgin.*—Three hundred days each time.

6. *The Sign of the Cross.*—Fifty days each time; with holy water, a hundred days.

7. Divers prayers. *My Jesus, mercy!*—A hundred days each time. *Jesus, meek and humble of heart, make my heart like unto Thine.*—Three hundred days, one a day. *Sweet Heart of Mary, be my salvation.*—Three hundred days each time.

8. *Praised be Jesus Christ.* ℞. *For ever and ever, Amen.*—Fifty days each time that two persons salute each other with these words.

9. *The Angelus.*—An indulgence of a hundred days each time it is recited, either in the morning, at noon, or in the evening, at the sound of the bell, kneeling, and with a contrite heart.

CHAPTER XXIX.

Relief of the Holy Souls—Alms—Raban-Maur and Edelard at the Monastery of Fulda.

IT remains for us to speak of a last and very powerful means of relieving the poor souls: viz., almsgiving. The Angelic Doctor, St. Thomas, gives the preference to alms before fasting and prayer, when there is a question of expiating past faults. "Almsgiving," he says, "possesses more completely the virtue of satisfaction than prayer, and prayer more completely than fasting. This is why the great servants of God and the great saints have chosen it as a principal means of assisting the dead. Amongst them we may mention as one of the most remarkable the holy Abbot Raban-Maur,[1] first Abbot of Fulda, in the tenth century, and afterwards Archbishop of Mayence.

Father Trithemius, a well-known writer of the Order of St. Benedict, caused abundant alms to be distributed for the dead. He had established a rule that whenever a Religious died, his portion of food should be distributed among the poor for thirty days, that the soul of the deceased might be relieved by the alms. It happened in the year 830 that the monastery of Fulda was attacked by a contagious disease, which carried off a large number of the Religious. Raban-Maur, full of zeal and charity for their souls, called Edelard, the Procurator of the monastery, and reminded him of the rule established regarding the alms for the departed. "Take great care," said he, "that our constitutions be faithfully observed, and that the poor be fed for a whole month with the food destined for the brethren we have lost."

[1] Feb. 4.

Edelard failed both in obedience and charity. Under pretext that such liberality was extravagant, and that he must economise the resources of the monastery, but in reality because he was influenced by a secret avarice, he neglected to distribute the food, or did so in a manner far short of the command he had received. God did not leave this disobedience unpunished.

A month elapsed, when one evening, after the community had retired, he walked across the chapter-room with a lamp in his hand. What was his astonishment when, at an hour that the room should be unoccupied, he found there a great number of Religious. His astonishment turned into fear when, looking at them attentively, he recognised the Religious lately deceased. Terror seized him, an icy coldness ran through his veins and riveted him to the spot like a lifeless statue. Then one of the dead brothers addressed him with terrible reproaches. "Unfortunate creature," said he, "why didst thou not distribute the alms which were destined to give relief to the souls of thy departed brethren? Why hast thou deprived us of that assistance amid the torments of Purgatory. Receive, from this moment, the punishment of thy avarice; another and more terrible chastisement is reserved for thee, when, after three days, thou shall appear before thy God."

At these words Edelard fell as though struck by a thunderbolt, and remained immovable until after midnight, at the hour when the community went to choir. There they found him half-dead, in the same condition as was Heliodorus of old, after he had been scourged by the angels in the temple of Jerusalem (2 Mach. iii.).

He was carried to the infirmary, where all possible care was lavished upon him, so that he recovered consciousness. As soon as he was able to speak, in the presence of the Abbot and of all his brethren, he related with tears the terrible occurence to which his sad condition but too evidently bore witness. Then adding that he was to die within three days, he asked for the last Sacraments, with all signs of humble repentance. He received them with sentiments of piety, and three days later expired, assisted by the prayers of his brethren.

Mass for the dead was immediately sung, and his share of food was distributed to the poor, for the benefit of his soul. Meanwhile, his punishment was not at an end. Edelard appeared to Abbot Raban, pale and disfigured. Touched with compassion, Raban inquired what he could do for him. "Ah!" replied the unfortunate soul, "nowithstanding the prayers of our holy community, I cannot obtain the grace of my deliverance until all my brethren, whom my avarice defrauded of the suffrages due to them, have been released. That which has been given to the poor for me has been of no profit but to them, and this by order of Divine Justice. I entreat you, therefore, O venerated and merciful Father, redouble your alms. I hope that by these powerful means Divine clemency will vouchsafe to deliver us all, my brethren first, and afterwards myself, who am the least deserving of mercy."

Raban-Maur increased his alms, and scarcely had another month elapsed, when Edelard again appeared; but clad in white, surrounded with rays of light and his countenance beaming with joy. He thanked, in the most touching manner, his Abbot and all the members of the monastery for the charity exercised towards him.[1]

What instruction does not this history contain! In the first place, the virtue of almsgiving for the dead shines forth in a most striking manner. Then we see how God chastises, even in this life, those who through avarice fear not to deprive the dead of their suffrages. I speak not here of those heirs who render themselves culpable, by neglecting to make the endowments which devolve upon them by last will and testament of their deceased relatives, a negligence which constitutes a sacrilegious injustice;

---

[1] *Vie de Raban-Maur*; Rossignoli, *Merv.*, 2.

PURGATORY, THE MYSTERY OF MERCY. 203

but of those children or relatives who, through miserable motives of interest, have as few Masses as possible celebrated, are sparing in the distribution of alms, having no pity for the souls of their departed relatives, which they leave to languish in the horrible torments of Purgatory. It is the blackest ingratitude, a hardness of heart entirely opposed to Christian charity, and which will meet its punishment perhaps even in this world.

CHAPTER XXX.

Relief of the Holy Souls—Almsgiving—Christian Mercy— St. Francis de Sales and the Widow at Padua.

CHRISTIAN *almsgiving*, that *mercy* which Jesus Christ so much recommends in the Gospel, comprises not only corporal assistance given to the needy, but also all the good we do for our neighbour by working for his salvation, supporting his defects, and pardoning his offences. All these works of charity may be offered to God for the dead, and contain great satisfactory virtue. St. Francis de Sales relates that at Padua, where he pursued part of his studies, there existed a detestable custom. The young men amused themselves by running through the streets at night armed with arquebuses, and crying out to all those they met, " *Who goes there?* "

People were obliged to answer, for they fired upon those who gave no reply, and many persons were thus wounded or killed. It happened one evening that a student, not having responded to the question, was struck in the head by a ball and mortally wounded. The perpetrator of this deed, seized with terror, took to flight and sought refuge in the house of a good widow whom he knew, and whose son was his fellow-student. He confessed to her with tears that he had just killed some one unknown to him, and begged her to give him an asylum in her house. Touched with compassion, and not suspecting that she had before her the murderer of her son, the lady concealed the fugitive in a place of safety where the officers of justice would be unable to discover him.

Half an hour had not elapsed, when a tumultuous noise was heard at the door; a corpse was carried in and placed before the eyes of the widow. Alas! it was her son who had been killed, and whose murderer now lay concealed in her house. The poor mother broke forth into heart-rending cries, and entering the hiding-place of the assassin, "Miserable man," said she, "what had my son done to you that you should thus cruelly have murdered him?"

The guilty wretch, learning that he had killed his friend, cried aloud, tearing his hair, and wringing his hands in despair. Then throwing himself upon his knees, he asked pardon of his protectress, and besought her to deliver him up to the magistrate, that he might expiate so horrible a crime.

The disconsolate mother remembered at this moment that she was a Christian, the example of Jesus Christ praying for His executioners stimulated her to heroic action. She replied that provided he asked pardon of God and amended his life, she would let him go, and stay all legal proceedings against him.

This pardon was so agreeable to God, that He wished to give the generous mother a striking proof thereof. He permitted that the soul of her son should appear to her, resplendent with glory, saying that he was about to enjoy eternal beatitude. "God has shown mercy to me, dear mother," said the blessed soul, "because you showed mercy towards my assassin. In consideration of the pardon which you granted, I have been delivered from

Purgatory, where, without the assistance which you have afforded me, I should have had to undergo long years of intense suffering."

CHAPTER XXXI.

Relief of the Holy Souls—The Heroic Act of Charity towards the Holy Souls—Father Mumford—Denis the Carthusian and St. Gertrude.

THUS far we have spoken of the different kinds of good works which we may offer to God as suffrages for the dead. It remains for us to make known an act which comprises all works and means, whereby we can most effectually assist the poor souls; it is *the heroic vow*, or, as others call it, *the Heroic act of Charity towards the souls in Purgatory*.

This act consists in ceding to them all our works of satisfaction, that is to say, the *satisfactory* value of all the works of our life and of all the suffrages which shall be given to us after our death, without reserving anything wherewith to discharge our own debts. We deposit them in the hands of the Blessed Virgin, that she may distribute them, according to her good pleasure, to those souls which she desires to deliver from Purgatory.

It is an absolute donation in favour of the souls of all that we can give them; we offer to God in their behalf all the good we do, of what kind soever, either in thought, words or works, all that we suffer meritoriously during this life, without excepting anything that we may reasonably give them, and adding even those suffrages which we may receive for ourselves after death.

It must be well understood that the matter of this holy

donation is the *satisfactory* value of our works,[1] and in no way the *merit* which has a corresponding degree of glory in Heaven ; for merit is strictly personal, and cannot be transferred to another.

Formula of the Heroic Act: "O Holy and Adorable Trinity, desiring to co-operate in the deliverance of the souls in Purgatory, and to testify my devotion to the Blessed Virgin Mary, I cede and renounce in behalf of those holy souls all the satisfactory part of my works, and all the suffrages which may be given to me after my death, consigning them entirely into the hands of the most Blessed Virgin, that she may apply them according to her good pleasure to those souls of the faithful departed whom she desires to deliver from their sufferings. Deign, O my God, to accept and bless this offering which I make to Thee at this moment. Amen."

The Sovereign Pontiffs, Benedict XIII., Pius VI., and Pius IX. have approved this heroic act, and have enriched it with indulgences and privileges, of which the principal are the following :—1. To priests who have made this act the indult of a privileged altar every day in the year. 2. The simple faithful can gain a plenary indulgence, applicable to the souls in Purgatory only, each time they communicate, provided they visit a church or public oratory, and there pray for the intention of His Holiness. 3. They may apply to the holy souls all those indulgences which are not otherwise applicable by virtue of concession, and which have been granted up to the present time, or which shall be granted in the future.[2]

"I advise all true Christians," says Father Mumford,[3] "to cede with holy disinterestedness to the faithful departed all the fruit of their good works which are at our disposal. I do not believe that they can make a better use of them, since they render them more meritorious and

---

[1] See Chap. ix.
[2] Pius IX., Decr. 30 Sept. 1852. [3] *Charity to the Departed.*

more efficacious, as well for obtaining grace from God as for expiating their own sins and shortening the term of their Purgatory, or even of acquiring an entire exemption therefrom."

These words express the precious advantages of the Heroic Act; and in order to dissipate all subsequent fear which might arise in the mind, we add three remarks: 1. This act leaves us perfect liberty to pray for those souls in whom we are most interested; the application of these prayers is subject to the disposition of the adorable will of God, which is always infinitely perfect and infinitely loving. 2. It does not oblige under pain of mortal sin, and can at any time be revoked. It may be made without using any particular formula; it suffices to have the intention, and to make it from the heart. Nevertheless it is useful to recite the formula of offering from time to time, in order to stimulate our zeal for the relief of the holy souls by prayer, penance, and good works. 3. The Heroic Act does not subject us to the direful consequences of having to undergo a long Purgatory ourselves; on the contrary, it allows us to rely with more assured coefidence on the mercy of God in our regard, as is shown by the example of St. Gertrude.

Venerable Denis, the Carthusian,[1] relates that the Virgin, St. Gertrude, had made a complete donation of all her works of satisfaction in favour of the faithful departed, without reserving anything wherewith to discharge the debts which she herself might have contracted in the sight of God. Being at the point of death, and, like all the saints, considering with much sorrow the great number of her sins on the one hand, and, on the other, remembering that she had employed all her works of satisfaction for the expiation of the sins of others, she was afflicted, lest, having given all to others and reserved nothing for herself, her soul, on its departure from this world, should be condemned to horrible suffering. In

[1] March 12.

the midst of her fears our Lord appeared to her and consoled her, saying: "Be reassured, my daughter, your charity towards the departed will be no detriment to you. Know that the generous donation you have made of all your works to the holy souls has been singularly pleasing to me; and to give you a proof thereof, I declare to you that all the pains you would have had to endure in the other life are now remitted; moreover, in recompense for your generous charity, I will so enhance the value of the merits of your works as to give you a great increase of glory in Heaven."

CHAPTER XXXII.

Relief of the Holy Souls—Which of them should be the Objects of our Charity—All the Faithful Departed—St. Andrew Avellino—Sinners dying without the Sacraments—St. Francis de Sales.

WE have seen the resources and the numerous means which Divine Mercy have placed in our hands for relieving the souls in Purgatory; but what souls are in those expiatory flames, and to what souls should we give our assistance? For what souls should we pray and offer our suffrages to God? To these questions we must answer that we should pray for the souls of all the faithful departed, *omnium fidelium defunctorum*, according to the expression of the Church. Although filial piety imposes special duties upon us with regard to parents and relations, Christian charity commands us to pray for all the faithful departed in general, because they are all our brethren in Jesus Christ, all are our neighbours, whom we must love as ourselves.

By these words, *faithful departed*, the Church means all

all those actually in Purgatory, that is to say, those who are neither in Hell, nor as yet worthy to be admitted into the glory of Paradise. But who are these souls? Can we know them? God has reserved this knowledge to Himself, and, except so far as He is pleased to show us, we should remain in total ignorance of the state of souls in the other life. Now, He rarely makes known that a soul is in Purgatory or in the glory of Heaven; still more rarely does He reveal the reprobation of a soul. In this uncertainty we must pray in general, as does the Church, *for all the departed*, without prejudice to those souls whom we wish to aid in particular.

We may evidently restrict our intention to those among the dead who are still in need of our assistance, if God grants us the privilege which He accorded to St. Andrew Avellino, of knowing the condition of souls in the other life. When this holy Religious of the Order of Theatines was, according to his pious custom, praying with angelic fervour for the departed, it sometimes happened that he experienced within himself a sort of resistance, a feeling of invincible repulsion; at other times it was, on the contrary, a great consolation and a particular attraction. He soon understood the meaning of these different impressions; the first signified that his prayer was useless, that the soul which he desired to assist was unworthy of mercy, and condemned to eternal fire; the other indicated that his prayer was efficacious for the relief of the soul in Purgatory. It was the same when he wished to offer the Holy Sacrifice for some one deceased. He felt, on leaving the sacristy, as though withheld by an irresistible hand, and understood that that soul was in Hell; but when he was inundated with joy, light, and devotion, he was sure of contributing to the deliverance of a soul.

This charitable saint prayed, therefore, with the greatest fervour for the dead whom he knew to be suffering, and ceased not to apply his suffrages until the souls came to thank him, giving him the assurance of their deliverance.[1]

As for us, who have not these supernatural lights, we must pray for all the departed, even for the greatest sinners and the most virtuous Christian. St. Augustine knew the great virtue of his mother, St. Monica; nevertheless, not content with offering his own suffrages for her to God, he asked his readers not to cease recommending her soul to Divine Mercy.

As regards great sinners, who die without being outwardly reconciled with God, we may not exclude them from our suffrages, because we have not the certainty of their interior impenitence. Faith teaches us that all men dying in the state of mortal sin incur eternal damnation; but who are those that in reality die in that state? God alone, who reserves to Himself the judgment of the living and the dead, knows this. As to ourselves, we can but draw a conjectural conclusion from exterior circumstances, and from this we must refrain. It must, however, be confessed that there is everything to be feared for those who die *unprepared for death*, and all hope seems to vanish for *those who refuse to receive the Sacraments*. The latter quit this life with exterior signs of reprobation. Nevertheless, we must leave the judgment to God, according to the words, *Dei judicium est*—"To God belongs judgment."[2] There is more to be hoped for those who are not positively hostile to religion, who are benevolent towards the poor, who retain some practice of Christian piety, or who at least approve and favour piety; there is more, I say, to hope for such persons when it happens that they die suddenly, without having had the time to receive the last Sacraments of the Church.

St. Francis de Sales will not have us despair of the conversion of sinners until their last breath, and even after their death he forbids us to judge evil of those who have

---

[1] Life of the Saint.   [2] Deut. i. 17.

led a bad life. With the exception of those sinners whose reprobation is made manifest by Holy Scripture, we may not, he says, conclude that a person is damned, but must respect the secret of God. His principal reason was, that as the first grace is gratuitous, so also is the last, which is final perseverance or a good death. This is why we must hope for the departed, how sad soever his death may have been, because our conjectures can be based on the exterior only, whereby the most clever may be deceived.

CHAPTER XXXIII.

Relief of the Holy Souls—For whom are we to Pray?— Great Sinners—Father Ravignan and General Exelmans —The Widow in Mourning and the Venerable Curé d'Ars—St. Catherine of St. Augustine and the Sinner Dead in a Grotto.

FATHER RAVIGNAN, an illustrious and holy preacher of the Society of Jesus, also cherished great hope for the welfare of sinners carried away by a sudden death, *when otherwise they had borne no hatred in the heart for the things of God.* He lived to speak of the supreme moment, and it seems to have been his opinion that many sinners are converted in their last moments, and are reconciled to God without being able to give any exterior sign thereof. In certain deaths there are mysteries of Mercy where the eye of man sees nothing but strokes of Justice. As a last glimmer of light, God sometimes reveals Himself to those souls whose greatest misfortune has been to ignore Him; and the lastt sigh, understood by Him who penetrates hearts, may be a groan that calls for pardon; that is to say, an act of perfect contrition. General Exelmans, a relative of this good father, was suddenly carried to the tomb by an accident, and unfortunately he had not been faithful in the practice of his religion. He had promised that he would one day make his confession, but had not had the opportunity to do so. Father Ravignan, who, for a long time had prayed and procured prayers for him, was filled with consternation when he heard of such a death. The same day, a person accustomed to receive supernatural communications thought he heard an interior voice, which said to him, "Who then knows the extent of God's mercy? Who knows the depth of the ocean, or how much water is contained therein? Much will be forgiven to those who have sinned through ignorance."

The biographer from whom we borrow this incident, Father de Ponlevoy, goes on to say, "Christians, placed under the law of Hope no less than under the law of Faith and Charity, we must continually lift ourselves up from the depths of our sufferings to the thought of the infinite goodness of God. No limit to the grace of God is placed here below; while there remains a spark of life there is nothing which it cannot effect in the soul. Therefore we must ever hope and petition God with humble persistency. We know not to what a degree we may be heard. Great saints and doctors have gone to great lengths in extolling the powerful efficacy of prayer for the dear departed, how unhappy soever their end may have been. We shall one day know the unspeakable marvels of Divine Mercy. We should never cease to implore it with the greatest confidence."

The following is an incident which our readers may have seen in the *Petit Messager du Cœur de Marie*, November 1880. A Religious, preaching a mission to the ladies at Nancy, had reminded them in a conference that we must never despair of the salvation of a soul, and that sometimes actions of the least importance in the eyes of man are rewarded by God at the hour of death. When he was about to leave the church, a lady dressed in mourning approached him and said, " Father, you just recommended to us confidence and hope ; what has just happened to me fully justifies your words. I had a husband who was most kind and affectionate, and who, although otherwise leading an irreproachable life, entirely neglected the practice of his religion. My prayers and exhortations remained without effect. During the month of May which preceded his death, I had erected in my room, as I was accustomed to do, a little altar of the Blessed Virgin, and decorated it with flowers, which I renewed from time to time. My husband passed the Sunday in the country, and each time he returned he brought me some flowers, which he himself had plucked, and with these I used to adorn my oratory. Did he notice this? Did he do this to give me pleasure, or was it through a sentiment of piety towards the Blessed Virgin? I know not, but he never failed to bring me the flowers.

" In the beginning of the following month he died suddenly, without having had time to receive the consolations of religion. I was inconsolable, especially as I saw all my hopes of his return to God vanish. In consequence of my grief, my health became completely shattered, and my family urged me to make a tour in the south. As I had to pass through Lyons, I desired to see the Curé d'Ars. I therefore wrote to him asking an audience, and recommending to his prayers my husband, who had died suddenly. I gave him no further details.

" Arrived at Ars, scarcely had I entered the venerable Curé's room than, to my great astonishment, he addressed me in these words: ' Madame, you are disconsolate ; but have you forgotten those bouquets of flowers which were brought to you each Sunday of the month of May?' It is impossible to express my astonishment on hearing M. Vianney remind me of a circumstance that I had not mentioned to any one, and which he could know only by revelation.

He continued, 'God has had mercy on him who honoured His Holy Mother. At the moment of his death your husband repented; his soul is in Purgatory; our prayers and good works will obtain his deliverance.'"

We read in the Life of a holy Religious, Sister Catherine of St. Augustine,[1] that in the place where she lived there was a woman named Mary, who in her youth had given herself up to a very disorderly life, and as age brought no amendment, but, on the contrary, she grew more obstinate in vice, the inhabitants, no longer willing to tolerate the scandal she gave, drove her from the city. She found no other asylum than a grotto in the forest, where, after a few months, she died without the assistance of the Sacraments. Her body was interred in a field, as though it were something contagious.

Sister Catherine, who was accustomed to recommend to God the souls of all those of whose death she heard, thought not of praying for this one, judging, as did every one else, that she was surely damned.

Four months later the servant of God heard a voice saying, "Sister Catherine, how unfortunate I am! You recommend to God the souls of all; I am the only one upon whom you take no pity!" "Who then are you?" replied the sister. "I am poor Mary, who died in the grotto." "What! Mary, are you saved?" "Yes, by the Divine Mercy I am. At the point of death, terrified by the remembrance of my crimes, and seeing myself abandoned by all, I called upon the Blessed Virgin. In her tender goodness she heard me, and obtained for me the grace of perfect contrition, with a desire of confessing, had it been in my power to do so. I thus recovered the grace of God and escaped Hell. But I was obliged to go to Purgatory, where I suffer terribly. My time will be shortened, and I shall soon be liberated, if a few Masses are offered for me. Oh! have them celebrated for me, dear

---

[1] St. Alphonsus, Paraph. of the *Salve Regina*.

sister, and I shall ever remember you before Jesus and Mary."

Sister Catherine hastened to fulfil this request, and after a few days the soul again appeared, brilliant as a star, and returning thanks for her charity.

CHAPTER XXXIV.

Motives for Assisting the Holy Souls—Excellence of this Work—St. Francis de Sales—St. Thomas of Aquin—St. Bridget.

WE have just passed in review the means and resources which Divine Mercy has placed in our hands for the relief of our brethren in Purgatory. These means are powerful, the resources rich; but do we make an abundant use thereof? Having it in our power to assist the poor souls, have we zeal enough to do so? Are we as rich in Charity as God is rich in mercy? Alas! how many Christians do little or nothing for the departed! And those who forget them not, those who have sufficient Charity to aid them by their suffrages, how often are they not lacking in zeal and fervour! Compare the care we bestow upon the sick with the assistance which we give to the suffering souls. When a father or mother is afflicted with some malady, when a child or any person dear to us is a prey to suffering, what care, what solicitude, what devotion on our part! But the holy souls, who are no less dear to us, languish under the weight, not of a painful malady, but of expiatory torments a thousand times more cruel. Are we equally fervent, solicitous, eager to procure them relief? "No," says St. Francis de Sales, "we do not sufficiently remember our dear departed friends. Their memory seems to perish with the sound of the funeral-bells, and we forget that the friendship which finds an end, even in death, was never genuine friendship."

From whence this sad and culpable forgetfulness? Its principal cause is want of reflection. *Quia nullus est qui recogitat corde*—" Because there is none that considereth in the heart."[1] We lose sight of the great motives which urge us to the exercise of this Charity towards the dead. It is, therefore, to stimulate our zeal that we are about to recall to mind these motives, and to place them in the strongest possible light.

We may say that all these motives are summed up in these words of the Holy Ghost : *It is a holy and wholesome thought to pray for the dead, that they may be loosed from their sins*, that is, from the temporal punishment due to their sins.[2] In the first place, it is a work, *holy* and excellent in itself, as also agreeable and meritorious in the sight of God. Accordingly, it is a *salutary* work, supremely profitable for our own salvation, for our welfare in this world and the next.

"One of the holiest works, one of the best exercises of piety that we can practise in this world," says St. Augustine, "is to offer sacrifices, alms, and prayers for the dead."[3] "The relief which we procure for the departed," says St. Jerome, "obtains for us a like mercy."

Considered in itself, prayer for the dead is a work of Faith, Charity, and frequently even of Justice.

1st, Who are, indeed, the persons whom there is question of assisting? Who are those holy, predestined souls, so dear to God and our Lord Jesus Christ, so dear to their Mother, the Church, who unceasingly recommends them to our charity; souls who are dear also to ourselves, that were, perhaps, intimately united to us upon earth, and who supplicate us in these touching words: *Have pity on me*,

---

[1] Jerem. xii. 11.   [2] 2 Machab. xii. 46.   [3] Homil. 16.

have pity on me, at least you my friends.[1] 2nd, In what necessities do they find themselves? Alas! their necessities being very great, the souls who thus suffer have a right to our assistance proportionate to their utter helplessness to do anything for themselves. 3rd, What good do we procure for the souls? The greatest good, since we put them in possession of eternal beatitude.

"To assist the souls in Purgatory," says St. Francis de Sales, "is to perform the most excellent of the works of Mercy, or rather it is to practise in a most sublime manner all the works of Mercy together: it is to visit the sick; it is to give drink to those who thirst for the vision of God; it is to feed the hungry, to ransom prisoners, to clothe the naked, to procure for poor exiles the hospitality of the Heavenly Jerusalem; it is to comfort the afflicted, to instruct the ignorant—in fine, to practise all works of Mercy in one." This doctrine agrees very well with that of St. Thomas, who says in his *Summa*, "Suffrages for the dead are more agreeable to God than suffrages for the living; because the former stand in more urgent need thereof, not being able to assist themselves, as are the living."[2]

Our Lord regards every work of Mercy exercised towards our neighbour as done to Himself. "*It is to Me*," says He, "*that you have done it,*"—*Mihi fecistis*. This is most especially true of Mercy practised towards the poor souls. It was revealed to St. Bridget that he who delivers a soul from Purgatory has the same merit as if he delivered Jesus Christ Himself from captivity.

[1] Job xix. 21.   [2] Supplem., q. 71. art. 5.

CHAPTER XXXV.

Motives for Aiding the Holy Souls—Excellence of the Work—Controversy between Brother Benedict and Brother Bertrand.

WHEN we so highly extol the merits of prayer for the dead, we do not in any way infer that other good works must be omitted; for all other works must be exercised according to time, place, and circumstances. The only intention we had in view was, to give a correct idea of Mercy towards the dead, and to inspire others with a desire to practise it.

Moreover, the spiritual works of Mercy, which have for object the salvation of souls, are all of equal excellency, and it is only in certain respects that we may place the assistance of the dead above zeal for the conversion of sinners.

It is related in the Chronicles of the Friars Preachers,[1] that a spirited controversy arose between two Religious of that Order, Brother Benedict and Brother Bertrand, on the subject of suffrages for the departed. It was occasioned by the following:—Brother Bertrand often celebrated Holy Mass for sinners, and prayed continually for their conversion, imposing upon himself the most severe penances; but he was rarely seen to say Mass in black for the dead. Brother Benedict, who had great devotion towards the souls in Purgatory, having remarked this conduct, asked him why he thus acted.

"Because," replied he, "the souls in Purgatory are sure of their salvation, while sinners are continually exposed to the danger of falling into Hell. What more deplorable condition

[1] Cf. Rossign., *Merv.* 1.

than that of a soul in the state of mortal sin? She is in enmity with God, and bound in the chains of the devil, suspended over the abyss of Hell by the frail thread of life, that may be broken at any moment. The sinner walks in the way of perdition; if he continues to advance, he will fall into the eternal abyss. We must, therefore, come to his assistance, and preserve him from this, the greatest of misfortunes, by labouring for his conversion. Moreover, was it not to save sinners that the Son of God came upon earth and died upon a cross? St. Denis also assures us that *the most divine of all divine things is to work with God for the salvation of souls.* As regards the souls in Purgatory, they are safe, their eternal salvation is secure. They suffer, they are a prey to great torments, but they have nothing to fear from Hell, and their sufferings will have an end. The debts they have contracted diminish each day, and they will soon enjoy eternal light; whilst sinners are continually menaced with damnation, the most terrible misfortune that can befall one of God's creatures."

"All that you have said is true," replied Brother Benedict, "but there is another consideration to be made. Sinners are slaves of Satan, of their own free will. Their yoke is of their own choosing, they could break their chains if they pleased; whereas the poor souls in Purgatory can but sigh and implore the assistance of the living. It is impossible for them to break the fetters which hold them captive in those penal flames. Suppose you met two beggars, the one sick, maimed, and helpless, absolutely incapable of earning his livelihood; the other, on the contrary, although in great distress, young and vigorous; which of the two would deserve the greater share of your alms?"

"Assuredly the one who was unable to work," answered Brother Bertrand.

"Well, my dear Father," continued Benedict, "this is just the case with regard to sinners and the holy souls. They can no longer help themselves. The time of prayer, confession, and good works is past for them; we alone are able to relieve them. It is true they have deserved these sufferings in punishment for their sins, but they now bewail and detest those sins. They are in the grace and friendship of God; whereas sinners are His enemies. Certainly we must pray for their conversion, but without prejudice to that which we owe to the suffering souls, so dear to the heart of Jesus. Let us compassionate sinners, but let us not forget that they have all the means of salvation at their disposal; they must break the bonds of sin and fly the danger of damnation which threatens them. Does it not appear evident that the suffering souls are in greater need and merit a larger share in our charity?"

Notwithstanding the force of these arguments, Brother Bertrand persisted in his first opinion. But the night following he had an apparition of a soul from Purgatory, which made him experience for a short time the pain which she herself endured. This suffering was so atrocious that it seemed impossible to bear it. Then, as Isaias says, torture gave him understanding: *Vexatio intellectum dabit*,[1] and he was convinced that he ought to do more for the suffering souls. The next morning, filled with compassion, he ascended the altar steps vested in black, and offered the Holy Sacrifice for the dead.

[1] Isaias xxviii. 19.

CHAPTER XXXVI.

Motives for Assisting the Holy Souls—Intimate Ties which Unite us to them—Filial Piety—Cimon of Athens and his Father in Prison—St. John of God saving the Sick from the Conflagration.

IF we are obliged to assist the holy souls because of the extreme necessity in which they are, how much greater does this motive become when we remember that these souls are united to us by the most sacred ties, the ties of blood, by the Blood of Jesus Christ, and by the ties of human flesh and blood, whence we have been brought forth according to the flesh?

Yes, there are in Purgatory souls united to us by the closest family ties. It may be a father or a mother, who, languishing in those horrible torments, extend their arms in supplication towards me. What would we not do for our father or for our mother, if we knew they were pining away in some loathsome dungeon? An ancient Athenian, the celebrated Cimon, had the grief to see his father imprisoned by heartless creditors whom he was unable to satisfy. What was worse, he could not raise a sum sufficient to effect his father's ransom, and the old man died in prison. Cimon hastened to the prison and requested that they would at least grant him the body of his father that he might give it burial. This was refused him, under pretext that, not having had wherewith to pay his debts, he could not be set at liberty. "Allow me first to bury my father," cried Cimon, "I will then return and take his place in prison."

We admire this act of filial piety, but are we not also bound to imitate it? Have we not also, perhaps, a father or a mother in Purgatory? Are we not obliged to deliver them at the cost of the greatest sacrifices? More fortunate than Cimon, we have wherewith to pay their debts; we need not take their place; on the contrary, to deliver them is to purchase our own ransom.

We admire, also, the charity of St. John of God,[1] who braved the fury of the flames to save the poor sick during a conflagration. This great servant of God died at Granada in the year 1550, kneeling before an image of Jesus crucified, which he embraced and continued to hold clasped tightly within his arms, even after he had breathed forth his soul to God. Born of very poor parents, and obliged to support himself by tending flocks, he was rich in faith and confidence in God. He took great delight in prayer and hearing the Word of God; this was the foundation of the great sanctity which he afterwards attained. A sermon by the Venerable Father John d'Avila, the Apostle of Andalusia, made such an impression upon him, that he resolved to consecrate his entire life to the service of the sick poor. Without other resource than his charity and confidence in God, he succeeded in purchasing a house, in which he assembled all poor abandoned sick, that he might give them nourishment for soul and body. This asylum soon developed into the Royal Hospital of Granada, an immense establishment, filled with a multitude of the aged and infirm. One day a fire having broken out in the hospital, many of the sick were in danger of perishing by a most horrible death. They were surrounded on all sides by flames, so that it was impossible for any one to attempt their rescue. They uttered the most heart-rending cries, calling Heaven and earth to their assistance. John sees them, his charity is inflamed, he rushes into the fire, battles through flame and smoke until he reaches the beds of the sick; then raising them upon his shoulders, he carries these unfortunate creatures one after another to a place of safety.

[1] March 8.

Obliged to traverse this vast furnace, working in the heat of the fire for a whole half-hour, the saint had not sustained the least injury; the flames respected his person, his clothing, and even the least hair of his head, God wishing to show by a miracle how pleasing to Him was the charity of His servant. And those who save, not the body, but souls from the flames of Purgatory, is their work less agreeable to God? Are the necessities, the cries and moans of those souls less touching to a heart of faith? Is it more difficult to aid them? Is it necessary to cast ourselves into the flames in order to rescue them?

Assuredly, we have every facility in our power for affording them relief, and God does not demand great efforts on our part. Yet the charity of fervent souls inspires them to make the most heroic sacrifices, and even to share the torments of their brethren in Purgatory.

CHAPTER XXXVII.

Motives for Assisting the Holy Souls—Facility in Relieving them—The Example of the Saints and of all Fervent Christians—The Servant of God, Mary Villani—The Burned Forehead.

WE have already seen how St. Catherine de Ricci and several others carried their heroism so far as to suffer instead of the souls in Purgatory. Let us add a few more, examples of this admirable Charity. The servant of God Mary Villani, of the Order of St. Dominic, whose life was written by Father Marchi,[1] applied herself day and night to the practice of satisfactory works in favour of the departed.

[1] Cf. Rossignoli, *Merv*., 41.

One day—it was the Vigil of the Epiphany—she remained a long time in prayer, beseeching God to alleviate their sufferings in consideration of those of Jesus Christ, offering to Him the cruel scourging of our Saviour, His crown of thorns, His cords, the nails and cross—in a word, all His bitter pains and all the instruments of His Passion. The following night God was pleased to manifest how agreeable to Him was this holy practice.

During her prayer she was rapt in ecstasy, and saw a long procession of persons robed in white garments and radiant with light. They were carrying the emblems of the Passion and entering into the glory of Paradise. The servant of God knew that they were the souls delivered by her fervent prayers and by the merits of the Passion of Jesus Christ.

On another occasion, the Feast of All-Souls, she was ordered to work at a manuscript, and to pass the day in writing. This task, imposed by obedience, was a trial to her piety: she experienced some repugnance to obey, because she wished to devote that whole day to prayer, penance, and pious exercises for the relief of the suffering souls. She forgot for a moment that obedience should take precedence over all else, as it is written, *Melior est obedientia quam victimæ*—" Obedience is better than sacrifice."[1] Seeing her great charity towards the poor souls, God vouchsafed to appear to her, in order to instruct and console her. "Obey, my daughter," He said to her; "do the work imposed upon you by Obedience, and offer it for the souls: each line which you shall write to-day in the spirit of Obedience and Charity, will procure the deliverance of a soul." It will be easily understood that she laboured with the greatest diligence, and wrote as many as possible of those lines, so acceptable to God.

Her charity towards the holy souls did not confine itself to prayer and fasting; she desired to endure a part of their

[1] 1 Kings xv. 22.

sufferings. One day, whilst praying for that intention, she was rapt in spirit and led into Purgatory. There, amongst the multitude of suffering souls, she saw one more grievously tormented than the others, and which excited her most tender compassion. "Why," she asked, "have you to suffer such excruciating torture? Do you receive no alleviation?" "I have been," replied the soul, "a great length of time in this place, enduring the most frightful torments, in punishment for my former vanity and scandalous extravagance. Thus far I have not received the least relief, because God has permitted that I should be forgotten by my parents, my children, my relatives, and friends: they offer not a single prayer for me. When I was upon earth, being exclusively occupied with my extravagant toilet and worldly vanities, with feasting and pleasure, I cast but a passing thought upon God and my duties. My only serious desire was to further the worldly interests of my family. I am well punished; for you see I am entirely forgotten by all."

These words made a painful impression upon Mary Villani. She begged this soul to allow her to feel something of what she suffered; and at the same instant it seemed as though a finger of fire touched her forehead, and the pain which she felt was so acute as to cause her ecstasy to cease. The mark remained so deeply impressed upon her forehead, that two months afterwards it was still visible, and caused her intolerable suffering. The servant of God offered this, together with prayers and other good works, for the soul to which we have just referred. This soul appeared to Mary at the end of two months, and said that having been delivered by her intercession, she was about to enter Heaven. At the same moment the scar on the forehead disappeared.

CHAPTER XXXVIII.

Motives for Assisting the Holy Souls—Examples of Holy Persons—Father James Laynez—Father Fabricius—Father Nieremberg, a Victim of his Charity.

"He who forgets his friend, after death has taken him away from his sight, never had a true friendship." These words Father Laynez, second General of the Society of Jesus, continually repeated to the sons of St. Ignatius. He desired that the interests of souls should be as dear to them after death as they were during life. Joining example to precept, Laynez applied to the souls in Purgatory a large part of his prayers, sacrifices, and the satisfaction which he merited before God by his labours for the conversion of sinners. The Fathers of the Society, faithful to his lessons of charity, ever manifested particular zeal for this devotion, as may be seen in the book entitled "Heroes and Victims of Charity in the Society of Jesus," from which I will here transcribe but one page.

"At Münster, in Westphalia, towards the middle of the seventeenth century, an epidemic broke out which each day swept away innumerable victims. Fear paralysed the charity of the greater part of the inhabitants, and few were found to devote themselves to the relief of the unfortunate plague-stricken creatures. Then Father John Fabricius, animated with the spirit of Laynez and Ignatius, rushed into the arena of self-sacrifice. Putting aside all personal precaution, he employed his time in visiting the sick, in procuring remedies for them, and in disposing them to die a Christian death. He heard their confessions, administered the other sacraments, buried them with his own hands, and finally celebrated the Holy Sacrifice for the repose of their souls.

"In fact, during his whole lifetime this servant of God had the greatest devotion towards the holy souls.

"Among all his exercises of piety, the one most dear to him, and which he always earnestly recommended, was that of offering the Holy Sacrifice of the Mass for the departed whenever the Rubrics permitted. As a result of this counsel, all the Fathers in Münster resolved to consecrate one day in each month to the faithful departed; they draped their church in black, and prayed with all solemnity for the dead.

"God deigned, as He often does, to recompense Father Fabricius, and encouraged his zeal by several apparitions of the suffering souls. Some besought him to hasten their deliverance, others thanked him for the relief he had procured for them; others, again, announced to him the happy moment of their deliverance.

"His greatest act of Charity was that which he accomplished at the moment of his death. With a generosity truly admirable, he made a sacrifice of all the suffrages, prayers, Masses, indulgences, and mortifications which the Society applies to her deceased members. He asked God to deprive him of them for the relief of the suffering souls most pleasing to his Divine Majesty."

We have already spoken of Father Nieremberg, renowned as well for the works of piety which he published as for the eminent virtue which he practised. His devotion for the holy souls, not content with sacrifices and frequent prayers, urged him to suffer for them with a generosity which often amounted to heroism.

There was among his penitents at the court of Madrid a lady of rank, who, under his wise direction, had attained a high degree of virtue in the midst of the world, but she was tormented with an excessive fear of death in view of Purgatory which follows it. She fell dangerously ill, and her fears increased to such a degree, that she almost lost her Christian sentiments. Her holy confessor employed every means that his zeal could suggest, but to no purpose; he could not succeed in restoring her to tranquillity, nor could he prevail upon her even to receive the last Sacraments.

To crown this misfortune, she suddenly lost consciousness, and was reduced to the last extremity. The Father, justly alarmed at the peril of this soul, retired into a chapel near the chamber of the dying woman. There he offered the Holy Sacrifice with the greatest fervour to obtain for the sick person time sufficient to receive the Sacraments of the Church. At the same time, prompted by truly heroic charity, he offered himself as a victim to Divine Justice, to undergo during this life all the sufferings reserved for that poor soul in the next.

His prayer was heard. The Mass was no sooner ended than the sick lady regained consciousness, and found that she was entirely changed. She was so well disposed that she asked for the last Sacraments, which she received with the most edifying fervour. Then her confessor, having told her that she had nothing to fear from Purgatory, she expired perfectly calm, and with a smile upon her lips.

From that hour, Father Nieremberg was afflicted with all manner of suffering, both of body and soul. The remaining sixteen years of his life was one long martyrdom and a most rigorous Purgatory. No human remedy could give him relief; his only consolation was in the remembrance of the holy cause for which he endured them. Finally, death came to terminate his terrible sufferings, and at the same time, we may reasonably believe, to open to him the gates of Paradise, since it is written, *Blessed are the merciful, for they shall obtain mercy.*

CHAPTER XXXIX.

Motives and Incentives to Devotion towards the Holy Souls—Examples of Generosity—St. Peter Damian and his Father—A Young Annamite—The Doorkeeper at the Seminary and the Propagation of the Faith.

EXAMPLES of generous Charity towards the departed are by no means rare, and it is always useful to recall them to mind. We may not omit the beautiful and touching example of St. Peter Damian,[1] Bishop of Ostia, Cardinal and Doctor of the Church, an example which never wearies by repetition. Whilst still young, Peter had the misfortune to lose his mother, and soon afterwards his father marrying again, he was left to the care of a stepmother. Although he showed all possible affection for her, this woman was incapable of returning the love of this dear child; she treated him with barbarous severity, and, in order to rid herself of him, sent him away to her eldest brother, who employed him to take care of the swine. His father, whose duty it was to have prevented this, left him to his unhappy fate. But the child lifted up his eyes to Heaven, where he saw another Father, in whom he placed all his confidence. He accepted all that happened as coming from His divine hands, and resigned himself to the hardships of his situation. "God," he said, "has His designs in all that He does, and they are designs of mercy; we have but to abandon ourselves into His hands, He will direct all things for our good." Peter was not deceived; it was in this painful trial that the future Cardinal of the Church, he who was to astonish his age by the extent of his learning, and to edify the world by the lustre of his virtues, laid the foundation of his future sanctity.

[1] Feb. 23.

Barely covered with rags, his biographer tells us that he had not always sufficient to appease his hunger, but he prayed to God and was satisfied.

Meanwhile his father died. The young saint forgot the harshness with which he had been treated, and, like a good son, prayed continually for the repose of his father's soul. One day he found upon the road a gold piece, which Providence seemed to have placed there for him. It was quite a fortune for the poor child. But, instead of making use of it to relieve his own misery, his first thought was to carry it to a priest, and beg him to celebrate the Holy Sacrifice of the Mass for the soul of his deceased father. Holy Church considers this trait of filial devotion so touching that she has inserted it at length in the Office of the feast.

"May I be allowed," says the missionary, Father Louvet, "to add one more incident of my own personal experience? When I was preaching the faith in Cochin-China, a poor little Annamite girl, who had just been baptized, lost her mother. At the age of fourteen she saw herself obliged to provide for her own support and that of her two younger brothers from her scanty earnings, which amounted to about eight sous, or about seven cents a day. What was my surprise when, at the end of the week, I saw her bring me the earnings of two days, that I might say Mass for the repose of their dear mother's soul. Those poor little ones had fasted during a part of the week to procure this humble suffrage for their departed mother. Oh, holy alms of the poor and the orphan! If my own heart was so deeply touched by it, how much more so the heart of our Heavenly Father, and what blessings it will have called down upon that mother and upon her children.

"Behold the generosity of the poor! What an example and reproach to so many of the rich, extravagant in luxury and pleasure, but miserly when there is question of giving an alms to have Masses celebrated for their deceased relatives.

PURGATORY, THE MYSTERY OF MERCY. 231

"Although before all other intentions they should devote part of their alms to have Masses offered for their own souls, or those of their friends, it is proper to use a portion for the relief of the poor, or for other good works, such as for the benefit of Catholic schools, the Propagation of the Faith, and other purposes, according to circumstances. This is a holy liberality, conformable to the spirit of the Church, and very profitable to the souls in Purgatory."

The Abbé Louvet, from whom we have taken the above, relates another incident which deserves a place here. It concerns a man in humble circumstances who made a generous sacrifice in favour of the Propagation of the Faith, but under circumstances which rendered this act particularly valuable for the future needs of his soul in Purgatory.

A poor porter at a seminary during his long life had, penny by penny, amassed the sum of eight hundred francs. Having no family, he destined this sum for the celebration of Masses after his death. But what can charity not effect when once it has inflamed the heart with its sacred fire? A young priest was on the point of quitting the seminary for the foreign missions. The old man felt himself inspired to give him his little treasure for the beautiful work of the Propagation of the Faith. He therefore gave it and said, "Dear sir, I beg you to accept this small alms to aid you in the work of spreading the Gospel. I kept it to have Masses said after my death, but I would rather remain a little longer in Purgatory that the name of the good God be glorified." The seminarian was moved even to tears. He would not accept the too generous offer of the poor man, but the latter insisted so earnestly that he had not the heart to refuse him.

A few months later the good old man died. No apparition has revealed his fate in the other world. But is he in need? Do we not know that the Heart of Jesus cannot allow itself to be surpassed in generosity? Do we not understand that a man who was generous enough to consign himself to the flames of Purgatory in order that Jesus Christ might be made known to infidel nations will surely have found abundant mercy before the Sovereign Judge?

CHAPTER XL.

Motives of Assisting the Holy Souls—Obligation not only of Charity, but also of Justice—Pious Legacies—Father Rossignoli and the Devastated Property—St. Thomas of Cantimpré and the Soldier of Charlemagne.

WE have just considered devotion to the souls in Purgatory as a work of Charity. Prayer for the dead, we have said, is a holy work, because it is a very salutary exercise of that most excellent of virtues, Charity. This Charity towards the departed is not only optional and of counsel, but it is also of precept, no less than to give alms to the poor. As there exists a general obligation of Charity for almsgiving, with how much greater reason are we not bound by the general law of Charity to assist our suffering brethren in Purgatory?

This obligation of Charity is often joined to an obligation of strict Justice. When a dying person, either by word of mouth or by written testament, expresses his last wishes in regard to works of piety; when he charges his heirs to have a certain number of Masses celebrated, to distribute a certain sum in alms, for any good work whatsoever, the heirs are obliged in strict justice, from the moment they come into possession of the property, to fulfil without delay the last wishes of the deceased.

This duty of Justice is the more sacred as these pious legacies are frequently but disguised restitutions. Now, what does daily experience teach us? Do people hasten with religious exactitude to acquit themselves of these pious obligations which concern the soul of the departed? Alas! quite the contrary. A family which comes into possession of a considerable fortune doles out to its poor departed relative the few suffrages that he has reserved for his own spiritual benefit; and if the subtilities of the civil law favour them, the members of this family are not ashamed, under the pretext of some informality, to fraudulently set aside the will in order to rid themselves of the obligation of making those pious legacies. It is not in vain that the author of the "Imitation" counsels us to make satisfaction for our sins during our life and not to depend too much upon our heirs, who often neglect to execute the pious endowments made by us for the relief of our poor souls.

Let such families beware! This is sacrilegious injustice combined with atrocious cruelty. To steal from a poor person, says the Fourth Council of Carthage, is to become his murderer (*Egentium necatores*). What, then, shall we say of those who rob the dead, who unjustly deprive them of their suffrages, and leave them without assistance in the terrible torments of Purgatory?

Moreover, those who render themselves guilty of this infamous theft are frequently most severely punished by God even in this life. We are sometimes astonished to see a considerable fortune melt away, as it were, in the hands of certain heirs; a sort of malediction seems to hover over certain inheritances. In the Day of Judgment, when that which is now hidden shall be made manifest, we shall see that the cause of this ruin has frequently been the avarice and injustice of the heirs, who neglected the obligations imposed upon them in regard to pious bequests when they succeeded to the property.

It happened in Milan, says Father Rossignoli, that a magnificent estate, situated a short distance from the city, was completely devastated by hail, whilst the neighbouring fields remained uninjured. This phenomenon attracted attention and astonishment ; it reminded one of the plagues of Egypt. The hail ravaged the fields of the Egyptians and respected the land of Gessen, inhabited by the children of Israel. This was looked upon as a similar scourge. The mysterious hail could not have confined itself exclusively within the limits of one property without obeying an intelligent cause. People knew not how to explain this phenomenon, when an apparition of a soul from Purgatory revealed that it was a chastisement inflicted upon ungrateful and culpable children, who had neglected to execute the last will of their departed father relative to certain works of piety.

We know that in all countries and in all places there are spoken of haunted houses, rendered uninhabitable, to the great loss of their proprietors. Now, if we try to fathom the cause of this, we shall generally find that a soul forgotten by its relatives returns to claim the suffrages justly due to it. Whether it be attributed to credulity, to the excitement of imagination, to hallucination, or even to deception, it will ever remain a well-proved fact to teach unfeeling heirs how God punishes such unjust and sacrilegious conduct even in this life.

The following incident, which we borrow from Thomas of Cantimpré,[1] proves clearly how culpable in the sight of God are those heirs who defraud the dead. During the wars of Charlemagne, a valiant soldier had served in the most important and honourable positions. His life was that of a true Christian. Content with his pay, he refrained from every act of violence, and the tumult of the camp never prevented him from the fulfilment of his essential duties, although in matters of minor importance he had been guilty of many little faults common to men of his profession. Having reached a very advanced

[1] Rossign. *Merv.*, 15.

age, he fell ill; and seeing that his last hour had come, he called to his bedside an orphan nephew, to whom he had been a father, and expressed to him his dying wishes. " My son," he said, "you know that I have no riches to bequeath to you: I have nothing but my weapons and my horse. My weapons are for you. As to my horse, sell it when I shall have rendered my soul to God, and distribute the money among the priests and the poor, that the former may offer the Holy Sacrifice for me, and the others may assist me by their prayers." The nephew wept, and promised to execute without delay the last wishes of his dying uncle and benefactor. The old man dying soon after, the nephew took possession of the weapons and led away the horse. It was a very beautiful and valuable animal. Instead of selling it immediately, as he had promised his deceased uncle, he began by using it for short journeys, and as he was well pleased with it, he did not wish to part with it so soon. He deferred under the double pretext that there was nothing that urged the prompt fulfilment of his promise, and that he would await a favourable opportunity to obtain a high price for him. Thus delaying from day to day, from week to week, and from month to month, he ended by stifling the voice of conscience, and forgot the sacred obligation which he had towards the soul of his benefactor.

Six months had elapsed, when one morning the deceased appeared to him addressing him in terms of severe reproach. "Unhappy man," he said, "thou hast forgotten the soul of thy uncle; thou hast violated the sacred promise which thou didst make at my deathbed. Where are the Masses which thou oughtest to have had offered? where the alms that thou shouldst have distributed to the poor for the repose of my soul? Because of thy guilty negligence I have suffered unheard-of torments in Purgatory. Finally, God has taken pity on me; to-day I am to enjoy the company of the blessed in Heaven. But thou, by a just judgment of God, shalt die in a few days, and be subjected to the same tortures which would have remained for me to endure had God not shown mercy to me. Thou shalt suffer for the same length of time that I should have suffered, after which thou shalt commence the expiation of thine own faults."

A few days later the nephew fell dangerously ill. He immediately called a priest, related to him the vision, and confessed his sins, weeping bitterly. "I shall soon die," said he, "and I accept death from the hands of God as a chastisement which I have but too well merited." He expired in sentiments of humble repentance. This was but the least part of the sufferings which had been announced to him in punishment of his injustice; we tremble with horror at the thought of the remaining portion which he was about to undergo in the other life.

CHAPTER XLI.

Motives of Justice—St. Bernardine of Sienna and the Unfaithful Widow—Disguised Restitutions—Neglect to Execute the Last Will.

ST. BERNARDINE relates that a married couple having no children made a contract that in case one should die before the other, the one who survived was to distribute the property left by the other, for the repose of the soul of the deceased. The husband died first and his widow neglected to fulfil her promise. The mother of the widow was still living, and the deceased appeared to her, begging her to go to her daughter and urge her in the name of God to fulfil her engagement. "If she delays," he said, "to distribute in alms the sum which I have destined for the poor, tell her on the part of God that in thirty days she will be struck by a sudden death." When the impious widow heard this solemn warning, she had the audacity to treat it as a dream, and persisted in her sacrilegious infidelity to her promise. Thirty days passed and the unfortunate woman having gone to an upper room in the house, fell through the window and was killed on the spot.

Injustice towards the dead, of which we have just spoken, and fraudulent manœuvres to escape the obligation of executing their pious legacies, are grievous sins, crimes which merit the eternal punishment of Hell. Unless a sincere confession and at the same time due restitution be made, this sin will meet its chastisement not in Purgatory but in Hell.

Alas! yes, it is especially in the other life that Divine Justice will punish the guilty usurpers of the property of the dead. *Judgment without mercy to him that hath not done mercy*, says the Holy Ghost.[1] If these words be true, how rigorous a judgment awaits those whose detestable avarice has left the soul of a parent, a benefactor, for months, years, perhaps even for centuries, in the frightful torments of Purgatory. This crime, as we have said above, is the more grievous, because in many cases these suffrages which the deceased asks for his soul are but disguised restitutions. This fact is in some families but too often overlooked. People find it very convenient to speak of intrigue and clerical avarice. The finest pretexts are made use of to invalidate a last will and testament, which often, perhaps in the majority of cases, involves a necessary restitution. The priest is but a medium in this indispensable act, bound to absolute secrecy by virtue of his sacramental ministry.

Let us explain this more clearly. A dying man has been guilty of some injustice during his life. This is of a more frequent occurrence than we imagine, even in regard to men

[1] James ii. 13.

who are most upright in the eyes of the world. At the moment when he is about to appear before God, this sinner makes his confession; he wishes to make a full reparation, as he is bound to do, of all the injury which he has caused his neighbour, but he has not the time left to do so himself, and is not willing to reveal the sad secret to his children. What does he do? He covers his restitution under the veil of a pious legacy.

Now, if this legacy is not paid, and consequently the injustice not repaired, what will become of the soul of the deceased? Will it be detained for an indefinite length of time in Purgatory? We know not all the laws of Divine Justice, but numerous apparitions serve to give us some idea of them, since they "all declare that they cannot be admitted into eternal beatitude so long as any part of the debt of Justice remains to be cancelled." Moreover, are not these souls culpable for having deferred until their death the payment of a debt of Justice which they had owed for so long a time? And if now their heirs neglect to discharge it for them, is it not a deplorable consequence of their own sin, of their own guilty delay? It is through their fault that these ill-gotten goods remain in the family, and they will not cease to cry out against them as long as restitution be not made. *Res clamat domino*, property cries out for its lawful owner; it cries out against its unjust possessor.

If, through the malice of the heirs, restitution is never made, it is evident that that soul cannot remain in Purgatory for ever; but in this case a long delay to his entrance into Heaven seems to be a fitting chastisement for an act of injustice, which the soul has retracted, it is true, but which still abides in its efficacious cause. Let us therefore think of these grave consequences when we allow days, weeks, months, and perhaps even years to elapse before discharging so sacred a debt.

Alas! how feeble is our faith! If a domestic animal,

a little dog, falls into the fire, do you delay to draw it out? And see, your parents, benefactors, persons most dear to you, writhe in the flames of Purgatory, and you do not consider it your urgent duty to relieve them; you delay, you allow long days of suffering to pass for those poor souls, without making an effort to perform those good works which will release them from their pains.

CHAPTER XLII.

Motives of Justice—Barren Tears—Thomas of Cantimpré and his Grandmother—Blessed Margaret of Cortona.

WE have just spoken of the obligation of Justice which is incumbent upon heirs for the execution of pious legacies. There is another duty of strict Justice which regards children; they are obliged to pray for their deceased parents. Reciprocally in their turn parents are bound by natural right not to forget before God those of their children who have preceded them into eternity. Alas! there are parents who are inconsolable at the loss of a son or of a dearly beloved daughter, and who, instead of praying for them, bestow upon them nothing but a few fruitless tears. Let us hear what Thomas of Cantimpré relates on this subject; the incident happened in his own family.

The grandmother of Thomas had lost a son in whom she had centred her fondest hopes. Day and night she wept for him and refused all consolation. In the excess of her grief she forgot the great duty of Christian love, and did not think of praying for that soul so dear to her. The unfortunate object of this barren tenderness languished amid the flames of Purgatory, receiving no alleviation in his sufferings. Finally God took pity on him. One day, whilst plunged in the depths of her grief, this woman had a miraculous vision. She saw on a beautiful road a procession of young men, as graceful as angels, advancing full of joy towards a magnificent city. She understood that they were souls from Purgatory making their triumphal entry into Heaven. She looked eagerly to see if among their ranks she could not discover her son. Alas! the child was not there; but she perceived him approaching far behind the others, sad, suffering, and fatigued, his garments drenched with water. "Oh, dear object of my grief," she cried out to him, "how is it that you remain behind that brilliant band? I should wish to see you at the head of your companions."

"Mother," replied the child in a plaintive tone, "it is you, it is these tears which you shed over me that moisten and soil my garments, and retard my entrance into the glory of Heaven. Cease to abandon yourself to a blind and useless grief. Open your heart to more Christian sentiments. If you truly love me, relieve me in my sufferings; apply some indulgences to me, say prayers, give alms, obtain for me the fruits of the Holy Sacrifice of the Mass. It is by this means that you will prove your love; for by so doing you will deliver me from prison where I languish, and bring me forth to eternal life, which is far more desirable than the life terrestrial which you have given me."

Then the vision disappeared, and that mother, thus admonished and brought back to true Christian sentiments, instead of giving way to immoderate grief, applied to the practice of every good work which could give relief to the soul of her son.

The great causes of this forgetfulness, this indifference, guilty neglect, and injustice towards the dead, is lack of faith. For do we not see that true Christians, those animated by a spirit of faith, make the most noble sacrifices in behalf of their departed friends? Descending in spirit into those penal flames, there contemplating the rigours of Divine Justice, listening to the voice of the dead who implore their compassion, they think only how to give relief to those poor souls, and consider it their most sacred duty to procure for their parents and departed friends all the suffrages possible, according to their means and condition. Happy are those Christians; they show their faith by their works; they are merciful, and in their turn they shall obtain mercy.

Blessed Margaret of Cortona was at first a great sinner; but after she had been sincerely converted, she blotted out her past disorders by great penances and works of mercy. Her charity towards the poor souls knew no bounds; she sacrificed everything, time, repose, satisfactions, to obtain their deliverance from Almighty God. Understanding that devotion towards the holy souls, when well directed, has for its first object our parents, her father and mother being dead, she never ceased to offer for them her prayers, mortifications, vigils, sufferings, Communions, and the Masses at which she had the happiness to assist. In reward for her filial piety, God revealed to her that by all her prayers she had shortened the long term of suffering which her parents would have had to endure in Purgatory; that she had obtained their complete deliverance and entrance into Paradise.

CHAPTER XLIII.

Motives of Justice—Prayer for Departed Parents—St. Catherine of Sienna and her Father Jacomo.

ST. CATHERINE of Sienna[1] has left us a similar example. It is thus related by her biographer, Blessed Raymond of Capua. "The servant of God," he writes, "had an ardent zeal for the salvation of souls. I will first speak of that which she did for her father, Jacomo, of whom we have already made mention. This excellent man had remarked the sanctity of his daughter, and was filled with respectful tenderness towards her; he advised every one in his house never to oppose her in anything, but to leave her perfect liberty in the practice of her good works. Thus the affection which united father and daughter increased day by day. Catherine constantly prayed for her father's salvation; Jacomo took a holy delight in the virtues of his daughter, hoping through her merits to obtain favour before God.

The life of Jacomo finally approached its end, and he was confined to bed by a dangerous illness. Seeing his condition, his daughter, as was her custom, betook herself to prayer, beseeching her Heavenly Spouse to cure him whom she so tenderly loved. He answered that Jacomo was at the point of death, and that to live longer would not be profitable to him. Catherine then went to her father, and found him so perfectly resigned to leave this world, and without any regret, that she thanked God with all her heart.

"But her filial love was not content; she returned to prayer in order to obtain from God, the Source of all grace,

[1] April 30.

to grant her father not only the pardon of all his faults, but also that at the hour of his death he might be admitted into Heaven, without so much as passing through the flames of Purgatory. She was answered that Justice could not sacrifice its rights; that the soul must be perfectly pure to enter the glory of Paradise. 'Your father,' said our Lord, 'has led a good life in the married state, and has done much that was very pleasing in My sight; above all, his conduct towards you has been most agreeable to Me; but My Justice demands that his soul should pass through fire, in order to purify it from the stains which it contracted in the world.' 'O my loving Saviour,' replied Catherine, 'how can I bear the thought of seeing him who has nourished me, who has brought me up with such tender care, who has been so good to me during his whole life, tormented in those cruel flames? I beseech your Infinite Goodness not to permit his soul to leave his body until in some way or another it shall have been so perfectly cleansed that it shall have no need to pass through the fires of Purgatory.'"

Admirable condescension! God yielded to the prayer and desire of His creature. The strength of Jacomo was exhausted, but his soul could not depart as long as the conflict lasted between our Lord, who alleged His Justice, and Catherine, who implored His Mercy. Finally, Catherine resumed: "If I cannot obtain this grace without satisfying Thy Justice, let, then, that Justice be exercised upon me; I am ready to suffer for my father all that Thy Goodness may be pleased to send me." Our Lord consented. "I will accept thy proposal," He said, "on account of thy love for Me. I exempt thy father's soul from all expiation, but thou shalt suffer as long as thou livest the pain that was destined for him." Full of joy, Catherine cried out, "Thanks for Thy word, O Lord, and may Thy wil be done!"

The saint immediately returned to her father, who had

just entered upon his agony. She filled him with courage and joy by giving him, on the part of God, the assurance of his eternal salvation, and she left him not until he had breathed forth his soul.

At the same moment that the soul of her father was separated from the body, Catherine was seized with most violent pains, which remained until her death, without allowing her one moment of repose. "She herself," adds Blessed Raymond, "often assured me of this, and indeed it was evident to all who saw her. But her patience was greater than her malady. All that I have related I learned from Catherine, when, touched at the sight of her sufferings, I asked her the cause thereof. I must not forget to say that at the moment her father expired she was heard to cry out, her face beaming with joy and a smile upon her lips, 'May God be praised! My dear father, how I wish I were like you.' During the celebration of the funeral obsequies, when all were in tears, Catherine seemed transported with delight. She consoled her mother and every one as though unaffected by her father's death. It was because she had seen that beloved soul come forth triumphant from the prison of the body and pass without any hindrance into eternal beatitude. This sight had inundated her with consolation, because a short time previous she herself had tasted the joys of eternal light.

"Let us here admire the wisdom of Providence. The soul of Jacomo could surely have been purified in another manner, and have been immediately admitted into Heaven, like the good thief who confessed our Saviour on the cross. But God willed that his purification should be effected through the sufferings of Catherine, as she herself had requested, and this not to try her, but to increase her merits and her crown.

"It was fitting that this holy maid, who so ardently loved the soul of her father, should receive some recompense for her filial affection; and since she had preferred the salvation of his soul to that of her own body, her bodily suffering contributed to the happiness of her soul. Thus she always spoke of her sweet, her dear sufferings. And she was right, for these afflictions augmented the sweetness of grace in this life and the delights of glory in the next. She confided to me that long after his death her father Jacomo continually came to thank her for the happiness she had procured for him. He revealed many hidden things to her, warned her of the snares of the demon, and preserved her from all danger."

CHAPTER XLIV.

Motives and Incentives to Devotion towards the Holy Souls— St. John of God—Give Alms for your Own Sake—St. Bridget—Blessed Peter Lefèvre.

WE have just seen how holy and meritorious Charity towards the holy souls is before God—*Sancta cogitatio.* It remains to show how salutary, at the same time, it is for ourselves—*Salubris cogitatio.* If the excellence of the work in itself is so powerful an incentive, the precious advantages which we derive from it are no less a stimulus. They consist, on the one hand, of the graces which we receive in recompense for our generosity, and, on the other, of the Christian fervour with which this good work inspires us.

Blessed, said our Saviour, *are the merciful, for they shall obtain mercy.*[1] *Blessed is he,* says the Holy Ghost, *that understandeth concerning the needy and the poor: the Lord will deliver him in the evil day.*[2] *As long as you did it to one of these My brethren, you did it to Me.*[3] *The Lord deal*

[1] Matt. v. 7.   [2] Ps. xl.   [3] Matt. xxv. 40.

mercifully with you, as you have dealt with the dead.[1] These different sentences express, in their strongest sense, Charity towards the departed.

All that we offer to God in Charity to the dead, says St. Ambrose in his book of *Offices*, is changed into merit for ourselves, and we shall find it after our death increased a hundredfold—*Omne quod defunctis impenditur, in nostrum tandem meritum commutatur, et illud post mortem centuplum recipimus duplicatum.* We can say that the spirit of the Church, the sentiments of the doctors and the saints, are expressed in these words: What you do for the dead, you do in a most excellent manner for yourself. The reason of this is, that this work of mercy will be returned to you increased a hundred-fold, in the day when you yourself shall be in distress. We may here apply the celebrated words of St. John of God when he asked the inhabitants of Granada to give him an alms for the love of themselves. To provide for the needs of the sick whom he took into his hospital, the charitable saint traversed the streets of Granada, crying, " *Give alms, my brethren, give alms for the love of yourselves.*" People were astonished at this new form of expression, because they had always been accustomed to hear: *alms for the love of God.* "Why," said they to the saint, "do you ask us to give alms for the love of ourselves?" "Because," replied he, "it is the great means of redeeming your sins, according to the words of the Prophet: *Redeem thou thy sins with alms, and thy iniquities with works of mercy to the poor.*"[4] In giving alms, you labour in your own interest, since you thereby diminish the terrible chastisements which your sins have merited. Must we not conclude that all this is true of alms bestowed upon the souls in Purgatory? To assist them is to preserve ourselves from those terrible expiations which we shall not otherwise escape. We may, therefore, cry with St. John of God, Give them the alms of your suffrages: *assist them for the*

[1] Ruth i. 8.   [4] Dan. iv. 24.

love of yourself. Generosity towards the departed is always repaid; it finds its recompense in all kinds of graces, the source of which is the gratitude of the holy souls and that of our Lord, who considers as done to Himself all that we do for the suffering souls.

St. Bridget declares in her Revelations, and her testimony is quoted by Benedict XIII.,[1] that she heard a voice from the depths of the Purgatorial flames pronouncing these words: "May those be blessed, may those be rewarded, who relieve us in these pains!" And on another occasion: "O Lord God, show Thy Almighty power in recompensing a hundred-fold those who assist us by their suffrages, and make the rays of the divine light to shine upon us." In another vision the saint heard the voice of an angel saying: "Blessed be upon earth those who, by their prayers and good works, come to the assistance of the poor suffering souls!"

Blessed Peter Lefèvre, of the Company of Jesus, so well known for his devotion towards the holy angels, had also a special devotion towards the souls in Purgatory. "Those souls," he said, "have bowels of Charity, which are ever open to those who still walk amidst the dangers of this life; they are filled with gratitude towards those who assist them. They can pray for us, and offer up their torments to God in our behalf. It is a most excellent practice to invoke the souls in Purgatory, that we may obtain from God, through their intercession, a true knowledge of our sins and a perfect contrition for them, fervour in the exercise of good works, care to produce worthy fruits of penance, and in general, all virtues, the absence of which has been the cause of their terrible chastisement.[2]

[1] Serm. iv. 12.
[2] Memorial of Blessed P. Lefèvre. See *Messenger of the S. Heart*, Nov. 1873.

CHAPTER XLV.

Advantages of Devotion towards the Holy Souls—Their Gratitude—St. Margaret of Cortona—St. Philip Neri—Cardinal Baronius and the Dying Woman.

Is it difficult to understand the gratitude of the holy souls? If you had ransomed a captive from the galling yoke of slavery, would he be grateful for such a benefit? When the Emperor Charles V. took possession of the city of Tunis, he restored to liberty twenty thousand Christian slaves, who before his victory had been reduced to a most deplorable condition. Penetrated with gratitude towards their benefactor, they surrounded him, blessing him and singing his praises. If you gave health to a person dangerously sick, fortune to an unhappy creature who had been reduced to poverty, would you not receive in return their gratitude and their benedictions? And those souls, so holy and so good, will they conduct themselves differently with regard to their benefactors?—those poor souls whose captivity, poverty, suffering, and necessity far surpass all captivity, indigence, or malady to be found upon earth. They come especially at the hour of death, to protect them, to accompany and introduce them into the happy abode of their eternal rest.

We have already spoken of St. Margaret of Cortona, and of her devotion to the holy souls. It is related in her biography that at her death she saw a multitude of souls that she had delivered from Purgatory form in procession to escort her to Paradise. God revealed this favour granted to Margaret of Cortona through the medium of a holy person in the city of Castello. This servant of God, wrapt in ecstasy at the moment when Margaret departed this life, saw her soul in the midst of this brilliant cortège, and on recovering from her rapture she related to her friends what our Lord had been pleased to manifest to her.

St. Philip Neri,[1] founder of the Congregation of the Oratory, had a most tender devotion towards the holy souls in Purgatory, and he felt a particular attraction to pray for those who had been under his spiritual direction. He considered himself under greatest obligation to them, because Divine Providence had confided them in a special manner to his zeal. It seemed to him that his charity ought to follow them until their final purification was accomplished, and they were admitted into the glory of Heaven. He confessed that many of his spiritual children appeared to him after their death, either to ask his prayers or to return him thanks for what he had already done for them. He declared also that by this means he had obtained more than one grace.

After his death, a Franciscan Father of great piety was praying in the chapel in which the venerated remains of the saint had been deposited, when the latter appeared to him surrounded with glory and in the midst of a brilliant train. Encouraged by the air of amiable familiarity with which the saint regarded him, he ventured to ask the meaning of that bright band of blessed spirits which accompanied him. The saint replied that they were the souls of those whose spiritual guide he had been during life, and whom by his suffrages he had delivered from Purgatory. He added that they had come to meet him on his departure from this world, that in their turn they might introduce him into the Heavenly Jerusalem.

"There is no doubt," says the devout Father Rossignoli, "that on their entrance into eternal glory the first favours which they ask of the Divine Mercy are for those who have opened to them the gates of Paradise, and they will never fail to pray for their benefactors, whenever they see them

[1] May 26.

in any necessity or danger. In reverses of fortune, sicknesses, and accidents of all kinds they will be their protectors. Their zeal will increase when the interests of the soul are at stake; they will powerfully assist them to vanquish temptation, to practise good works, to die a Christian death, and to escape the sufferings of the other life."

Cardinal Baronius, whose authority as historian is well known, relates that a person who was very charitable towards the holy souls was afflicted with a terrible agony when on her deathbed. The spirit of darkness suggested to her the most gloomy fears, and veiled from her sight the sweet light of Divine Mercy, endeavouring to drive her into despair; when suddenly Heaven seemed to open before her eyes, and she saw thousands of defenders fly to her aid, reanimating her courage, and promising her the victory. Comforted by this unexpected assistance, she asked who were her defenders? "We are," they replied, "the souls which you have delivered from Purgatory; we, in our turn, come to help you, and very soon we shall conduct you to Paradise." At these consoling words the sick person felt that her fears were changed into the sweetest confidence. A short time afterwards she tranquilly expired, her countenance serene and her heart filled with joy.

CHAPTER XLVI.

Advantages—Gratitude of the Souls—The Return of an Exiled Priest—Father Mumford and the Printer, William Freyssen.

In order to understand the gratitude of the souls, it is necessary that we should have a most clear conception of the benefit they receive from their liberators; that we should know what it is to enter Heaven. "Who will make known to us," says the Abbé Louvet, "the joys of that blessed hour! Represent to yourself the happiness of an exile who at length returns to his fatherland. During the Reign of Terror, a poor priest of La Vendée was condemned to be drowned. Having escaped by miracle, he was obliged to emigrate in order to save his life. When peace was restored to the Church and to France, he hastened to return to his beloved parish.

"It was a festival day in the village. All the parishioners went to meet their pastor and father; the bells in the old tower rang joyously, and the church was decorated as upon days of great solemnity. The old man advanced smiling in the midst of his children, but when the doors of the holy place opened before him, when he beheld again the altar that had so long rejoiced the days of his youth, his heart, too weak to bear such transports of joy, broke within his bosom. With a trembling voice he intoned the *Te Deum*, but it was the *Nunc Dimittis* of his priestly life; he fell dying at the foot of the altar. The exile had not the strength to support the joys of his return."

If such are the joys of the return of an exile to his terrestrial fatherland, who will make known to us the transports we shall experience upon entering Heaven, the true home of our souls? And how can we wonder at the gratitude of the blessed whom we have caused to enter there?

Father James Mumford, of the Society of Jesus, who was born in England in 1605, and who struggled during forty years in the cause of the Church in that country, given up to heresy, composed a remarkable work on Purgatory, which he had printed at Cologne by William Freyssen, a well-known Catholic publisher. This book obtained a large circulation, and effected a great good among souls, the publisher, Freyssen, being one of those who derived the greatest advantage from it. This is what he wrote to Father Mumford in 1649 :—

"I write, Father, to inform you of the miraculous and twofold cure of my son and my wife. During the holidays, whilst my office was closed, I set to work reading the book, 'Mercy Exercised towards the Souls in Purgatory,' which you have sent me to print. I was still engaged in reading the work when I was informed that my young son, four years of age, showed symptoms of a serious illness. The malady made rapid progress, the physician lost hope, and preparations for his burial were already thought of. It occurred to me that I might perhaps save him by making a vow in favour of the souls in Purgatory.

"I went to church early in the morning, and fervently besought God to have pity on me, promising by a vow to distribute a hundred copies of your book among the ecclesiastics and Religious free of charge, in order to remind them of the zeal with which they should interest themselves in behalf of the Chuch Suffering, and of the practices that are best suited to fulfil this duty.

"I acknowledge that I was full of hope. Upon my return home I found the child better. He already asked for nourishment, although for several days he had been incapable of swallowing even a single drop of liquid. The following day his cure was complete; he arose, went out for a walk, and ate with as good an appetite as if he had never been sick. Penetrated with gratitude, my most urgent desire was to fulfil my promise. I went to the College of the Society of Jesus and besought the Fathers to accept my hundred copies, to keep what they wanted for themselves, and to distribute the remainder among the other communities and ecclesiastics of their acquaintance, that the suffering souls, my benefactors, might be comforted by new suffrages.

"Three weeks later, another and not less serious accident happened to me. My wife upon entering the house was suddenly seized with a violent trembling in all her limbs, which caused her to fall insensible to the ground. She soon lost her appetite and the power of speech. All manner of remedies were employed, but in vain. The malady only increased, and all hope seemed lost. Her confessor, seeing her reduced to this condition, sought words to console me, exhorting me to be resigned to the will of God. As for myself, after the protection I had experienced from the good souls in Purgatory, I could not think of despairing. I returned to the same church, prostrated myself before the Blessed Sacrament, and renewed my supplication with all the fervour of which I was capable. 'O my God,' I exclaimed, 'thy mercy is without limit! In the name of thine Infinite Goodness, permit not that the restoration of my son to health be atoned for by the death of my wife!' I then made a vow to distribute two hundred copies of your book in order to obtain copious relief for the suffering souls. At the same time I besought the souls that had formerly been delivered to unite their prayers to those of the others still retained in Purgatory. After this prayer I returned home, and saw my servants running to meet me. They told me that my dear wife was considerably better, that the delirium had ceased and her speech had returned. I hastened to her side and found all was true. I offered her nourishment, which she took with relish. A very short time afterwards she was so completely restored that she accompanied me to the church to return thanks to God for all His mercy.

"Your Reverence may place entire confidence in this statement. I pray you to aid me in thanking our Lord for this double miracle. FREYSSEN."[1]

[1] See Rossignoli, *Merv.*, 16.

CHAPTER XLVII.

Advantages—Temporal Favours—L'Abbé Postel and the Servant of Paris.

THE following is related as a fact by the Abbé Postel, the translator of F. Rossignoli's work. It took place in Paris, he says, about the year 1827, and is inserted as No. 27 in the *Merveilles du Purgatoire*.

A poor servant, who had been brought up as a good Christian in her native village, had adopted the pious practice of having a Mass said every month for the suffering souls. Her employers, having taken her with them to the capital, she never once neglected it, and furthermore made it her rule to assist at the Divine Sacrifice, and to unite her prayers with those of the priest, especially for the soul that had most nearly completed its expiation. This was her ordinary intention.

God soon tried her by a long illness, that not only occasioned her cruel suffering, but also caused her to lose her place and draw upon her last resources. On the day that she was able to leave the hospital, she had but twenty sous left. After addressing a fervent prayer to Heaven, full of confidence, she went in search of a situation. She was told that she would probably find employment in a certain family at the other end of the city, whither she went, and as she was obliged to pass by the Church of St. Eustache, she entered. The sight of a priest at the altar reminded her that this month she had forgotten her usual Mass for the dead, and that this was the very day upon which, for many years, she had been accustomed to do this good work. But what was she to do? If she disposed of her last franc, she would have nothing left, even to satisfy her hunger.

It was a struggle between devotion and human prudence. Devotion gained the day. "After all," she said to herself, " the good God knows it is for Him, and He will not forsake me!" Entering the sacristy, she gave her offering for a Mass, at which she assisted with her usual fervour.

A few moments after, she continued on her way, full of anxiety as may be readily understood. Being absolutely destitute of means, what was she to do if she failed to obtain employment? She was still occupied with these thoughts when a pale young man of a slight figure and distinguished appearance approached her and said, " Are you in search of a situation?" " Yes, sir." " Well, go to a certain street and number, to the house of Madame ———. I think you will suit her, and that you will be satisfied there." Having spoken these words, he disappeared in the passing crowd, without waiting to receive the poor girl's thanks.

She found the street, recognised the number, and ascended to the apartments. A servant came out carrying a package under her arm and uttering words of complaint and anger. " Is Madame there?" asked the newcomer. "She may or she may not be," replied the other. "What does it matter to me? Madame will open the door herself if it suits her; I will trouble myself no longer about it. Adieu!" And she descended the steps.

Our poor girl rang the bell with trembling hand, and a sweet voice bade her enter. She found herself in the presence of an old lady of venerable appearance, who encouraged her to make known her wishes.

"Madame," said the servant, "I learned this morning that you are in need of a servant, and I came to offer my services. I was assured that you would receive me kindly." "Oh, but, my dear child, what you tell me is very extraordinary. This morning I had no need of one; it is only within the last half-hour that I have discharged an insolent domestic, and there is not a soul in the world except her and myself who know it. Who sent you, then?" "It was a gentleman, Madame; a young gentleman whom I met on the street, who stopped me for this purpose, and I praised God for it, for it is absolutely necessary for me to find a place to-day; I have not a penny in my pocket."

The old lady could not understand who the person was, and was lost in conjecture, when the servant raising her eyes to the furniture of the little parlour, perceived a portrait. "Wait, Madame," she said immediately, "do not puzzle yourself any more; this is the exact picture of the young man who spoke to me. It is on his account that I am come."

At these words the lady uttered a loud cry and seemed to lose consciousness. She made the girl repeat the story of her devotion to the souls in Purgatory, of the morning Mass, and her meeting with the stranger; then throwing herself on the neck of the girl, she embraced her amid a flood of tears and said, "You shall not be my servant from this moment; you are my daughter. It is my son, my only son, whom you saw—my son, dead for the past two years, who owes to you his deliverance, whom God directed to send you here. I cannot doubt it. May you, then, be blessed, and let us pray continually for all those who suffer before entering into a blessed eternity."

CHAPTER XLVIII.

Advantages—Temporal Favours—The Neapolitan Woman and the Mysterious Note.

To prove that the souls in Purgatory show their gratitude even by temporal favours, Father Rossignoli relates a fact that happened at Naples, which bears some resemblance to that which we have just read.

If it is not given to all to offer to God the abundant alms of Judas Machabeus, who sent twelve thousand drachms to Jerusalem for sacrifices and prayers to be offered in behalf of the dead, there are, very few who cannot at least make the offering of the poor widow of the Gospel, who was praised by our Saviour Himself. She gave only two mites, but, said Jesus, "these two mites were of more value than all the gold of the rich, because *she of her want cast in all she had, even her whole living.*"[1] This touching example was imitated by a humble Neapolitan woman, who had the greatest difficulty in providing for the wants of her family. The resources of the house depended upon the daily earnings of the husband, who each evening brought home the fruit of his labours.

Alas! one day this poor father was imprisoned for debt, so that the responsibility of supporting the family rested upon the unhappy mother, who possessed nothing but her confidence in God. With faith she besought Divine Providence to come to her aid, and especially to deliver her husband, who languished in prison for no other crime than his poverty.

' She went to a wealthy and benevolent 'gentleman, and, relating to him the sad story of her woes, entreated him with tears to assist her. God permitted that she should

[1] St. Mark xii. 44.

receive but a trifling alms, *a carlin*, a piece of money worth about ten cents of our coin. Deeply afflicted, she entered a church to implore the God of the indigent to succour her in her distress, since she had nothing to hope from earth. She was absorbed in her prayers and tears, when, by an inspiration, no doubt, of her good angel, it occurred to her to interest the sympathy of the holy souls in her behalf, for she had heard much of their sufferings, and of their gratitude towards those who befriend them. Full of confidence, she went into the sacristy, offered her little piece of money, and asked if a Mass could be celebrated for the dead. The good priest, who was there, hastened to say Mass for her intention, and ascended the altar for that purpose, whilst the poor woman, prostrate on the pavement, assisted at the Holy Sacrifice, offering her prayers for the departed.

She returned quite consoled, as though she had received the assurance that God had heard her prayer. Whilst traversing the populous streets of Naples, she was accosted by a venerable old man, who inquired whence she came and whither she was going? The unfortunate woman explained her distress, and the use she had made of the small alms she had received. The old man seemed deeply touched by her misery, spoke some words of encouragement, and gave her a note enclosed in an envelope, which he directed her to take to a gentleman whom he designated, and then left her.

The woman went in all haste to deliver the note to the gentleman indicated. The latter, on opening the envelope, was seized with astonishment, and was on the point of fainting away; he recognised the handwriting of his father, who had died some time previous. "Where did you get this letter?" he cried, quite beside himself. "Sir," replied the good woman, "it was from an old man who accosted me in the street. I told him of my distress, and he sent me to give you this note in his name. As regards his features, he very much resembles that portrait which you have there over the door." More and more impressed by these circumstances, the gentleman again took up the note, and read aloud:— " My son, your father has just been delivered from Purgatory, thanks to a mass which the bearer has had celebrated this morning. She is in great distress, and I recommend her to you." He read and re-read those lines, traced by that hand so dear to him, by a father who was now among the number of the elect. Tears of joy coursed down his cheeks as he turned towards the woman. "Poor woman," he said, " by your trifling alms you have secured the eternal felicity of him who gave me life. In my turn I will secure your temporal happiness. I take upon myself to supply all the needs of yourself and your whole family."

What joy for that gentleman! what joy for that poor woman! It is difficult to say on which side was the greatest happiness. What is most important and most easy is, to see the instruction to be derived from this incident; it teaches us that the smallest act of charity towards the members of the Church Suffering is precious in the sight of God, and draws down upon us miracles of mercy.

CHAPTER XLIX.

Advantages—Spiritual and Temporal Favours—Christopher Sandoval at Louvain—The Lawyer Renouncing the World—Brother Lacci and Dr. Verdiano.

LET us here cite another example, the more worthy of mention as a great Pope, Clement VIII., saw therein the finger of God, and recommended its publication for the edification of the Church. "Several authors," says Father Rossignoli, "have related the marvellous assistance which Christopher

Sandoval, Archbishop of Seville, received from the souls in Purgatory. Whilst still a child, he was accustomed to distribute part of his pocket-money in alms for the benefit of the holy souls. His piety increased with his age; for the sake of the poor suffering souls he gave away all that he could dispose of, and even went so far as to deprive himself of a thousand little things which were useful or necessary. When he was pursuing his studies at the University of Louvain, it happened that some letters which he expected from Spain were delayed, in consequence of which he found himself reduced to such pecuniary straits that he had scarcely wherewith to purchase food. At this moment a poor person asked of him an alms for love of the souls in Purgatory, and, what had never happened to him before, he was obliged to refuse.

"Afflicted by this circumstance, he went into a church. 'If,' said he, 'I cannot give an alms for my poor souls, I can at least give them the assistance of my prayers.'

"Scarcely had he finished his prayer when, on leaving the church, he was accosted by a beautiful young man, dressed as a traveller, who saluted him with respectful affability. Christopher experienced a feeling of religious awe, as though he were in the presence of a spirit in human form. But he was soon reassured by his amiable interlocutor, who spoke to him with the greatest gentleness of the Marquis of Dania, his father, his relatives and friends, just as a Spaniard who had recently arrived from the Peninsula. He ended by begging him to accompany him to an hotel, where they could dine together and be more at their ease. Sandoval, who had not eaten anything since the previous day, gladly accepted the gracious offer. They therefore seated themselves at table, and continued to converse most pleasantly together. After the repast, the stranger gave Sandoval a sum of money, entreating him to accept it, and to make use of it for any purpose he pleased, adding that the Marquis, his father, would make him compensation on his return to Spain. Then, under pretext of transacting some business, he withdrew, and Christopher never saw him again. Notwithstanding all his inquiries concerning the stranger, he never succeeded in obtaining any information regarding him. No one, neither in Louvain nor Spain, had ever seen or known a young man corresponding to his description. As regards the sum of money, it was exactly the amount which the pious Christopher needed to defray expenses until the arrival of his letters, and this money was never afterwards claimed from his family.

He was, therefore, convinced that Heaven had worked a miracle in his favour, and had sent to his assistance one of those souls that he himself had relieved by his prayers and alms. He was confirmed in this opinion by Pope Clement VIII., to whom he related the incident when he went to Rome to receive the Bulls raising him to the Episcopate. This Pontiff, struck by the extraordinary circumstances of the case, advised him to make it known for the edification of the faithful; he looked upon it as a favour from Heaven, which proved how precious in the sight of God is charity towards the departed.

Such is the gratitude of the holy souls which have left this world, that they testify it even for favours bestowed upon them whilst they were still in this life. It is related in the Annals of the Friars Preachers[1] that among those who went to receive the habit from the hands of St. Dominic in 1241, there was a lawyer who had quitted his profession under extraordinary circumstances. He was united by ties of friendship to a young man of great piety, whom he charitably assisted during the sickness of which he died. This was sufficient to move the deceased to procure for him the greatest of all benefits, that of conversion and vocation to a religious life. About thirty days after his death he appeared to the lawyer, and implored his assistance, because he was in Purgatory. "Are your

[1] Malvenda, an. 1241.

sufferings intense?" he asked of his friend. "Alas!" replied the latter, "if the whole earth with its forests and mountains were on fire, it would not form a furnace such as the one into which I am plunged." Seized with fear, his faith revived, and thinking only of his own soul, he asked, "In what state am I in the eyes of God?" "In a bad state," replied the deceased, "and in a dangerous profession." "What have I to do? What advice do you give me?" "Quit the perverse world in which you are engaged, and occupy yourself only with the affairs of your soul." The lawyer, following this counsel, gave all his goods to the poor and took the habit of St. Dominic.

Let us see how a holy Religious of the Society of Jesus showed his gratitude, even after death, to the physician who had attended him during his last illness. Francis Lacci, a Brother Coadjutor, died in the College of Naples in 1598. He was a man of God, full of charity, patience, and tender devotion towards the Blessed Virgin. . Some time after his death, Dr. Verdiano entered the church of the College to assist at Mass before beginning his visits. It was the day on which were celebrated the obsequies of King Philip II., who had died four months previous. When, on leaving the church, he was about to take holy water, a Religious approached and asked him why the catafalque had been prepared, and whose was the service about to be celebrated. "It is that of King Philip II.," he replied.

At the same time Verdiano, astonished that a Religious should ask such a question of a stranger, and not distinguishing the features of his interlocutor in the obscurity of the place where he stood, asked who he was. "I am," he answered, "Brother Lacci, whom you attended during my last illness." The doctor looked at him attentively, and recognised perfectly the features of Lacci. Stupefied with astonishment, he said, "But you died of that disease! Are you then suffering in Purgatory, and do you come to ask our suffrages?" "Blessed be God, I am no longer in pain nor sorrow. I need not your suffrages. I am in the joys of Paradise." "And King Philip, is he also already in Paradise?" "Yes, he is there, but placed as much below me as he was elevated above me upon earth. As for you, Dr. Verdiano, where do you propose to make your first visit to-day?" Verdiano having replied that he was then going to the Patrician di Maio, who was dangerously ill, Lacci warned him to guard against a great danger which menaced him at the door of the house. In fact, the doctor found there a large stone so placed, that on being shaken, it would have fallen and mortally injured him.

This material circumstance seems to have been designed by Providence to prove to Verdiano that he had not been the sport of an illusion.

CHAPTER L.

Advantages—Prayers of the Souls for us—Suarez—St. Bridget—St. Catherine of Bologna—Venerable Vianney.

WE have just spoken of the gratitude of the holy souls. This they sometimes manifest, as we have seen, in a clearly visible manner, but most frequently they exercise it invisibly by their prayers. The souls pray for us not only when, after their deliverance, they are with God in Heaven, but even in their place of exile and in the midst of their sufferings. Although they cannot pray for themselves, yet, by their supplications, they obtain great grace for us. Such is the express doctrine of two eminent theologians, Bellarmine and Suarez. "These souls are holy," says Suarez, "and dear to God. Charity urges them to love us, and they know, at least in a general way, to what dangers we are exposed, and what need we have of the Divine assistance. Why, then, would they not pray for their benefactors?

Why? But it will be answered because they know them not. In that dismal abode, in the midst of their torments, how can they know who are those that assist them by their suffrages?

To this objection it may be replied, the souls feel at least the alleviation which they receive and the assistance which is given them; this suffices, even should they be ignorant of the source whence it came, to call down the benedictions of Heaven upon their benefactors, whosoever they may be, and who are known to God.

But in reality do they not know from whom they receive assistance in their sufferings? Their ignorance of this is nowise proved, and we have strong reason to believe that no such ignorance exists. Would their angel-guardian, who dwells there with them to give them all the consolation in his power, deprive them of this consoling knowledge? Is this knowledge not conformable to the doctrine of the Communion of Saints? Would the intercourse which exists between us and the Church Suffering not be the more perfect for its being reciprocal, and that the souls know their benefactors better?

This doctrine is confirmed by a great number of particular revelations, and by the practice of several holy persons. We have already said that St. Bridget, in one of her ecstasies, heard several souls cry aloud, "Lord God all-powerful, reward a hundred-fold those who assist us by their prayers, and who offer to you their good works, in order that we may enjoy the light of your Divinity."

We read in the Life of St. Catherine of Bologna[1] that she had a most tender devotion towards the holy souls in Purgatory; that she prayed for them very frequently, and

[1] March 9.

with the greatest fervour; that she recommended herself to them with the greatest confidence in her spiritual necessities, and advised others to do the same, saying, "When I wish to obtain any favour from our Father in Heaven, I have recourse to the souls that are detained in Purgatory; I entreat them to present my request to the Divine Majesty in their own name, and I feel that I am heard through their intercession." A holy priest of our own day, the cause of whose beatification has been commenced in Rome, Venerable Vianney, Curé of Ars, said to an ecclesiastic who consulted him, "Oh! if it were but known how great is the power of the good souls in Purgatory with the Heart of God, and if we knew all the graces we can obtain through their intercession, they would not be so much forgotten. We must, therefore, pray much for them, that they may pray much for us."

These last words of Venerable Vianney indicate the true manner of having recourse to the souls in Purgatory; we must assist them, to obtain their prayers and the effects of their gratitude in return— *We must pray much for them that they may pray much for us.*

There is no question here of invoking them as we invoke the saints in Heaven. Such is not the spirit of the Church, which, before all else, prays for the departed, and assists them by her suffrages. But it is nowise contrary to the spirit of the Church nor to Christian piety to procure relief for the souls, with the intention of obtaining in return, through the assistance of their prayers, the favours which we desire. Thus it is a laudable and pious act to offer a Mass for the departed when we are in need of any particular grace. If, when the holy souls are still in their sufferings, their prayers are so powerful, we may easily conceive that they will be much more efficacious when, being entirely purified, these souls stand before the throne of God.

CHAPTER LI.

Advantages—Gratitude of the Divine Spouse of Souls—Venerable Archangela Panigarola and her Father, Gothard.

IF the souls are so grateful towards their benfeactors, our Lord Jesus Christ, who loves those souls, who receives as done to Himself all the good which we procure for them, will bestow an abundant recompense, very often even in this life, and always in the next. He regards those who show mercy, and punishes those who forget to show it, towards the suffering souls.

Let us first see an example of chastisement. Venerable Archangela Panigarola, a Dominican Religious and Prioress of the Monastery of St. Martha in Milan, had extraordinary zeal for the relief of the souls in Purgatory. She prayed, and obtained prayers for all her deceased friends, and even for those unknown to her, but of whose death she had been notified. Her father, Gothard, whom she tenderly loved, was one of those Christians of the world who seldom thought of praying for the dead. He himself died, and, quite disconsolate, Archangela understood that her dear father stood more in need of her prayers than of her tears. She therefore took the resolution of recommending him to God by special suffrages. But, strange to say, this resolution was scarcely ever carried into effect; this girl, so pious and devoted to her father, did very little for his soul. God permitted that, notwithstanding her holy resolutions, she continually forgot him, and interested herself in behalf of others. Finally, an unexpected event explained this unwonted forgetfulness, and aroused her devotion in behalf of her father. On the Feast of All Souls she remained secluded in her cell, exclusively occupied in exercises of piety and penance for the relief of the poor souls. Suddenly her angel appeared to her, took her by the hand, and conducted her in spirit into Purgatory. Among the first souls which she saw, she recognised that of her father, plunged in a pond of icy water. Scarcely had Gothard seen his daughter than, coming towards her, he reproached her sorrowfully for having abandoned him in his sufferings, whilst she showed so much Charity towards others, whom she constantly relieved, and frequently delivered those who were strangers to her.

Archangela stood for some time confused by these reproaches, which she knew she had merited; soon, however, shedding a torrent of tears, she replied, "I will do, my dear father, all that you ask of me. May it please God to give ear to my supplications and speedily deliver you." Meanwhile she could not recover from her astonishment, nor understand how she could thus have forgotten her beloved father. Having taken her back, her angel told her that this forgetfulness had happened by a disposition of Divine Justice. "God," he said, "has permitted it in punishment for the little zeal which, during life, your father manifested for God, his own soul, and that of his neighbour. You saw how he was tormented and benumbed in a lake of ice; this was the chastisement of his tepidity in the service of God, and his indifference with regard to the salvation of souls. Your father was not an immoral man, it is true, but he showed little inclination for the acquirement of virtue and for the practice of those works of piety and charity to which the Church exhorts the faithful. . . . This is the reason why God permitted that he should be forgotten, even by you, who would have given him too much relief. This is the chastisement ordinarily inflicted by Divine Justice upon those who are lacking in fervour and charity. He permits that others should conduct themselves in their regard as they have acted towards God and towards their brethren." Moreover, this is the rule of Justice which our Saviour has established in the Gospel, *With what measure you mete, it shall be measured to you again.*[1]

CHAPTER LII.

Advantages—Charity towards the Holy Souls recompensed by Jesus Christ—St. Catherine of Sienna and Palmerine—St. Magdalen de Pazzi and her Mother.

GOD is more inclined to reward than to punish, and if He inflict a chastisement upon those who forget the souls so dear to His Heart, He shows Himself truly grateful towards those who assist Him in the person of His suffering spouses. In recompense He will one day say to them, *Come, ye blessed of my Father, possess the kingdom which is prepared for you.* You have exercised mercy towards your necessitous and suffering brethren; *Amen, I say to you, as long as you did it to one of these my least brethren, you did it to Me.*[2] Very often in this life Jesus rewards compassionate and charitable souls by the bestowal of many favours. St. Catherine of Sienna by her charity had converted a sinner named Palmerine, who died and went to Purgatory. The saint gave herself no rest until she had delivered this soul. In recompense, our Lord permitted her to appear to the saint, or rather our Saviour Himself showed her to His servant, as a glorious conquest of her Charity. Blessed Raymond thus gives the details:—In the middle of the fourteenth century, when St. Catherine edified her native city by all

[1] Matt. vii. 2.   [2] Matt. xxv. 40.

sorts of works of mercy, a woman named Palmerine, after having been the object of her tenderest charity, conceived a secret aversion towards her benefactors, which even degenerated into implacable hatred. No longer able to see or listen to the saint, the ungrateful Palmerine, embittered against the servant of God, ceased not to blacken her reputation by the most atrocious calumnies. Catherine did all in her power to conciliate her, but in vain. Then, seeing that her kindness, her humility, her benefits served but to excite the fury of this unfortunate woman, she earnestly implored God to vouchsafe Himself to move her obdurate heart.

God heard her prayer by striking Palmerine with a mortal malady; but this chastisement did not suffice to make her enter into herself. In return for all the tender care which the saint lavished upon her, the wretched woman loaded her with insults and drove her from her presence. Meanwhile, her end approached, and a priest was called to administer the last Sacraments. The sick person was unfit to receive them, on account of the hatred which she nourished, and which she refused to give up. On hearing this, and seeing that the unfortunate creature had already one foot in Hell, Catherine shed a torrent of tears and was inconsolable. For three days and three nights she ceased not to supplicate God on her behalf, adding fasting to prayer. "What! Lord," she said, "will you allow this soul to be lost on my account? I conjure you, grant me at any price her conversion and her salvation. Punish me for her sin, of which I am the occasion: it is not her, but me, the chastisement should strike. Lord, refuse me not the grace which I ask of you: I shall not leave you until I shall have obtained it. In the name of your Goodness, of your Mercy, I conjure you, most merciful Saviour, not to permit the soul of my sister to leave her body until it has been restored to your grace."

Her prayer, adds her biographer, was so powerful, that

she prevented the sick woman from dying. Her agony lasted for three days and three nights, to the great astonishment of her nurses. Catherine during this time continued to intercede, and ended by gaining the victory. God could no longer resist, and worked a miracle of mercy. A ray of heavenly light penetrated the heart of the dying woman, showed her her fault, and nerved her to repentance. The saint, to whom God revealed this, hastened to her side. As soon as the sick person saw her, she gave her every possible mark of friendship and respect, accused herself aloud of her fault, received with piety the last Sacraments, and died in the grace of God.

Notwithstanding the sincerity of her conversion, it was to be feared that a sinner who had barely escaped Hell would have to undergo a severe Purgatory. The charitable Catherine continued to do all in her power to hasten the moment when Palmerine would be admitted to the glory of Paradise.

So much Charity could not fail to meet its reward. "Our Lord," writes Blessed Raymond, "showed to His spouse that soul saved by her prayers. It was so brilliant, that she told me she could find no words capable of expressing its beauty. It was not yet admitted to the glory of the beatific vision, but had that brightness which creation and the grace of baptism imparts. Our Lord said to her, '*Behold, My daughter, this lost soul which you have found:*' And He added, '*Does she not appear to you most beautiful and precious? Who would not endure all sorts of suffering to save a creature so perfect and introduce it into eternal life? If I, who am the Supreme Beauty, from whom all beauty emanates, have been so far captivated by the beauty to souls as to descend upon earth and shed My Blood to redeem them; with how much greater reason should you not labour one for another, that such admirable creatures be not lost. If I have showed you this soul, it was that you should be all the more zealous in all that concerns the salvation of souls.*'"

St. Magdalen of Pazzi, so full of devotion for the dead, exhausted all the resources of Christian Charity on behalf of her mother, after the latter had departed this life. A fortnight after her death, Jesus, wishing to console His spouse, showed her the soul of her beloved parent. Magdalen saw her in Paradise, arrayed in dazzling splendour, and surrounded by saints, who appeared to take great interest in her. She heard the blessed soul give her three commands, which ever remained impressed upon her memory: "Take care, my daughter," she said, "to descend as low as possible in humility, to observe religious obedience, and to carry out with prudence all that it prescribes." Saying this, Magdalen saw her blessed mother vanish from sight, and she remained inundated with the sweetest consolation.[1]

CHAPTER LIII.

Advantages—Charity towards the Dead Rewarded—St. Thomas of Aquin, his Sister, and Brother Romano—The Archpriest Ponzoni and Don Alphonso Sanchez—Blessed Margaret Mary and Mother Greffier.

THE Angelic Doctor, St. Thomas of Aquin, was likewise very devout towards the suffering souls, who appeared to him several times, and we know of them by the testimony of the illustrious Doctor himself.[2]

He offered his prayers and sacrifices to God, particularly for the departed souls whom he had known or who were related to him. When he was Professor of Theology at the University of Paris he lost a sister, who died in Capua, at the convent of St. Mary, of which she was Abbess. As soon

[1] Cepari, Life of St. Mag. de Pazzi.   [2] March 7.

as he heard of her decease, he recommended her soul to God with great fervour. Some days later she appeared to him, conjuring him to have pity on her, and to redouble his suffrages, because she suffered cruelly in the flames of the other life. Thomas hastened to offer for her all the satisfaction in his power, and solicited also the suffrages of several of his friends. He thus obtained the deliverance of his sister, who came herself to announce the glad tidings.

Some time after this, having been sent to Rome by his superiors, the soul of this sister appeared to him in all the glory of triumphant joy. She told him that his prayers had been heard, that she was freed from suffering, and was going to enjoy eternal repose in the bosom of God. Familiarised with these supernatural communications, the saint feared not to interrogate the apparition, and asked what had become of his two brothers, Arnold and Landolph, who had died some time previous. "Arnold is in Heaven," replied the soul, "and there enjoys a high degree of glory for having defended the Church and the Sovereign Pontiff against the aggressions of the Emperor Frederic. As to Landolph, he is still in Purgatory, where he suffers much, and is greatly in need of assistance. As regards yourself, my dear brother," she added, "a magnificent place awaits you in Paradise, in recompense for all you have done for the Church. Hasten to put the last stroke to the different works which you have undertaken, for you will soon join us." History tells us that, in fact, he lived but a short time after this event. On another occasion, the same saint being in prayer in the Church of St. Dominic at Naples, saw approaching him Brother Romano, who had succeeded him at Paris in the chair of theology. The saint thought at first that he had just arrived from Paris, for he was ignorant of his death. He, therefore, arose, went to meet him, saluted him and inquired of him concerning his health and the motive of his journey. "I am no longer of this world," said the Religious with a smile, "and by the mercy of God I am already in the enjoyment of eternal beatitude. I come by the command of God to encourage you in your labours." "Am I in the state of grace?" asked Thomas immediately. "Yes, dear brother, and your works are very agreeable to God." "And you, had you to suffer Purgatory?" "Yes, for fourteen days, on account of little infidelities which I had not sufficiently expiated on earth."

Then Thomas, whose mind was constantly occupied with questions of theology, profited by the opportunity to penetrate the mystery of the beatific vision; but he was answered with this verse of Psalm xlvii., *Sicut audivimus, sic vidimus in civitate Dei nostri*—"As we have learned by faith, we have seen with our eyes in the city of our God." Saying these words, the apparition vanished, leaving the Angelic Doctor inflamed with the desire of the Eternal Good.

More recently, in the sixteenth century, a favour of the same nature, but perhaps more wonderful, was granted to a zelator of the souls in Purgatory, an intimate friend of St. Charles Borromeo. Venerable Gratian Ponzoni, Archpriest of Arona, interested himself in the cause of the poor suffering souls throughout his whole lifetime. During the pest which carried off so many victims in the diocese of Milan, Ponzoni, not content with administering the Sacraments to the plague-stricken, hesitated not to become sexton, and to bury the dead bodies; for fear had paralysed the courage of all, and no one would take upon themselves that terrible task. With a zeal and charity truly apostolic, he had assisted a large number of the unfortunate victims in Arona in their last moments, and had interred them in the cemetery near his church of St. Mary. One day, after the office of Vespers, as he was passing by the cemetery in company with Don Alphonso Sanchez, then governor of Arona, he stopped suddenly, struck with an extraordinary vision. Fearing some delusion, he turned towards Sanchez and said, "Sir, do you see the same spectacle which presents itself to my view?" "Yes," replied the governor, who had the same vision, "I see a procession of the dead, advancing from their graves towards the church; and I avow that until you spoke I could not believe my eyes." Assured of the reality of the apparition, the Archpriest added, "They are probably the recent victims of the pest, who wish to make known that they are in need of our prayers." He immediately caused the bells to be rung, and invited the parishioners to assemble on the following morning for a solemn service for the dead.[1]

We see here two persons whose sound judgment guarded them against all danger of illusion, and who, both struck at the same time, seeing the same apparition, hesitate to give credence to it until they were convinced that their eyes saw the same phenomenon. There is not the least room for hallucination, and every sensible man must admit the reality of a supernatural occurrence, attested by such witnesses. Nor can we call in question those apparitions based upon the testimony of a St. Thomas of Aquin, as related above. We must also guard against too easily rejecting other facts of the same nature, from the moment they are attested by persons of recognised sanctity and truly worthy of belief. We must be prudent, no doubt, but ours must be a Christian prudence, equally removed from credulity and from that proud, conceited spirit with which, as we have remarked elsewhere, Jesus reproached His Apostles, "*Noli esse incredulus, sed fidelis.*"[2]

Monseigneur Languet, Bishop of Soissons, makes the same remark with reference to a circumstance which he relates in the Life of Blessed Margaret Alacoque. Madame Billet, wife of the doctor of the house—that is to say, of the convent of Paray—where the blessed sister resided, had just died. The soul of the deceased appeared to the

---

[1] Life of Ven. Ponzoni; cf. Ross., *Merv.*, 75.
[2] John xx. 27.

servant of God, asking her prayers, and charging her to warn her husband of two secret affairs that concerned his salvation. The holy sister gave an account of what had taken place to her Superior, Mother Greffier. The Superior ridiculed the vision, and the one who related it to her; she imposed silence upon Margaret, forbidding her to say or do anything regarding what had been asked of her. "The humble Religious obeyed with simplicity; and with the same simplicity she related to Mother Greffier the second solicitation which she received from the deceased some days later; but the Superior treated this with the same contempt. However, the following night she herself was aroused by such a horrible noise in her room that she thought she would die from fright. She called the sisters, and when assistance came, she was on the point of swooning away. When she somewhat recovered, she reproached herself with her incredulity, and no longer delayed to acquaint the doctor with what had been revealed to Sister Margaret.

"The doctor recognised the warning as coming from God, and profited by it. As for Mother Greffier, she learned by experience that if distrust is ordinarily the wisest policy, it is sometimes wrong to carry it too far, especially when the glory of God and the good of our neighbour is concerned."

CHAPTER LIV.

Advantages—Salutary Thoughts—Make Satisfaction in this Life rather than in the Next—St. Augustine and St. Louis Bertrand—Brother Lourenco—Father Michel de la Fontaine.

BESIDES the advantages which we have already considered, Charity towards the departed is very salutary to those who practise it, because it stimulates them to fervour in the service of God, and inspires the holiest thoughts. To think of the souls in Purgatory is to think of the sufferings of the other life; it is to call to mind that all sin demands expiation, either in this life or the next.

Now, who does not understand that it is better to make satisfaction here, since future chastisements are so terrible? A voice seems to come forth from Purgatory, repeating these words of the "Imitation," "Better is it to purge away our sins and to cut off our *vices* now, than to keep them for purgation hereafter."[1]

We call to mind, also, this other sentence, of which we read in the same chapter, "There, one hour of punishment will be more grievous than a hundred years of the most bitter penance here." Then, penetrated with salutary fear, we willingly endure the sufferings of the present life, and we say to God with St. Augustine and St. Louis Bertrand, *Domine, hic ure, hic seca, hic non parcas, ut in æternum parcas—*" Lord, apply here iron and fire; spare me not in this life, in order that you may spare me in the next."

Penetrated with these thoughts, the Christian regards the tribulations of the present life, and especially the sufferings of a painful malady, as a Purgatory upon earth which will dispense him from Purgatory after death.

[1] Imit., i. 24.

On January 6, 1676, there died in Lisbon, at the age of sixty-nine years, the servant of God, Gaspar Lourenco, Brother Coadjutor of the Society of Jesus, and porter of the professed house of that Institute. He was full of charity towards the poor and towards the souls in Purgatory. He knew not how to spare himself in the service of the unfortunate, and was marvellously ingenious in teaching them to bless God for their misery, which was to purchase Heaven for them. He himself was so penetrated with the happiness of suffering for our Lord, that he crucified his flesh almost without measure, and added other austerities on the vigils of Communion days. At the age of seventy-eight, he would accept of no dispensation from the fasts and abstinences of the Church, and allowed no day to pass without taking the discipline at least twice. Even in his last illness, the Brother Infirmarian said that the approach of death did not make him divest himself of his hair-shirt, so great was his desire to die upon the cross. The sufferings of his agony, which were most cruel, might have taken the place of the most rigorous penances. When asked if he suffered much, "*I am undergoing my Purgatory before departing for Heaven,*" he replied with a joyous air. Brother Lourenco was born on the day of Epiphany; and our Lord had revealed to him that this beautiful day was to be also that of his death. He designated the hour on the previous night; and when the Infirmarian visited him at daybreak, he said to him with a smile expressive of doubt, "Is it not to-day, brother, that you expect to go and enjoy the vision of God?" "Yes," he replied, "as soon as I shall have received the Body of my Saviour for the last time." In fact, he received Holy Communion and expired without struggle and without agony.

There is, then, every reason to believe that he spoke with a supernatural knowledge of the truth when he said, "*I am undergoing my Purgatory before departing for Heaven.*"

Another servant of God received from the Blessed Virgin

herself the same assurance that her earthly suffering would take the place of Purgatory. I speak of Father Michel de la Fontaine, who slept sweetly in the Lord on February 11, 1606, at Valencia, in Spain. He was one of the first missionaries who laboured for the salvation of the people of Peru. His greatest care when instructing the new converts was to inspire them with a sovereign horror of sin, and to lead them to great devotion towards the Mother of God, by speaking of the virtues of that admirable Virgin, and teaching them to recite the beads in her honour.

Mary, on her part, did not refuse the favours asked of her. One day when, exhausted with fatigue, he lay prostrate in the dust, not having strength to rise, he was visited by her whom the Church styles with reason *Comforter of the Afflicted.* She reanimated his courage, saying to him, "*Confidence, my son; your fatigues will take the place of Purgatory for you; bear your sufferings patiently, and on leaving this life your soul will be received into the abode of the blessed.*"

This vision was for Father de la Fontaine during life, but especially at the hour of his death, a source of abundant consolation. In gratitude for this favour, he each week practised some particular penance. At the moment when he expired, a Religious of eminent virtue saw his soul take its flight to Heaven in company of the Blessed Virgin, the Prince of the Apostles, St. John the Evangelist, and of St. Ignatius, the founder of the Company of Jesus.

CHAPTER LV.

Advantages—Salutary Instruction—Blessed Mary of the Angels—St. Peter Claver and the Sick Negro—The Negro and the Rosary.

BESIDES the holy thoughts which devotion to the holy souls suggests, the latter sometimes contribute directly to the spiritual welfare of their benefactors. In the Life of Blessed Mary of the Angels, of the Order of Mount Carmel, it is said that it is almost beyond belief how frequent were the apparitions of the souls of Purgatory who came to implore her assistance, and afterwards to thank her for their deliverance. Very often they conversed with the blessed sister, giving her useful advice for herself or for her sisters, and revealing things relating to the other world. "On the Wednesday within the Octave of the Assumption," she writes, "whilst saying the evening prayers, one of our good sisters appeared to me. She was clad in white, surrounded with glory and splendour, and so beautiful that I know of nothing here below to which I could compare her. Fearing some illusion of the devil, I armed myself with the sign of the cross; but she smiled, and disappeared shortly after. I begged our Lord not to permit me to be deceived by the demon. The following night the sister again appeared, and calling me by my name, said, 'I come on the part of God to let you know that I am in the enjoyment of eternal bliss. Tell our Mother Prioress that it is not the design of God to reveal to her the destiny that awaits her; tell her to place her confidence in St. Joseph and in the souls in Purgatory.' Having said this, she disappeared."

St. Peter Claver, Apostle of the Negroes of Carthagena, was aided by the souls in Purgatory in this work of the apostolate. He did not abandon the souls of his dear negroes after their death; penances, prayers, masses, indulgences, as far as depended upon himself, he applied to them, says Father Fleurian, his biographer. Thus it often happened that those poor afflicted souls, sure of his power with God, came to ask the assistance of his prayers.

The fastidiousness and incredulity of our century, says the same author, does not prevent us from relating some few additional facts. They may perhaps appear worthy of the raillery of freethinkers, but does it not suffice to know that God is the Master of these occurrences, and that they are, moreover, so well authenticated as to deserve a place in a history written for Christian readers?

A sick negro, whom he had taken into his room and laid upon his own bed, having heard a noise as of loud moaning during the night, fear made him run to Father Claver, who was kneeling in prayer. "Oh, Father!" he cried, "what is that dreadful noise, which terrifies me and prevents me from sleeping?" "Return, my son," replied the holy man, "and go to sleep without fear." Then, having assisted him to get into bed, he opened the door of the chamber, said a few words, and immediately the moaning ceased.

Several other negroes, being occupied in repairing a house at some distance from the city, one of them went out to cut wood upon a neighbouring mountain. As he approached the forest he heard himself called by his name from the top of a tree. He raised his eyes in the direction whence the voice came, and not seeing any one, was about to take to flight and join his companions, but he was stopped in a narrow path by a frightful spectre, who discharged a shower of blows upon him with a whip furnished with pieces of red-hot iron, and saying, "Why have you not got your rosary? Carry it about you in future, and say it for the souls in Purgatory." The phantom then ordered him to ask of the mistress of the house for three gold pieces which were due to him, and which he was to take to Father Claver, that Masses might be offered for his intention, after which he disappeared.

In the meantime the noise of the blows and the cries of the negro had brought his companions to the spot, where they found him more dead than alive, covered with the wounds he had received, and unable to utter a word. They carried him to the house, where the mistress acknowledged that in reality she owed the sum of money in question to a negro who had died some time previous. Father Claver, on being informed of what had occurred, said the Masses which were asked of him, and gave a rosary to the negro, who ever afterwards wore it, and never omitted to say it daily.

CHAPTER LVI.

Advantages—Salutary Instructions—St. Magdalen de Pazzi and Sister Benedicta—Father Paul Hoffée—Venerable Father de la Colombière—Louis Corbinelli.

ST. MAGDALEN DE PAZZI, in an apparition of a departed soul, received the most wholesome instruction on religious virtues. There was in her convent a sister named Mary Benedicta, who was distinguished for her piety, her obedience, and all other virtues which are the ornament of holy souls. She was so humble, says Father Cepari, and had such contempt for herself, that, without the guidance of her Superiors, she would have gone to extremes, with the sole view of acquiring the reputation of being a person without prudence and without judgment. She therefore said that she could not help feeling jealous of St. Alexis, who found a means of living a hidden life, contemptible in the eyes of the world. She was so docile and prompt in obedience, that she ran like a little child at the least sign of the will of her Superiors, and the latter were obliged to use great circumspection in the orders which they gave her, lest she should go beyond their desires. In fact, she had gained such control over her passions and appetites, that it would be difficult to imagine a more perfect mortification.

This good sister died suddenly, having had but a few hours of sickness. The following morning, which was Saturday, when, during the Mass which was celebrated, the Religious were singing the *Sanctus*, Magdalen was rapt in ecstasy. During the rapture, God showed her this soul under a corporal form in the glory of Heaven. She was adorned with a golden star, which she had received in recompense for her ardent charity. All her fingers were covered with costly rings, on account of her fidelity to all the rules, and the care she had taken to sanctify her most ordinary actions. Upon her head she wore a very rich crown, because she had always loved obedience and suffering for Jesus Christ. In fact, she surpassed in glory a great multitude of virgins, and she contemplated her Spouse Jesus with singular familiarity, because she had so loved humiliation, according to these words of our Saviour, *He that humbleth himself shall be exalted*. Such was the sublime lesson which the saint received in reward for her charity towards the departed.

The thought of Purgatory incites us to labour zealously, and to fly the least faults, in order to avoid the terrible expiations of the other life. Father Paul Hoffée, who died a holy death at Ingolstadt in the year 1608, made use of this thought for his own benefit and that of others. He never lost sight of Purgatory, nor ceased to relieve the poor souls who frequently appeared to him to solicit his suffrages.

PURGATORY, THE MYSTERY OF MERCY.

As he was Superior of his brethren in religion, he often exhorted them, first to sanctify themselves, the better to be able afterwards to sanctify others, and never to neglect the smallest prescription of their rules; then he would add with great simplicity, "Otherwise I fear you will come, like several others have done, to ask my prayers that you may be delivered from Purgatory." In his last moments he was wholly occupied in loving colloquies with our Lord, His Blessed Mother, and the Saints. He was sensibly consoled by a visit of a very holy soul, who had preceded him to Heaven but two or three days previous, and who now invited him to go and enjoy the eternal love of God.[1]

When we say that the thought of Purgatory makes us use all means to avoid it, it is evident that we have reason to fear that we shall go there. Now on what is this fear based? If we but reflect a little upon the sanctity required to enter Heaven, and the frailty of human nature, which is the source of so many faults, we easily understand that this fear is but too well founded. Moreover, do not the examples we have read above show us clearly that very often even the holiest souls have sometimes to undergo expiation in the other life?

Venerable Father Claude de la Colombière died in the odour of sanctity at Paray, February 15, 1682, as Blessed Margaret Mary had predicted to him. As soon as he had expired, a pious girl came to announce his death to Sister Margaret. The holy Religious, without showing any disturbance or breaking forth into vain regrets, said simply to that person, "Go and pray to God for him, and cause prayers to be everywhere offered for the repose of his soul." The Father had died at five o'clock in the morning. That same evening she wrote a note to the same person in these terms: "*Cease to be afflicted; invoke Him. Fear nothing. He is more powerful to aid us than ever.*" These words give

[1] Menology of the Society of Jesus, Dec. 17.

us to understand that she had been supernaturally enlightened regarding the death of this holy man, and of the state of his soul in the other life.

Sister Margaret's peace and tranquillity at the death of a director who had been useful to her was another sort of miracle. The blessed sister loved nothing except in God and for God; God held the place of all else in her heart, and consumed by the fire of His love all other attachment. The Superior was surprised at her perfect tranquillity on the death of the holy missionary, and still more so that Margaret did not ask to do any extraordinary penance for the repose of his soul, as was her custom on the death of any one of her acquaintances in whom she was particularly interested. The Mother Superior asked the servant of God the reason of this, and she replied quite simply, "He is in no need of it; he is in a condition to pray for us, since he is exalted in Heaven by the Sacred Heart of our Divine Lord. Only to expiate some slight negligence in the practice of Divine Love," she added, "his soul was deprived of the vision of God from the time it left his body until the moment when his remains were consigned to the tomb."

Let us add one example more, that of Father Corbinelli. This holy person was not exempted from Purgatory. It is true he was not detained there, but he had to pass through the flames before being admitted into the presence of God. Louis Corbinelli, of the Company of Jesus, died in the odour of sanctity at the professed house in Rome, in the year 1591, almost at the same time with St. Aloysius Gonzaga. The tragic death of Henry II., king of France, gave him a disgust for the world, and he decided to consecrate himself entirely to the service of God. In the year 1559 the marriage of the Princess Elizabeth was celebrated with great pomp in the city of Paris. Among other amusements, a tournament was organised, in which figured the flower of the French nobility and chivalry. The King himself appeared in the midst of his brilliant court. Among the spectators, gathered even from foreign lands, was young Louis Corbinelli, who had come from his native city, Florence, to assist at the festival. Corbinelli contemplated with admiration the glory of the French monarch, now at the zenith of his grandeur and prosperity, when suddenly he saw him fall, struck by a fatal blow aimed by an imprudent tilter. The lance badly directed by Montgomery transpierced the King, who expired bathed in his blood.

In the twinkling of an eye all his glory vanished and the royal magnificence was covered with a shroud. This event made a salutary impression upon Corbinelli; seeing the vanity of human greatness thus exposed, he renounced the world and embraced a religious life in the Society of Jesus. His life was that of a saint, and his death filled with joy all those who were witnesses of it. It took place a few days before that of St. Aloysius, who was then sick in the Roman College. The young saint announced to Cardinal Bellarmine that the soul of Father Corbinelli had entered into glory; and when the Cardinal asked him if it had not passed through Purgatory, "It passed through," he replied, "but it did not stay."

CHAPTER LVII.

Advantages—Stimulant to Fervour—Cautions to us—Probability of going to Purgatory—Means of Escaping it—Employment of those Means—St. Catherine of Genoa.

IF holy Religious pass through Purgatory, although not detained there, have we not to fear that we shall not only pass through it, but also remain for a longer or shorter time? Can we live in a security that would be, to say the least, very imprudent? Our faith and our conscience tell us that our fear of Purgatory is well grounded. I go still further, dear reader, and say that with a little reflection you yourself must acknowledge that it is very probable, and almost certain, that you will go to Purgatory. Is it not true that on leaving this earth your soul will enter into one of those three abodes pointed out to us by faith, Hell, Heaven, or Purgatory? Will you go to Hell? It is not probable, because you have a horror of mortal sin, and for nothing in the world would you commit one, or keep it upon your conscience after having committed it. Will you go to Heaven? You answer immediately that you think yourself unworthy of such a favour. There remains, then, but Purgatory; and you must own that it is very probable, almost certain, that you will go into that place of expiation.

By setting this grave truth before your eyes, do not think, dear reader, that we wish to frighten you, or take from you all hope of entering Heaven without Purgatory. On the contrary, this hope must ever remain deeply impressed upon our hearts, for it is the spirit of Jesus Christ, who nowise desires that His disciples should stand in need of future expiation. He even instituted Sacraments and established all sorts of means to assist us to make full satisfaction in this world. But these means are too often neglected; and it is especially by a salutary fear that we are stimulated to make use of them.

Now, what are those means which we have to employ in order to avoid, or at least shorten, our Purgatory and mitigate its rigour? They are evidently those exercises and good works which most assist us to satisfy for our faults in this world and to find mercy before God, namely, the following: devotion to the Blessed Virgin Mary, and fidelity in wearing her scapular; charity towards the living and the dead; mortification and obedience; a pious reception of the Sacraments, especially on the approach of death; confidence in the Divine Mercy; and, finally, the holy acceptation of death in union with the death of Jesus upon the cross.

These means are sufficiently powerful to preserve us from Purgatory, but we must make use of them. Now, to employ them seriously and with perseverance, one condition is necessary: it is to form a firm resolution of satisfying in this world rather than in the next. This resolution must be based upon faith, which teaches us how easy is satisfaction in this life, how terrible is Purgatory. *Be at agreement with thy adversary betimes,* says Jesus Christ, *whilst thou art in the way with him: lest, perhaps, thy adversary deliver thee to the judge, and the judge deliver thee to the officer, and thou be cast into prison. Amen, I say to thee, thou shalt not go out from thence till thou repay the last farthing.*[1]

To be reconciled with our adversary in the way, signifies, in the mouth of our Lord, to appease Divine Justice, and to make satisfaction on our way through life, before reaching that unchangeable end, that eternity where all penance is impossible, and where we shall have to submit to all the rigours of Justice. Is not this counsel of our Divine Saviour most wise?

Can we appear before the tribunal of God burdened with an enormous debt, which we might so easily have discharged by some works of penance, and which we shall then have to pay by years of torment? "He who purifies himself from his faults in the present life," says St. Catherine of Genoa, "satisfies with a penny a debt of a thousand ducats; and he who waits until the other life to discharge his debts, consents to pay a thousand ducats for that which he might before have paid with a penny. We must, therefore, begin with the firm and efficacious resolution of making

[1] Matt. v. 25.

satisfaction in this world; that is the foundation-stone. This foundation once laid, we must employ the means enumerated above.

CHAPTER LVIII.

Means to Avoid Purgatory—Great Devotion to the Blessed Virgin—Father Jerome Carvalho—St. Bridget—The Scapular of Mount Carmel.

A SERVANT of God sums up these means, and reduces them to two, saying, "*Let us cleanse our souls by water and by fire;*" that is to say, by the water of tears, and by the fire of charity and good works. In fact, we may classify them all under these two exercises, and this is conformable to Holy Scripture, where we see that souls are cleansed from their stains, and purified like gold in the crucible. But since we must seek above everything to be practical, let us follow the method we have indicated, and which has been practised, with so much success, by the saints and by all fervent Christians.

In the first place, in order to obtain great purity of soul, and in consequence to have little reason to fear Purgatory, we must cherish a great devotion towards the Blessed Virgin Mary. This good Mother will so assist her dear children in cleansing their souls and in shortening their Purgatory, that they may live in the greatest confidence. She even desires that they should not trouble themselves on this subject, and that they should not allow themselves to be discouraged by excessive fear, as she herself deigned to declare to her servant, Jerome Carvalho, of whom we have already spoken. "*Have confidence, my son,*" she said to him. "*I am the Mother of Mercy for my dear children in*

Purgatory, *as well as for those still living upon earth.*" In the Revelations of St. Bridget we read something similar: "*I am*," said the Blessed Virgin to her, "*the Mother of all those who are in the place of expiation; my prayers mitigate the chastisements inflicted upon them for their faults.*"[1]

Those who wear the holy scapular have a special right to the protection of Mary. The devotion of the holy scapular, unlike that of the Rosary, does not consist in prayer, but in the pious practice of wearing a sort of habit, which is as the livery of the Queen of Heaven. The scapular of Our Lady of Mount Carmel, of which we here speak, traces its origin back to the thirteenth century, and was first preached by Blessed Simon Stock, fifth General of the Order of Mount Carmel. This celebrated servant of Mary, born in Kent, England, in the year 1100, whilst yet young, retired into a solitary forest to apply himself to prayer and penance. He chose as his dwelling the hollow of a tree, to which he attached a crucifix and a picture of the Blessed Virgin, whom he honoured as his Mother, and ceased not to invoke with the tenderest affection. For twelve years he entreated her to make known to him what he could do that would be most agreeable to her Divine Son, when the Queen of Heaven told him to enter the Order of Mount Carmel, which was particularly devoted to her service. Simon obeyed; and, under the protection of Mary, became an exemplary Religious and the ornament of the Order of Mount Carmel, of which he was elected Superior General in 1245.

One day—it was the 16th July 1251—the Blessed Virgin appeared to him surrounded by a multitude of heavenly spirits, and, with a countenance radiant with joy, she presented to him a scapular of a brown colour, saying, "Receive, my dear son, this scapular of thy Order; it is the badge of my Confraternity and the pledge of a privilege which I have obtained for thee and for thy brethren of

[1] Book iv. chap. i.

Mount Carmel. Those who die devoutly clothed in this habit shall be preserved from eternal fire. It is the sign of salvation, a safeguard in peril, a pledge of peace and special protection, until the end of time." The happy old man everywhere published the favour he had received, showing the scapular, healing the sick, and working other miracles in proof of his marvellous mission. Immediately, Edward I., king of England, Louis IX., king of France, and after their example almost all the sovereigns of Europe, as also a great number of their subjects, received the same habit. From that time commenced the celebrated *Confraternity of the Scapular*, which was soon afterwards canonically erected by the Holy See.

Not content with granting this first privilege, Mary made another promise in favour of the members of the Confraternity of the Scapular, by assuring them of a speedy deliverance from the sufferings of Purgatory. About fifty years after the death of Blessed Simon, the illustrious Pontiff, John XXII., whilst at prayer in the early morning, saw the Mother of God appear surrounded with light, and bearing the habit of Mount Carmel. Among other things she said to him, "If among the Religious or members of the Confraternity of Mount Carmel there are any who, on account of their faults, are condemned to Purgatory, I will descend into the midst of them like a tender Mother on the Saturday after their death: I will deliver them and conduct them to the holy mount of eternal life." These are the words which the Pontiff places in the lips of Mary in his celebrated Bull of 3rd March 1322, commonly called the *Sabbatine Bull*. He concludes in these words: "I therefore accept this holy indulgence; I ratify and confirm it upon earth, as Jesus Christ has graciously granted it in Heaven through the merits of the most Blessed Virgin." This privilege was afterwards confirmed by a great many Bulls and Decrees of the Sovereign Pontiffs.

Such is the devotion of the holy scapular. It is sanctioned by the practice of pious souls throughout the Christian world, by the testimony of twenty-two Popes, by the writings of an incalculable number of pious authors, and by multiplied miracles during the past 600 years; so that, says the illustrious Benedict XIV., "he who dares call in question the validity of the devotion of the scapular, or deny its privileges, would be a proud despiser of religion."

CHAPTER LIX.

Means to Avoid Purgatory—Privileges of the Holy Scapular—Venerable Father De la Colombière—The Hospital at Toulon—The Sabbatine—St. Teresa—A Lady at Otranto.

ACCORDING to what we have said, the Blessed Virgin has attached two great privileges to the holy scapular; on their part, the Sovereign Pontiffs have added to them the richest indulgences. We shall not speak here of the two indulgences; but we consider it useful to make these two precious privileges thoroughly known, the one under the name of *Preservation*, the other under that of *Deliverance*.

The first is the exemption from the torments of Hell: *In hoc moriens æternum non patietur incendium*—"He who dies wearing this habit shall not suffer the fire of Hell." It is evident that he who dies in mortal sin, even whilst wearing the scapular, will not be exempt from damnation; and such is not the meaning of Mary's promise. This good Mother has promised mercifully so to dispose all things that he who dies wearing that holy habit will receive an efficacious grace worthily to confess and bewail his faults; or, if he is surprised by sudden death, he will have the time and will to make an act of perfect contrition. We might fill a volume with the miraculous events which prove the fulfilment of this promise. Let it suffice to relate a few of them.

Venerable Father de la Colombière tells us that a young person, who was at first pious and wore the holy scapular, had the misfortune to stray from the path of virtue. In consequence of bad literature and dangerous company, she fell into the greatest disorders, and was about to lose her honour. Instead of turning to God and having recourse to the Blessed Virgin, who is the refuge of sinners, she abandoned herself to despair. The demon soon suggested a remedy to her evils—the frightful remedy of suicide, which would put an end to her temporal miseries to plunge her into eternal torments. She ran to the river, and, still wearing the scapular, threw herself into the water. But, oh, wonder! she floated instead of sinking, and could not find the death she sought. A fisherman, who saw her, hastened to give her assistance, but the wretched creature prevented him: tearing off her scapular, she cast it far from her and sank immediately. The fisherman was unable to save her, but he found the scapular, and recognised that this sacred livery while she wore it had prevented the sinner from committing suicide.

In the hospital at Toulon there was an officer, a most impious man, who refused to see a priest. Death approached, and he fell into a sort of lethargy. The attendants profited by this to place a scapular about his neck, without his knowledge. On recovering soon after, he cried out in a fury, "Why have you put fire upon me, a fire which burns me? Take it away, take it away!" Then they invoked the Blessed Virgin, and tried again to put on the scapular. He perceived this, tore it off in a rage, threw it far away from him, and with a horrible blasphemy upon his lips he expired.

The second privilege, that of the *Sabbatine* or *Deliver-*

PURGATORY, THE MYSTERY OF MERCY. 293

ance, consists in being released from Purgatory by the Blessed Virgin on the first Saturday after death. To enjoy this privilege, certain conditions are to be fulfilled:— 1st, To observe the chastity of our state. 2nd, To recite the Little Office of the Blessed Virgin. Those who recite the Canonical Office satisfy this condition. Those who are unable to read must, instead of saying the Office, observe the fasts prescribed by the Church, and abstain from flesh-meat on all Wednesdays, Fridays, and Saturdays. 3rd, In case of necessity, the obligation of reciting the Office, the abstinence and fasting, may be commuted into other pious works, by those who have the power to grant such dispensations. Such is the privilege of the *Sabbatine* or *Deliverance*, with the conditions necessary to enjoy it. If we remember what has been said of the rigours of Purgatory and its duration, we shall find that this privilege is most precious, and its conditions very easy.

We know that doubts have been raised concerning the authenticity of the Sabbatine Bull, but besides constant tradition and the pious practice of the faithful, the great Pope, Benedict XIV., whose eminent learning and moderation of opinions are well known, has pronounced in its favour.

At Otranto, a city in the kingdom of Naples, a lady of high rank experienced great pleasure in assisting at the sermons of a Carmelite Father who was a great promoter of the devotion to Mary. He assured his auditors that all Christians who piously wore the scapular, and fulfilled the prescribed conditions, would see the Divine Mother at their departure from this world, and that this great consoler of the afflicted would come on the Saturday after their death to deliver them from Purgatory, and take them into the abode of the Blessed. Struck with these precious advantages, this lady immediately put on the livery of the Blessed Virgin, firmly resolved to observe faithfully the rules of the Confraternity. Her piety made rapid progress. She prayed to Mary day and night, placed all her confidence in her, and rendered her all possible homage. Among other favours which she asked, she implored that of dying on a Saturday, in order that she might be the sooner delivered from Purgatory. Her prayers were heard. Some years later, having fallen ill, notwithstanding the contrary opinion of her physician, she declared that her malady would carry her to the grave. "I bless God," she added, "in the hope of being soon united with Him in Heaven." Her sickness made such rapid progress that the doctors unanimously declared that she was at the point of death, and that she could not live through the day, which was Wednesday. "You are again mistaken," said the sick lady; "I shall live three days more, and shall not die until Saturday." The event justified her words. Regarding the days of suffering which remained to her as an inestimable treasure, she profited of them to purify her soul and to increase her merits. When Saturday came, she rendered her soul into the hands of her Creator.

Her daughter, who was also very pious, was inconsolable in her bereavement. Whilst praying in her oratory for the soul of her dear mother, and shedding abundant tears, a great servant of God, who was habitually favoured with supernatural communications, went to her and said, "Cease to weep, my child, or rather let your grief be turned into joy. I come to assure you, on the part of God, that to-day, Saturday, thanks to the privileges granted to the members of the Confraternity of the Scapular, your mother has gone to Heaven, and is numbered among the elect. Be consoled and bless the most August Virgin, the Mother of Mercy."

CHAPTER LX.

Means to Avoid Purgatory — Charity and Mercy — The Prophet Daniel and the King of Babylon—St. Peter Damian and John Patrizzi.

WE have just seen the first means of avoiding Purgatory, a tender devotion towards Mary; the second consists in Charity and works of Mercy of every kind. *Many sins are forgiven her,* said our Lord, speaking of Magdalen, *because she hath loved much.*[1] *Blessed are the merciful: for they shall obtain mercy.*[2] *Judge not, and you shall not be judged. Condemn not, and you shall not be condemned. Forgive, and you shall be forgiven.*[3] *If you forgive men their offences, your Heavenly Father will forgive you also your offences.*[4] *Give to every one that asketh of thee: give, and it shall be given to you: for with the same measure that you shall mete withal, it shall be measured to you again.*[5] *Make unto you friends of the mammon of iniquity, that when you shall fail (when you leave this world) they may receive you into everlasting dwellings.*[6] And the Holy Ghost says by the mouth of the Royal Prophet, *Blessed is he that understandeth concerning the needy and the poor: the Lord will deliver him in the evil day.*[7] All these words indicate clearly that Charity, Mercy, and Benevolence, whether towards the poor or towards sinners, towards our enemies and those who injure us, or towards the departed who are in great need of our assistance, we shall find mercy at the tribunal of the Sovereign Judge.

The rich of this world have much to fear. *Woe to you that are rich,* says the Son of God, *for you have had your*

---

[1] Luke vii. 47.   [2] Matt. v. 7.   [3] Luke vi. 37.   [4] Matt. vi. 14.
[5] Luke vi. 30, 38.   [6] Luke xvi. 9.   [7] Ps. xl.

consolation. Woe to you that are filled: for you shall hunger. Woe to you that laugh now: for you shall mourn and weep.[1] Certainly, these words of God should cause the wealthy votaries of this world to tremble; but if they wished, their wealth itself could become for them a great means of salvation; they might redeem their sins and pay their terrible debts by abundant alms. *Let my counsel, O king, be acceptable to thee,* said Daniel to the proud Nabuchodonosor, *and redeem thy sins with alms, and thy iniquities with works of mercy to the poor.*[2] *For alms deliver from all sin and from death, and will not suffer the soul to go into darkness. Alms shall be a great confidence before the Most High God to all them that give it,* said Tobias to his son.[3] Our Saviour confirms all this, and goes even further when He says to the Pharisees, *But yet that which remaineth, give alms; and behold all things are clean unto you.* How great, then, is the folly of the rich, who have in hand so easy a means of ensuring their future spiritual welfare, and yet neglect to employ it! What folly not to make a good use of that fortune of which they shall have to render an account to God! What folly to go and burn in Hell or Purgatory, and leave a fortune to avaricious and ungrateful heirs, who will not bestow upon the departed so much as a prayer, a tear, or even a passing thought! But, on the contrary, how happy are those Christians who understand that they are but the dispensers, before God, of the goods which they have received from Him, who think only of disposing of them according to the designs of Jesus Christ, to whom they must render an account, and, in fine, who make use of them only to procure friends, defenders, and protectors in eternity!

St. Peter Damian, in one of his treatises, relates the following.[4] A Roman lord, named John Patrizzi, died. His life, although Christian, had been like that of the

---

[1] Luke vi. 24. [2] Dan. iv. 24.
[3] Tob. iv. 11, 12. [4] Tracts, 34.

generality of the rich, far different from that of his Divine Master, poor, suffering, crowned with thorns. Fortunately, however, he had been very charitable towards the poor, even so far as to give away his garments to clothe them. A few days after his death, a holy priest, being in prayer, was wrapt in ecstasy, and transported to the Basilica of St. Cecilia, one of the most celebrated in Rome. He there saw a number of heavenly virgins, St. Cecilia, St. Agnes, St. Agatha, and others, grouped around a magnificent throne, upon which sat the Queen of Heaven, surrounded by angels and blessed spirits.

At this moment appeared a poor woman, dressed in a miserable garment, but having a cape of costly fur upon her shoulders. She knelt humbly at the feet of the Heavenly Queen, and joining her hands, her eyes filled with tears, she said with a smile, "Mother of Mercy, in the name of thy ineffable goodness, I beg thee to have pity on the unfortunate John Patrizzi, who has just died, and who suffers most cruelly in Purgatory." Three times she repeated the same prayer, each time with more fervour, but without receiving any answer. "Thou knowest well, O most merciful Queen, that I am that beggar who, at the entrance to your great Basilica, asked alms in the depth of winter with nothing to cover me but my rags. Oh, how I trembled with cold! Then John, whom I petitioned in the name of Our Lady, took from his shoulder this costly fur and gave it to me, depriving himself of it in order to give it to me. Does so great an act of charity, performed in thy name, O Mary, not merit some indulgence?"

At this touching appeal the Queen of Heaven cast a glance of love upon the supplicant. "The man for whom you pray," she replied, "is condemned for a long time to the most terrible suffering, on account of his numerous sins. But since he had two special virtues, mercy towards the poor and devotion for my altars, I will condescend to give him my assistance." At these words the holy assembly testified its joy and gratitude towards the Mother of Mercy. Patrizzi was brought in; he was pale, disfigured, and loaded with chains, which had made deep wounds. The Holy Virgin looked upon him for a moment with tender compassion, then ordered that his chains should be taken off, and garments of glory to be put upon him, in order that he might join the saints and blessed spirits who surrounded her throne. This order was immediately executed, and all disappeared.

The holy priest who had enjoyed this vision ceased not from that moment to preach the clemency of Our Lady towards the poor suffering souls, especially towards those who had been devoted to her service, and who had had great charity towards the poor.

CHAPTER LXI.

Means to Avoid Purgatory—Blessed Margaret Mary and the Suffering Souls—The Novice and her Father—A Soul that had Suffered without Complaint.

AMONG the revelations of our Lord to Margaret Mary on the subject of Purgatory there is one which shows how particularly severe are the punishments inflicted for faults against Charity. " One day," relates Monseigneur Languet, " our Lord showed His servant a number of souls deprived of the assistance of the Blessed Virgin and the saints, and even of the visits of their angel-guardians; this was," said her Divine Master, " in punishment for their want of union with their superiors, and certain misunderstandings. Many of those souls were destined to remain for a great length of time in horrible flames. The blessed sister recognised also many souls who had lived in religion, and who, on account of their lack of union and charity with their brethren, were deprived of their suffrages and received no alleviation."

If it is true that God punishes thus severely those that have failed in Charity, He will be infinitely merciful towards those who have practised this virtue so dear to His Heart. *But before all things*, He says to us by the mouth of His Apostle, St. Peter, *have a constant mutual charity among yourselves, for charity covereth a multitude of sins.*[1]

Let us hear Monseigneur Languet again in the Life of Margaret Mary. It is Mother Greffier, he says, who, in the memoir she wrote after the death of the blessed sister, attests the following fact. " I cannot omit the cause of certain particular circumstances which manifest the truth of a revelation made on this occasion to the servant of God. The father of one of the novices was the cause of it. This gentleman had died some time previous, and had been recommended to the prayers of the community. The charity of Sister Margaret, then Mistress of Novices, urged her to pray more especially for him.

"Some days later the novice went to recommend him to her prayers. 'My daughter,' said her holy mistress, 'be perfectly tranquil; your father is rather in a condition to pray for us. Ask your mother what was the most generous action your father performed before his death; this action has obtained for him from God a favourable judgment.'

"The action to which she alluded was unknown to the novice; no one in Paray knew the circumstance of a death which had happened so far away from that town. The novice did not see her mother until long afterwards, on the day of her profession. She then asked what was that generous Christian action which her father had performed before dying. 'When the Holy Viaticum was brought to him,' replied her mother, 'the butcher joined those who accompanied the Blessed Sacrament, and placed

---
[1] Peter iv. 8.

himself in a corner of the room. The sick, on perceiving him, called him by his name, told him to approach, and, pressing his hand with a humility uncommon in persons of his rank, asked pardon for some hard words which he had addressed to him from time to time, and desired that all present should be witness of the reparation which he made.' Sister Margaret had learned from God alone what had taken place, and the novice knew by that the consoling truth of what she had told her concerning her father's happy state in the other life."

Let us add that God, by this revelation, has shown us once more how *Charity covereth a multitude of sins*, and will cause us to find Mercy in the day of Justice.

Blessed Margaret Mary received from our Divine Lord another communication relative to Charity. He showed her the soul of a deceased person who had to undergo but a light chastisement, and he told her that among all the good works which this person had performed in the world, He had taken into special consideration certain humiliations to which she had submitted in the world, because she had suffered them in the spirit of charity, not only without murmuring, but even without speaking of them. Our Lord added, that, in recompense, He had given her a mild and favourable judgment.

CHAPTER LXII.

Means to Avoid Purgatory — Christian Mortification — St. John Berchmans — Blessed Emily de Verceil and the Religious who was Weary of Choir.

THE third means of satisfying in this world is the practice of Christian mortification and religious obedience. We

PURGATORY, THE MYSTERY OF MERCY. 301

bear about in our body the mortification of Jesus, says the Apostle, *that the life also of Jesus may be made manifest in our bodies.*[1] This mortification of Jesus, which the Christian must bear about in him, is, in its broadest sense, the part that he must take in the sufferings of his Divine Master, by bearing in union with Him the trials he may have to encounter in this life, or the suffering which he voluntarily inflicts upon himself. The first and best mortification is that which is attached to our daily duties, the pains we have to take, the effort we must make to acquit ourselves properly of the duties of our state, and to bear the contradictions of each day. When St. John Berchmans said that *his chief mortification was the common life,* he said nothing else than this, because for him the common life embraced all the duties of his state.

Moreover, he who sanctifies the duties and sufferings of each day, and who thus practises fundamental mortification, will soon advance, and impose voluntary privations and sufferings upon himself in order to escape the pains of the other life.

The slightest mortifications, the most trifling sacrifice, especially when done through obedience, are of great value in the sight of God.

Blessed Emily, a Dominican, and Prioress of the Monastery of St. Mary at Vercelli, inspired her Religious with a spirit of perfect obedience in view of Purgatory. One of the points of the Rule prohibited the Religious to drink between meals without express permission of the Superior. Now, the latter, knowing, as we have seen, the value of the sacrifice of a glass of water in the eyes of God, was generally accustomed to refuse this permission, that she might afford her sisters an opportunity to practise an easy mortification, but she sweetened her refusal by telling them to offer their thirst to Jesus, tormented by a cruel thirst upon the cross. She then advised them to suffer this slight privation with a

[1] 2 Cor. iv. 10.

view of diminishing their torments in the expiatory flames of Purgatory.

There was in her community a sister named Mary Isabella, who was too prone to levity, being fond of conversation and other exterior distractions. The consequence was that she had little relish for prayer, was negligent in reciting the Office, and only acquitted herself of this her chief duty with the greatest repugnance. Thus she was never in any haste to go to choir, and as soon as the office was ended she was the first to go out. One day whilst she was hurrying to leave the choir, she passed by the stall of the Prioress, who stopped her. "Where are you going in such haste, my good sister?" she said to her, "and why are you so anxious to get out before the other sisters?" The sister, taken by surprise, at first observed a respectful silence, then she acknowledged with humility that the Office was wearisome to her and seemed too long. "That is all very well," replied the Prioress, "but if it costs you so much to chant the praises of God seated comfortably in the midst of your sisters, what will you do in Purgatory, where you will be obliged to remain in the midst of flames? To spare you that terrible trial, my daughter, I order you to leave your place the last of all." The sister submitted with simplicity, like a truly obedient child; she was recompensed. The disgust which she had experienced thus far for the things of God was changed into devotion and spiritual joy. Moreover, as God revealed to Blessed Emily, having died some time afterwards, she obtained a great diminution of the suffering which awaited her on the other life. God counted as so many hours in Purgatory the hours which she passed in prayer through a spirit of obedience.[1]

[1] *Diario Dominicano*, May 3; *Merv.*, 60.

CHAPTER LXIII.

Means to Avoid Purgatory—The Sacraments—Receiving them Promptly—Medicinal Effect of Extreme Unction —St. Alphonsus Liguori.

WE have indicated, as a fourth means of satisfying in this world, the use of the Sacraments, and especially a holy and Christian reception of the last Sacraments on the approach of death.

The Divine Master admonishes us in the Gospel to prepare ourselves well for death, in order that it may be precious in His eyes and the worthy crowning of a Christian life. His love for us makes Him desire ardently that we should leave this world entirely purified, divested of all debt towards Divine Justice; and that on appearing before God, we should be found worthy to be admitted among the elect, without need of passing through Purgatory. It is for this end that He ordinarily sends us the pains of sickness before death, and that He has instituted the Sacraments, to aid us in sanctifying our sufferings, and the more perfectly to dispose us to appear before His face.

The Sacraments which we receive in time of sickness are three : Confession, which we may receive as soon as we wish; Holy Viaticum and Extreme Unction, which we may receive as soon as there is danger of death. This circumstance of the danger of death must be taken in the broad sense of the word.

It is not necessary that there should be an imminent danger of dying, and that all hope of recovery be lost; it is not even necessary that the danger of death be certain; it suffices that it be probable, and prudently presumed, even when there is no other infirmity than old age.[1]

The effects of the Sacraments, well received, correspond to all the needs, all the lawful desires of the sick. These divine remedies purify the soul from her sins, and increase her treasure of sanctifying grace; they fortify the sick person, and enable him to bear his sufferings with patience, to triumph over the assaults of the demon at the last moment, and to make a generous sacrifice of his life to God. Moreover, besides the effects which they produce upon the soul, the Sacraments exert a salutary influence upon the body. Extreme Unction especially comforts the sick person and alleviates his sufferings; it even restores him to health, if God judges it expedient for his salvation.

The Sacraments are, then, for the faithful, an immense assistance, an inestimable benefit. It is not, therefore, surprising that the enemy of souls makes it his first object to deprive them of so great a good. Not being able to rob the Church of her Sacraments, he endeavours to keep them from the sick, either by making them entirely neglect to receive them, or that they receive them so late as to lose all their benefit. Alas! how many souls allow themselves to be taken in this snare! How many souls for not promptly receiving the Sacraments fall into hell, or into the deepest abyss of Purgatory!

To avoid this misfortune, the first care of a Christian, in case of sickness, must be to think of the Sacraments, and to receive them as promptly as possible. We say, that he should receive them promptly, whilst he is still in possession of the use of his faculties, and we dwell upon this circumstance for the following reasons. 1. In receiving the Sacraments promptly, the patient having yet sufficient strength to prepare himself properly, derives all the fruit of them. 2. He needs to be provided as soon

---

[1] See a pamphlet, approved by all the Bishops of Belgium, and entitled *Les Médicins et les Familles*. Brussels, Maison Goemaere.

as possible with the Divine assistance, in order to support his sufferings, to overcome temptation, and to sanctify the precious time of sickness. 3. It is only by receiving the holy oils in time, that we can experience the effects of a bodily cure. For we must here remark an important point: the sacramental remedy of the holy unction produces its effect upon the sick person in the same manner as medical remedies. It resembles an exquisite medicine that assists nature, in which there is still supposed to be a certain vigour; so that extreme unction cannot exercise a medicinal virtue when nature has become too feeble, and life is almost extinguished. Thus a great number of sick persons die because they put off receiving the Sacraments until they are at the last extremity; whilst it is not unusual to see those entirely recover who hasten to receive them.

St. Alphonsus[1] speaks of a sick man who delayed to receive extreme unction until it was almost too late, for he died shortly afterwards. Now, God made known by way of revelation, says the holy doctor, that if he had received that Sacrament earlier, he would have been restored to health. However, the most precious effect of the last Sacraments is that which it produces upon the soul; they purify it from the remains of sin, and take away, or at least diminish, its debt of temporal punishment; they strengthen it to bear suffering in a holy manner; they fill it with confidence in God, and assist it to accept death from His hands in union with that of Jesus Christ.

[1] Praxis Confess., n. 274.

CHAPTER LXIV.

Means to Avoid Purgatory—Confidence in God—St. Francis de Sales—St. Philip Neri and Sister Scholastica.

THE fifth means for obtaining favour before the tribunal of God is to have great confidence in His Mercy. *In Thee, O Lord, have I hoped; let me never be confounded*, says the Prophet.[1] Surely He who said to the good thief, "This day thou shalt be with Me in Paradise," well merits that we should have an unbounded confidence in Him. St. Francis de Sales avowed that if he considered his misery only, he deserved Hell; but full of humble confidence in the mercy of God and in the merits of Jesus Christ, he firmly hoped to share the happiness of the elect. "And what would our Lord do with His eternal life," said he, "if not to give it to us, poor, little, insignificant creatures as we are, who have no hope but in His goodness? Blessed be God! I have this firm confidence in the depth of my heart, that we shall live eternally with God. We shall one day be all united in Heaven. Take courage; we shall soon be there above."

"We must," he said again, "die between two pillows; the one, of the humble confession that we merit nothing but Hell; the other, of an entire confidence that God, in His mercy, will give us Paradise." Having one day met a gentleman who was filled with excessive fear of the judgments of God, he said to him, "He who has a true desire to serve God and to avoid sin, must in nowise allow himself to be tormented by the thought of death and judgment. If they are to be feared, it is not with that fear which dejects and depresses the vigour of the soul; but a fear tempered with confidence, and therefore salutary. Hope in God: who hopes in Him shall never be confounded."

[1] Ps. xxx.

We read in the Life of St. Philip Neri, that having gone one day to the Convent of St. Martha in Rome, one of the Religious, named Scholastica, desired to speak to him in private. This lady had been tormented for a long time with a thought of despair, which she had not dared to make known to any one; but, full of confidence in the saint, she resolved to open her heart to him. When she went to him, before she had time to say a word, the man of God said to her with a smile, "You are very wrong, my daughter, to believe that you are destined for eternal flames: Paradise belongs to you!" "I cannot believe it, Father," she replied with a deep sigh. "You do not believe it? That is folly on your part, you will see. Tell me, Scholastica, for whom did Jesus die?" "He died for sinners." "And now tell me are you a saint?" "Alas!" replied she weeping, "I am a great sinner." "Therefore Jesus died for you, and most assuredly it was to open Heaven for you. It is thus clear that Heaven is yours. For as to your sins, you detest them, I have no doubt." The good Religious was touched by these words. Light entered her soul, the temptation vanished, and from that moment those sweet words, *Paradise is yours*, filled her with confidence and joy.

CHAPTER LXV.

Means to Avoid Purgatory—Holy Acceptation of Death—Father Aquitanus—St. Alphonsus Liguori—Venerable Frances of Pampeluna and the Person who was not Resigned to Die—Father Vincent Caraffa and the Condemned Man—Sister Mary of St. Joseph and Mother Isabella—St. John of the Cross—Sweetness of the Death of the Saints.

THE sixth means to avoid Purgatory is the humble and submissive acceptation of death in expiation of our sins: it is a generous act, by which we make a sacrifice of our life to God, in union with the sacrifice of Jesus Christ upon the cross.

Do you desire an example of this holy resignation of life into the hands of the Creator? On December 2, 1638, there died at Brisach, on the right bank of the Rhine, Father George Aquitanus, of the Society of Jesus. Twice he had devoted his life to the service of the plague-stricken. It happened that on two different occasions the pest raged with such fury that it was almost impossible to approach the sick without being attacked by the contagion. Every one fled and abandoned the dying to their unhappy fate. But Father Aquitanus, placing his life in the hands of God, made himself the servant and the apostle of the sick; he employed himself exclusively in relieving their sufferings and in administering to them the Sacraments.

God preserved him during the first visitation of the pest; but when it again broke out with renewed violence, and the man of God was called upon for the second time to devote himself to the care of the sick, God this time accepted his sacrifice.

When, a victim of his Charity, he lay extended upon his bed of death, he was asked if he willingly made the sacrifice of his life to God. "Oh!" he replied full of joy, " if I had a million lives to offer to Him, He knows how readily I would give them to Him." Such an act, it is easy to understand, is very meritorious in the sight of God. Does it not resemble that supreme act of charity accomplished by the martyrs who died for Jesus Christ, and which, like Baptism, effaces all sin and cancels all debts? *Greater love than this,* says our Lord. *no man hath, that a man lay down his life for his friend.*[1]

To make this act in time of sickness, it is useful, not to say necessary, that the patient should understand his condition, and know that his end is approaching. It is therefore to do him great injury to withhold this knowledge from him through a false delicacy. " *We must,*" says St. Alphonsus, "*prudently impart to the sick person the knowledge of his danger.*"

If the patient endeavours to deceive himself with illusions, if, instead of resigning himself into the hands of God, he thinks only of his cure, even when he receives all the Sacraments, he does himself a deplorable wrong.

We read in the Life of Venerable Mother Frances of the Blessed Sacrament, a Religious of Pampeluna,[2] that a soul was condemned to a long Purgatory for not having had a true submission to the Divine will upon her deathbed. She was otherwise a very pious young person, but when the icy hand of death came to touch her in the flower of her youth, nature recoiled, and she had not the courage to resign herself into the ever-loving hands of her Heavenly Father —she would not die yet. She expired, nevertheless, and the Venerable Mother Frances, who received frequent visits from the souls of the departed, learned that this soul had

[1] John xv. 13.
[2] By Joachim of St. Mary ; Rossign., *Merv.,* 26.

to expiate by long sufferings her want of submission to the decrees of her Creator.

The Life of Venerable Father Caraffa [1] furnishes us with a more consoling example.

Father Vincent Caraffa, General of the Society of Jesus, was called to prepare for death a young nobleman who was condemned to be executed, and who thought himself condemned to death unjustly. To die in the flower of one's age, when one is rich, happy, and when the future smiles upon us, is hard, we must own; yet a criminal who is a prey to remorse of conscience may resign himself to it, and accept it as a chastisement in expiation for his crime. But what shall we say of a person who is innocent?

The Father had, therefore, a difficult task to accomplish. Nevertheless, assisted by grace, he knew so well how to manage this unhappy man, he spoke with such unction of the faults of his past life and of the necessity of making satisfaction to Divine Justice, he made him understand so thoroughly how God permitted this temporal chastisement for his good, that he crushed rebellious nature and completely changed the sentiments of his heart. The young man looked upon his sentence as an expiation which would obtain for him the pardon of God, mounted the scaffold not only with resignation, but also with a truly Christian joy. Up to the last moment, even under the axe of the executioner, he blessed God and implored His Mercy, to the great edification of all those who assisted at his execution.

At the moment when his head fell, Father Caraffa saw his soul rise triumphantly to Heaven. He immediately went to the mother of the young man to console her by relating what he had seen. He was so transported with joy, that on returning to his cell he ceased not to cry aloud, "O happy man! O happy man!"

The family wished to have a great number of Masses

---

[1] By Father Bartoli; Rossign., *Merv.*, 97.

celebrated for the repose of his soul. "It is superfluous," replied the Father; "we must rather thank God and rejoice, for I declare to you that his soul has not even passed through Purgatory." Another day, whilst engaged in some work, he suddenly stopped, his countenance changed, and he looked towards Heaven; then he was heard to cry out, "*O happy lot! O happy lot!*" And when his companion asked him an explanation of these words, "Ah! my dear Father," he replied, "it was the soul of that condemned man which appeared to me in glory. Oh, how profitable to him has been his resignation!"

Sister Mary of St. Joseph, one of the four first Carmelites who embraced the reform of St. Teresa, was a Religious of great virtue. The end of her career approached, and our Lord, wishing that His spouse should be received into Heaven in triumph on breathing her last sigh, purified and adorned her soul by the sufferings which marked the end of her life.

During the four last days which she passed upon earth, she lost her speech and the use of her senses; she was a prey to frightful agony, and the Religious were heart-broken to see her in that state. Mother Isabella of St. Dominic, Prioress of the convent, approached the sick Religious, and suggested to her to make many acts of resignation, and total abandonment of herself into the hands of God. Sister Mary of St. Joseph heard her, and made these acts interiorly, but without being able to give any exterior sign thereof.

She died in these holy dispositions, and, on the very day of her death, whilst Mother Isabella was hearing Mass and praying for the repose of her soul, our Lord showed her the soul of His faithful spouse crowned in glory, and said, "*She is of the number of those who follow the Lamb.*" Sister Mary of St. Joseph, on her part, thanked Mother Isabella for all the good she had procured for her at the hour of death. She added that the acts of resignation which she had suggested to her had merited for her great glory in Paradise and had exempted her from the pains of Purgatory.[1] What happiness to quit this miserable life, to enter the only true and blessed one! We all may enjoy this happiness, if we employ the means which Jesus Christ has given us for making satisfaction in this world, and for preparing our souls perfectly to appear in His presence. The soul thus prepared is filled in her last hour with the sweetest confidence; she has, as it were, a foretaste of Heaven; the experiences which St. John of the Cross has written on the death of a saint in his *Living Flame of Love*.

"Perfect love of God," he says, "renders death agreeable, making the soul taste the greatest sweetness therein. The soul that loves is inundated with a torrent of delights at the approach of that moment when she is about to enjoy the full possession of her Beloved. On the point of being delivered from this prison of the body, she seems already to contemplate the glories of Paradise, and all within her is transformed into love."

[1] Life of Mother Isabella, lib. iii. c. 7.

THE END.

BURNS AND OATES, LIMITED, LONDON.

FROM

BURNS & OATES'

Catalogue

OF

PUBLICATIONS.

LONDON: BURNS AND OATES, Ld.
28 ORCHARD ST., W., & 63 PATERNOSTER ROW, E.C.
NEW YORK, CINCINNATI, CHICAGO: BENZIGER BROTHERS.

1893.

Latest Publications.

Pastime Papers. By CARDINAL MANNING. Cloth, 2s. 6d.

The Life of Father Augustus Law, S.J. By ELLIS SCHREIBER. Quarterly Series. Cloth, 6s.

God's Birds (Birds mentioned in the Bible). By JOHN PRIESTMAN. Quarto, tastefully bound, 3s. 6d.

Life of Mère Marie Thérèse, Foundress and First Superior-General of the Daughters of the Cross. From the French. By a Daughter of the Cross. With Preface by CARDINAL VAUGHAN. Cloth, 4s.

Primer of Church Latin. For converts and others. By RENÉ F. R. CONDER, B.A., Oxon. Cloth, 2s.

An Architect in Exile, and other Essays. By BERNARD WHELAN. Cloth, 2s. 6d.

The Blessed Virgin Mary in the Fathers of the First Six Centuries. By the REV. THOMAS LIVIUS, C.SS.R., M.A. With a Preface by CARDINAL VAUGHAN. Cloth, 12s.

Memorials of Mr. Sergeant Bellasis (1800-1873). By Edward Bellasis. With Portraits and Illustrations. Half-bound, 10s. 6d.

Messrs. BURNS & OATES have recently acquired the Stock and Copyrights of:—

Ceremonial according to the Roman Rite. Translated from the Italian of JOSEPH BALDESCHI, Master of Ceremonies of the Basilica of St. Peter at Rome; with the Pontifical Offices of a Bishop in his own diocese, compiled from the "Cæremoniale Episcoporum"; to which are added various other Functions and copious explanatory Notes; the whole harmonized with the latest Decrees of the Sacred Congregation of Rites. By the Rev. J. D. HILARIUS DALE. New Edition. Cloth, 6s. 6d.

The Sacristan's Manual; or, Handbook of Church Furniture, Ornament, &c. Harmonized with the most approved commentaries on the Roman Ceremonial and latest Decrees of the Sacred Congregation of Rites. By the Rev. J. D. HILARIUS DALE. New Edition, with numerous Additions. Cloth, 2s. 6d.

Perry's Practical Sermons for all the Sundays of the Year. FIRST AND SECOND SERIES. Sixth Edition. In Two Volumes. Cloth. Price 3s. 6d. per Volume.

Controversial Catechism; or, Protestantism refuted and Catholicism established by an appeal to the Holy Scriptures, the testimony of the Holy Fathers, and the Dictates of Reason; in which such portions of Scheffmacher's Catechism as suit modern Controversy are embodied. By the Rev. STEPHEN KEENAN. New Edition, Revised and Enlarged. Cloth, 2s.

No. 2.   1893.
SELECTION
FROM
BURNS AND OATES' CATALOGUE OF PUBLICATIONS.

ALLIES, T. W. (K.C.S.G.)

Formation of Christendom. Vols. I., II. (out of print).
Vol. III. £0 12 0
Church and State as seen in the Formation of Christendom, 8vo, pp. 472, cloth . (out of print.)
The Throne of the Fisherman, built by the Carpenter's Son, the Root, the Bond, and the Crown of Christendom. Demy 8vo 0 10 6
The Holy See and the Wandering of the Nations. Demy 8vo. 0 10 6
Peter's Rock in Mohammed's Flood. Demy 8vo. . 0 10 6

"It would be quite superfluous at this hour of the day to recommend Mr. Allies' writings to English Catholics. Those of our readers who remember the article on his writings in the *Katholik*, know that he is esteemed in Germany as one of our foremost writers."—*Dublin Review.*

ALLIES, MARY.

Leaves from St. John Chrysostom, With introduction by T. W. Allies, K.C.S.G. Crown 8vo, cloth . 0 6 0

"Miss Allies' 'Leaves' are delightful reading; the English is remarkably pure and graceful; page after page reads as if it were original. No commentator, Catholic or Protestant, has ever surpassed St. John Chrysostom in the knowledge of Holy Scripture, and his learning was of a kind which is of service now as it was at the time when the inhabitants of a great city hung on his words."—*Tablet.*

History of the Church in England, from the beginning of the Christian Era to the accession of Henry VIII. Crown 8vo, cloth 0 6 0

"Miss Allies has in this volume admirably compressed the substance, or such as was necessary to her purpose, of a number of authorities, judiciously selected. . . . Considering how scanty was the material available for the due performance of much of her task, she has secured a proportion and continuity which is surprising. . . . As a narrative the volume is capitally written, as a summary it is skilful, and not its least excellence is its value as an index of the best available sources which deal with the period it covers."—*Birmingham Daily Gazette.*

ANNUS SANCTUS:

Hymns of the Church for the Ecclesiastical Year. Translated from the Sacred Offices by various Authors, with Modern, Original, and other Hymns, and an Appendix of Earlier Versions. Selected and Arranged by ORBY SHIPLEY, M.A.
Plain Cloth, lettered 0 5 0
Edition de luxe 0 10 6

ANSWERS TO ATHEISTS: OR NOTES ON

Ingersoll. By the Rev. A. Lambert, (over 100,000 copies sold in America). Tenth edition. Paper. . . . £0 0 6
Cloth 0 1 0

B. N.

The Jesuits: their Foundation and History. 2 vols. crown 8vo, cloth, red edges 0 15 0

"The book is just what it professes to be—*a popular history*, drawn from well-known sources," &c.—*Month*.

BAKER, VEN. FATHER AUGUSTIN.

Holy Wisdom; or, Directions for the Prayer of Contemplation, &c. Extracted from Treatises written by the Ven. Father F. Augustin Baker, O.S.B., and edited by Abbot Sweeney, D.D. Beautifully bound in half leather 0 6 0

"We earnestly recommend this most beautiful work to all our readers. We are sure that every community will use it as a constant manual. If any persons have friends in convents, we cannot conceive a better present they can make them, or a better claim they can have on their prayers, than by providing them with a copy."—*Weekly Register*.

BOWDEN, REV. H. S. (of the Oratory) Edited by.

Dante's Divina Commedia: Its scope and value. From the German of FRANCIS HETTINGER, D.D. With an engraving of Dante. Crown 8vo . . 0 10 6

"All that Venturi attempted to do has been now approached with far greater power and learning by Dr. Hettinger, who, as the author of the 'Apologie des Christenthums,' and as a great Catholic theologian, is eminently well qualified for the task he has undertaken."—*The Saturday Review*.

Natural Religion. Being Vol. I. of Dr. Hettinger's Evidences of Christianity. With an Introduction on Certainty. Second edition. Crown 8vo, cloth 0 7 6

"As an able statement of the Catholic Doctrine of Certitude, and a defence, from the Romanist point of view, of the truth of Christianity, it was well worth while translating Dr. Franz Hettinger's 'Apologie des Christenthums,' of which the first part is now published."—*Scotsman*.

BRIDGETT, REV. T. E. (C.SS.R.).

Discipline of Drink 0 3 6

"The historical information with which the book abounds gives evidence of deep research and patient study, and imparts a permanent interest to the volume, which will elevate it to a position of authority and importance enjoyed by few of its compeers."—*The Arrow*.

Our Lady's Dowry; how England Won that Title. New and Enlarged Edition. 0 5 0

"This book is the ablest vindication of Catholic devotion to Our Lady, drawn from tradition, that we know of in the English language."—*Tablet*.

BRIDGETT REV. T. E. (C.SS.R.)—*continued*.

Ritual of the New Testament. An essay on the principles and origin of Catholic Ritual in reference to the New Testament. Third edition . . . £0 5 0

The Life of the Blessed John Fisher. With a reproduction of the famous portrait of Blessed JOHN FISHER by HOLBEIN, and other Illustrations. 2nd Ed. 0 7 6

"The Life of Blessed John Fisher could hardly fail to be interesting and instructive. Sketched by Father Bridgett's practised pen, the portrait of this holy martyr is no less vividly displayed in the printed pages of the book than in the wonderful picture of Holbein, which forms the frontispiece."—*Tablet.*

The True Story of the Catholic Hierarchy deposed by Queen Elizabeth, with fuller Memoirs of its Last Two Survivors. By the Rev. T. E. BRIDGETT, C.SS.R., and the late Rev. T. F. KNOX, D.D., of the London Oratory. Crown 8vo, cloth, 0 7 6

"We gladly acknowledge the value of this work on a subject which has been obscured by prejudice and carelessness."—*Saturday Review.*

The Life and Writings of Blessed Thomas More, Lord Chancellor of England and Martyr under Henry VIII. With Portrait of the Martyr taken from the Crayon Sketch made by Holbein in 1527. 2nd Ed. 0 7 6

"Father Bridgett has followed up his valuable Life of Bishop Fisher with a still more valuable Life of Thomas More. It is, as the title declares, a study not only of the life, but also of the writings of Sir Thomas. Father Bridgett has considered him from every point of view, and the result is, it seems to us, a more complete and finished portrait of the man, mentally and physically, than has been hitherto presented."—*Athenæum.*

The Wisdom and Wit of Blessed Thomas More . . 0 6 0

"It would be hard to find another such collection of true wisdom and keen, pungent, yet gentle wit and humour, as this volume contains."—*American Catholic Quarterly.*

BRIDGETT, REV. T. E. (C.SS.R.), Edited by.

Souls Departed. By CARDINAL ALLEN. First published in 1565, now edited in modern spelling by the Rev. T. E. Bridgett 0 6 0

BROWNLOW, VERY REV. CANON

A Memoir of the late Sir James Marshall, C.M.G., K.C.S.G., taken chiefly from his own letters. With Portrait. Crown 8vo, cloth . . 0 3 6
Lectures on Slavery and Serfdom in Europe. Cloth 0 3 6

"The general impression left by the perusal of this interesting book is one of great fairness and thorough grasp of the subject."—*Month.*

CASWALL, FATHER.

Catholic Latin Instructor in the Principal Church Offices and Devotions, for the Use of Choirs, Convents, and Mission Schools, and for Self-Teaching. 1 vol., complete 0 3 6
Or Part I., containing Benediction, Mass, Serving at Mass, and various Latin Prayers in ordinary use . 0 1 6

CASWALL, FATHER.—*continued.*
  May Pageant : A Tale of Tintern. (A Poem) Second
    edition £0 2 0
  Poems 0 5 0
  Lyra Catholica, containing all the Breviary and Missal
    Hymns, with others from various sources. 32mo,
    cloth, red edges 0 2 6

CATHOLIC BELIEF : OR, A SHORT AND
  Simple Exposition of Catholic Doctrine. By the
  Very Rev. Joseph Faà di Bruno, D.D. Twelfth
  edition . . . . . Price 6d. ; post free, 0 0 8½
    Cloth, lettered, ... 0 0 10
  Also an edition on better paper and bound in cloth, with
  gilt lettering and steel frontispiece 0 2 0

CHALLONER, BISHOP.
  Meditations for every day in the year. New edition.
  Revised and edited by the Right Rev. John Virtue,
  D.D., Bishop of Portsmouth. 8vo. 6th edition . 0 3 0
  And in other bindings.

COLERIDGE, REV H. J. (S.J.) *(See Quarterly Series.)*

DEVAS, C. S.
  Studies of Family Life : a contribution to Social
    Science. Crown 8vo 0 5 0
  "We recommend these pages and the remarkable evidence brought
  together in them to the careful attention of all who are interested in
  the well-being of our common humanity."—*Guardian.*
  "Both thoughtful and stimulating."—*Saturday Review.*

DRANE, AUGUSTA THEODOSIA, Edited by.
  The Autobiography of Archbishop Ullathorne. Demy
  8vo., cloth. Second edition 0 7 6
  "As a plucky Yorkshireman, as a sailor, as a missionary, as a
  great traveller, as a ravenous reader, and as a great prelate, Dr,
  Ullathorne was able to write down most fascinating accounts of his
  experiences. The book is full of shrewd glimpses from a Roman point
  of view of the man himself, of the position of Roman Catholics in this
  country, of the condition of the country, of the Colonies, and of the
  Anglican Church in various parts of the world, in the earlier half of
  this century."—*Guardian.*
  The Letters of Archbishop Ullathorne. (Sequel
    to the *Autobiography.*) Demy 8vo, cloth . . 0 9 0
  "Compiled with admirable judgment for the purpose of displaying
  in a thousand various ways the real man who was Archbishop
  Ullathorne."—*Tablet.*

EYRE MOST REV. CHARLES, (Abp. of Glasgow).
  The History of St. Cuthbert : or, An Account of his
  Life, Decease, and Miracles. Third edition. Illustrated with maps, charts, &c., and handsomely
  bound in cloth. Royal 8vo 0 14 0
  "A handsome, well appointed volume, in every way worthy of its
  illustrious subject. . . . The chief impression of the whole is the
  picture of a great and good man drawn by a sympathetic hand."—
  Spectator.

FABER, REV. FREDERICK WILLIAM, (D.D.)

All for Jesus	£0	5 0
Bethlehem	0	7 0
Blessed Sacrament	0	7 6
Creator and Creature	0	6 0
Ethel's Book of the Angels	0	5 0
Foot of the Cross	0	6 0
Growth in Holiness	0	6 0
Hymns	0	6 0
Notes on Doctrinal and Spiritual Subjects, 2 vols. each	0	5 0
Poems	0	5 0
Precious Blood	0	5 0
Sir Lancelot	0	5 0
Spiritual Conferences	0	6 0
Life and Letters of Frederick William Faber, D.D., Priest of the Oratory of St. Philip Neri. By John Edward Bowden of the same Congregation	0	6 0

FOLEY, REV. HENRY, (S.J.)

Records of the English Province of the Society of Jesus. Vol. I., Series I. . . . . net	1	6 0
Vol. II., Series II., III., IV. . . . net	1	6 0
Vol. III., Series V., VI., VII., VIII. . . net	1	10 0
Vol. IV. Series IX., X., XI. . . . net	1	6 0
Vol. V., Series XII. with nine Photographs of Martyrs . . . . net	1	10 0
Vol. VI., Diary and Pilgrim-Book of the English College, Rome. The Diary from 1579 to 1773, with Biographical and Historical Notes. The Pilgrim-Book of the Ancient English Hospice attached to the College from 1580 to 1656, with Historical Notes . . . . net	1	6 0
Vol. VII. Part the First: General Statistics of the Province; and Collectanea, giving Biographical Notices of its Members and of many Irish and Scotch Jesuits. With 20 Photographs . . . . . net	1	6 0
Vol. VII. Part the Second: Collectanea, Completed; With Appendices. Catalogues of Assumed and Real Names: Annual Letters; Biographies and Miscellanea. . . . . net	1	6 0

"As a biographical dictionary of English Jesuits, it deserves a place in every well-selected library, and, as a collection of marvellous occurrences, persecutions, martyrdoms, and evidences of the results of faith, amongst the books of all who belong to the Catholic Church."—*Genealogist.*

FORMBY, REV. HENRY.

Monotheism: in the main derived from the Hebrew nation and the Law of Moses. The Primitive Religion of the City of Rome. An historical Investigation. Demy 8vo.	0	5 0

FRANCIS DE SALES, ST.: THE WORKS OF.
Translated into the English Language by the Very Rev. Canon Mackey, O.S.B., under the direction of the Right Rev. Bishop Hedley, O.S.B.

Vol. I. Letters to Persons in the World. Cloth . £0 6 0
"The letters must be read in order to comprehend the charm and sweetness of their style."—*Tablet.*

Vol. II.—The Treatise on the Love of God. Father Carr's translation of 1630 has been taken as a basis, but it has been modernized and thoroughly revised and corrected. 0 9 0
"To those who are seeking perfection by the path of contemplation this volume will be an armoury of help."—*Saturday Review.*

Vol. III. The Catholic Controversy. . . . 0 6 0
"No one who has not read it can conceive how clear, how convincing, and how well adapted to our present needs are these controversial 'leaves.'"—*Tablet.*

Vol. IV. Letters to Persons in Religion, with introduction by Bishop Hedley on "St. Francis de Sales and the Religious State." 0 6 0
"The sincere piety and goodness, the grave wisdom, the knowledge of human nature, the tenderness for its weakness, and the desire for its perfection that pervade the letters, make them pregnant of instruction for all serious persons. The translation and editing have been admirably done."—*Scotsman.*

*** Other vols. in preparation.

GALLWEY, REV. PETER, (S.J.)
Precious Pearl of Hope in the Mercy of God, The. Translated from the Italian. With Preface by the Rev. Father Gallwey. Cloth. 0 4 6
Lectures on Ritualism and on the Anglican Orders. 2 vols. (Or may be had separately.) 0 8 0
Salvage from the Wreck. A few Memories of the Dead, preserved in Funeral Discourses. With Portraits. Crown 8vo. 0 7 6

GIBSON, REV. H.
Catechism Made Easy. Being an Explanation of the Christian Doctrine. Eighth edition. 2 vols., cloth. 0 7 6
"This work must be of priceless worth to any who are engaged in any form of catechetical instruction. It is the best book of the kind that we have seen in English."—*Irish Monthly.*

GILLOW, JOSEPH.
Literary and Biographical History, or, Bibliographical Dictionary of the English Catholics. From the Breach with Rome, in 1534, to the Present Time. Vols. *I., II. and III. cloth, demy 8vo . . each.* 0 15 0
*** Other vols. in preparation.
"The patient research of Mr. Gillow, his conscientious record of minute particulars, and especially his exhaustive bibliographical information in connection with each name, are beyond praise."—*British Quarterly Review.*

The Haydock Papers. Illustrated. Demy 8vo. . 0 7 6
' We commend this collection to the attention of every one that is interested in the records of the sufferings and struggles of our ancestors to hand down the faith to their children. It is in the perusal of such details that we bring home to ourselves the truly heroic sacrifices that our forefathers endured in those dark and dismal times."—*Tablet.*

GLANCEY, REV. M. F.
Characteristics from the Writings of Archbishop Ullathorne, together with a Bibliographical Account of the Archbishop's Works. Crown 8vo, cloth . . £0 6 0

"The Archbishop's thoughts are expressed in choice, rich language, which, pleasant as it is to read, must have been additionally so to hear. We have perused this book with interest, and have no hesitation in recommending our readers to possess themselves of it."—*Birmingham Weekly Mercury.*

GRADWELL, MONSIGNOR.
Succat, The Story of Sixty Years of the Life of St. Patrick. Crown 8vo, cloth 0 5 0

"A work at once bright, picturesque, and truthful."—*Tablet.*

"We most heartily commend this book to all lovers of St. Patrick."—*Irish Ecclesiastical Record.*

GROWTH IN THE KNOWLEDGE OF OUR LORD.
Meditations for every Day in the Year, exclusive of those for Festivals, Days of Retreat, &c. Adapted from the original of Abbé de Brandt, by Sister Mary Fidelis. A new and Improved Edition, in 3 Vols. Sold only in sets. Price per set, ... 1 2 6

"The praise, though high, bestowed on these excellent meditations by the Bishop of Salford is well deserved. The language, like good spectacles, spreads treasures before our vision without attracting attention to itself."—*Dublin Review.*

HEDLEY, BISHOP.
Our Divine Saviour, and other Discourses. Crown 8vo. 0 6 0

"A distinct and noteworthy feature of these sermons is, we certainly think, their freshness—freshness of thought, treatment, and style; nowhere do we meet pulpit commonplace or hackneyed phrase —everywhere, on the contrary, it is the heart of the preacher pouring out to his flock his own deep convictions, enforcing them from the 'Treasures, old and new,' of a cultivated mind."—*Dublin Review.*

KING, FRANCIS.
The Church of my Baptism, and why I returned to it. Crown 8vo, cloth 0 2 6

"Altogether a book of an excellent spirit, written with freshness and distinction."—*Weekly Register.*

LEDOUX, REV. S. M.
History of the Seven Holy Founders of the Order of the Servants of Mary. Crown 8vo, cloth . . 0 4 6

"Throws a full light upon the Seven Saints recently canonized, whom we see as they really were. All that was marvellous in their call, their works, and their death is given with the charm of a picturesque and speaking style."—*Messenger of the Sacred Heart.*

LEE, REV. F. G., D.D. (of All Saints, Lambeth.)
Edward the Sixth : Supreme Head. Second edition.
Crown 8vo . . . . . . , . . £0 6 0
"In vivid interest and in literary power, no less than in solid historical value, Dr. Lee's present work comes fully up to the standard of its predecessors ; and to say that is to bestow high praise. The book evinces Dr. Lee's customary diligence of research in amassing facts, and his rare artistic power in welding them into a harmonious and effective whole."—*John Bull.*

LIGUORI, ST. ALPHONSUS.
New and Improved Translation of the Complete Works of St. Alphonsus, edited by the late Bishop Coffin :—
Vol. I. The Christian Virtues, and the Means for Obtaining them. Cloth 0 3 0
Or separately :—
  1. The Love of our Lord Jesus Christ . . . 0 1 0
  2. Treatise on Prayer. *(In the ordinary editions a great part of this work is omitted)* . . 0 1 0
  3. A Christian's rule of Life 0 1 0
Vol. II. The Mysteries of the Faith—The Incarnation; containing Meditations and Devotions on the Birth and Infancy of Jesus Christ, &c., suited for Advent and Christmas. 0 2 6
Vol. III. The Mysteries of the Faith—The Blessed Sacrament 0 2 6
Vol. IV. Eternal Truths—Preparation for Death . 0 2 6
Vol. V. The Redemption—Meditations on the Passion. 0 2 6
Vol. VI. Glories of Mary. New edition . . . 0 3 6
Reflections on Spiritual Subjects . . . 0 2 6

LIVIUS, REV. T. (M.A., C.SS.R.)
St. Peter, Bishop of Rome ; or, the Roman Episcopate of the Prince of the Apostles, proved from the Fathers, History and Chronology, and illustrated by arguments from other sources. Dedicated to his Eminence Cardinal Newman. Demy 8vo, cloth . 0 12 0
"A book which deserves careful attention. In respect of literary qualities, such as effective arrangement, and correct and lucid diction, this essay, by an English Catholic scholar, is not unworthy of Cardinal Newman, to whom it is dedicated."—*The Sun.*
Explanation of the Psalms and Canticles in the Divine Office. By ST. ALPHONSUS LIGUORI. Translated from the Italian by THOMAS LIVIUS, C.SS.R. With a Preface by his Eminence Cardinal MANNING. Crown 8vo, cloth 0 7 6
"To nuns and others who know little or no Latin, the book will be of immense importance."—*Dublin Review.*
"Father Livius has in our opinion even improved on the original, so far as the arrangement of the book goes. New priests will find it especially useful."—*Month.*
Mary in the Epistles ; or, The Implicit Teaching of the Apostles concerning the Blessed Virgin, set forth in devout comments on their writings. Illustrated from Fathers and other Authors, and prefaced by introductory Chapters. Crown 8vo. Cloth 0 5 0

MANNING, CARDINAL. Popular Edition of the Works of

Four Great Evils of the Day. 6th edition.	£0	2	6
Fourfold Sovereignty of God. 3rd edition.	0	2	6
Glories of the Sacred Heart. 5th edition	0	4	0
Grounds of Faith. 10th edition.	0	1	6
Independence of the Holy See. 2nd edition	0	2	6
Internal Mission of the Holy Ghost. 5th edition	0	5	0
Miscellanies. 3 vols. . . . . the set	0	18	0
Pastime Papers	0	2	6
Religio Viatoris. 4th edition,	0	1	6
Sermons on Ecclesiastical Subjects. Vol. I.	0	6	0
(Vols. II. and III. out of Print.)			
Sin and its Consequences. 7th edition	0	4	0
Temporal Mission of the Holy Ghost. 3rd edition	0	5	0
True Story of the Vatican Council. 2nd edition	0	2	6
The Eternal Priesthood. 10th edition	0	2	6
The Office of the Church in the Higher Catholic Education. A Pastoral Letter	0	0	6
Workings of the Holy Spirit in the Church of England. Reprint of a letter addressed to Dr. Pusey in 1864	0	1	6
Lost Sheep Found. , A Sermon	0	0	6
Rights and Dignity of Labour	0	0	1

The Westminster Series
In handy pocket size. All bound in cloth.

The Blessed Sacrament, the Centre of Immutable Truth	0	1	0
Confidence in God.	0	1	0
Holy Gospel of Our Lord Jesus Christ according to St. John.	0	1	0
Love of Jesus to Penitents.	0	1	0
Office of the Holy Ghost under the Gospel	0	1	0
Holy Ghost the Sanctifier	0	2	0

MANNING, CARDINAL, Edited by.
Life of the Curé of Ars. Popular edition . . . 0 2 6

MEDAILLE, REV. P.
Meditations on the Gospels for Every Day in the Year. Translated into English from the new Edition, enlarged by the Besançon Missionaries, under the direction of the Rev. W. H. Eyre, S.J. Cloth 0 6 0
(This work has already been translated into Latin, Italian, Spanish, German, and Dutch.)

"We have carefully examined these Meditations, and are fain to confess that we admire them very much. They are short, succinct, pithy, always to the point, and wonderfully suggestive."—*Tablet.*

MIVART, PROF. ST. GEORGE (M.D., F.R.S.)
Nature and Thought. Second edition . . . 0 4 0
"The complete command of the subject, the wide grasp, the subtlety, the readiness of illustration, the grace of style, contrive to render this one of the most admirable books of its class."— *British Quarterly Review.*

A Philosophical Catechism. Fifth edition . . 0 1 0
"It should become the *vade mecum* of Catholic students."—*Tablet.*

MONTGOMERY, HON. MRS.
Approved by the Most Rev. G. Porter, Achbp. of Bombay.
The Eternal Years. With an Introduction by the
Most Rev. G. Porter, Achbp. of Bombay. Cloth. £0 3 6
The Divine Ideal. Cloth 0 3 6
"A work of original thought carefully developed and expressed in lucid and richly imaged style."—*Tablet.*
"The writing of a pious, thoughtful, earnest woman."—*Church Review.*
"Full of truth, and sound reason, and confidence."—*American Catholic Book News.*

MORRIS, REV. JOHN (S.J., F.S.A.)
Letter Books of Sir Amias Poulet, keeper of Mary
Queen of Scots. Demy 8vo 0 10 6
Two Missionaries under Elizabeth 0 14 0
The Catholics under Elizabeth 0 14 0
The Life of Father John Gerard, S.J. Third edition,
rewritten and enlarged 0 14 0
The Life and Martyrdom of St. Thomas Becket. Second
and enlarged edition. In one volume, large post 8vo,
cloth, pp. xxxvi., 632, ... 0 12 6
or bound in two parts, cloth 0 13 0
"Father Morris is one of the few living writers who have succeeded in greatly modifying certain views of English history, which had long been accepted as the only tenable ones. . . To have wrung an admission of this kind from a reluctant public, never too much inclined to surrender its traditional assumptions, is an achievement not to be underrated in importance."—*Rev. Dr. Augustus Jessopp, in the Academy.*

MORRIS, REV. W. B. (of the Oratory.)
The Life of St. Patrick, Apostle of Ireland. Fourth
edition. Crown 8vo, cloth 0 5 0
"Promises to become the standard biography of Ireland's Apostle. For clear statement of facts, and calm judicious discussion of controverted points, it surpasses any work we know of in the literature of the subject."—*American Catholic Quarterly.*
Ireland and St. Patrick. A study of the Saint's
character and of the results of his apostolate.
Second edition. Crown 8vo. Cloth. . . 0 5 0
"We read with pleasure this volume of essays, which, though the Saint's name is taken by no means in vain, really contains a sort of discussion of current events and current English views of Irish character."—*Saturday Review.*

NEWMAN, CARDINAL.
Church of the Fathers 0 4 0
Prices of other works by Cardinal Newman on application.

PAGANI, VERY REV. JOHN BAPTIST,
The Science of the Saints in Practice. By John Baptist Pagani, Second General of the Institute of
Charity. Complete in three volumes. Vol. 1,
January to April (out of print). Vol. 2, May to
August. Vol. 3, September to December . each 0 3 0
"'The Science of the Saints' is a practical treatise on the principal Christian virtues, abundantly illustrated with interesting examples from Holy Scripture as well as from the Lives of the Saints. Written chiefly for devout souls, such as are trying to live an interior and supernatural life by following in the footsteps of our Lord and His saints, this work is eminently adapted for the use of ecclesiastics and of religious communities."—*Irish Ecclesiastical Record.*

PAYNE, JOHN ORLEBAR, (M.A.)

Records of the English Catholics of 1715. Demy 8vo. Half-bound, gilt top £0 15 0

"A book of the kind Mr. Payne has given us would have astonished Bishop Milner or Dr. Lingard. They would have treasured it, for both of them knew the value of minute fragments of historical information. The Editor has derived nearly the whole of the information which he has given, from unprinted sources, and we must congratulate him on having found a few incidents here and there which may bring the old times back before us in a most touching manner."—*Tablet.*

English Catholic Non-Jurors of 1715. Being a Summary of the Register of their Estates, with Genealogical and other Notes, and an Appendix of Unpublished Documents in the Public Record Office. In one Volume. Demy 8vo. . . 1 1 0

"Most carefully and creditably brought out . . . From first to last, full of social interest and biographical details, for which we may search in vain elsewhere."—*Antiquarian Magazine.*

Old English Catholic Missions. Demy 8vo, half-bound. 0 7 6

"A book to hunt about in for curious odds and ends."—*Saturday Review.*

"These registers tell us in their too brief records, teeming with interest for all their scantiness, many a tale of patient heroism."—*Tablet.*

St. Paul's Cathedral in the time of Edward VI. Being a detailed Account of its Treasures from a Document in the Public Record Office. Tastefully printed on imitation hand-made paper, and bound in cloth 0 2 6

PORTER, ARCHBISHOP.

The Letters of the late Father George Porter, S.J., Archbishop of Bombay. Demy 8vo. Cloth. . 0 7 6

"Brimful of good things . . . . . In them the priest will find a storehouse of hints on matters spiritual; from them the layman will reap crisp and clear information on many ecclesiastical points; the critic can listen to frank opinions of literature of every shade; and the general reader can enjoy the choice bits of description and morsels of humour scattered lavishly brough the book."—*Tablet.*

QUARTERLY SERIES. Edited by the Rev. John Morris, S.J. 84 volumes published to date.

Selection.

The Life and Letters of St. Francis Xavier. By the Rev. H. J. Coleridge, S.J. 2 vols. . . . 0 10 6

The History of the Sacred Passion. By Father Luis de la Palma, of the Society of Jesus. Translated from the Spanish. 0 5 0

The Life of Dona Louisa de Carvajal. By Lady Georgiana Fullerton. Small edition . . . 0 3 6

The Life and Letters of St. Teresa. 3 vols. By Rev. H. J. Coleridge, S.J. . . . . . each 0 7 6

The Life of Mary Ward. By Mary Catherine Elizabeth Chalmers, of the Institute of the Blessed Virgin. Edited by the Rev. H. J. Coleridge, S.J. 2 vols. 0 15 0

The Return of the King. Discourses on the Latter Days. By the Rev. H. J. Coleridge, S.J. . . 0 7 6

QUARTERLY SERIES—(*selection*) *continued.*
Pious Affections towards God and the Saints. Meditations for every Day in the Year, and for the Principal Festivals. From the Latin of the Ven. Nicolas Lancicius, S.J. £0 7 6
The Life and Teaching of Jesus Christ in Meditations for Every Day in the Year. By Fr. Nicolas Avancino, S.J. Two vols. 0 10 6
The Baptism of the King: Considerations on the Sacred Passion. By the Rev. H. J. Coleridge, S.J. . . 0 7 6
The Mother of the King. Mary during the Life of Our Lord. 0 7 6
The Hours of the Passion. Taken from the *Life of Christ* by Ludolph the Saxon 0 7 6
The Mother of the Church. Mary during the first Apostolic Age 0 6 0
The Life of St. Bridget of Sweden. By the late F. J. M. A. Partridge 0 6 0
The Teachings and Counsels of St. Francis Xavier. From his Letters 0 5 0
Garcia Moreno, President of Ecuador. 1821—1875. From the French of the Rev. P. A. Berthe, C.SS.R. By Lady Herbert 0 7 6
The Life of St. Alonso Rodriguez. By Francis Goldie, of the Society of Jesus . . . 0 7 6
Letters of St. Augustine. Selected and arranged by Mary H. Allies 0 6 6
A Martyr from the Quarter-Deck—Alexis Clerc, S.J. By Lady Herbert 0 5 0
Acts of the English Martyrs, hitherto unpublished. By the Rev. John H. Pollen, S.J. . . 0 7 6
Life of St. Francis di Geronimo, S.J. By A. M. Clarke. 0 7 6
Aquinas Ethicus; or the Moral Teaching of St. Thomas By the Rev. Joseph Rickaby, S.J. 2 vols. . 0 12 0
The Spirit of St. Ignatius, Founder of the Society of Jesus. From the French of the Rev. Fr. Xavier de Franciosi, S.J. 0 6 0
Jesus, the All-Beautiful. A devotional Treatise on the character and actions of Our Lord. Edited by Rev. J. G. MacLeod, S.J. 0 6 6
The Manna of the Soul. By Fr. Paul Segneri. New edition. In two volumes. . . . 0 12 0
Saturday dedicated to Mary. From the Italian of Fr. Cabrini, S.J. 0 6 0

VOLUMES ON THE LIFE OF OUR LORD.
The Holy Infancy.
The Preparation of the Incarnation . . . 0 7 6
The Nine Months. The Life of our Lord in the Womb. 0 7 6
The Thirty Years. Our Lord's Infancy and Early Life. 0 7 6
The Public Life of Our Lord.
The Ministry of St. John Baptist . . . 0 6 6
The Preaching of the Beatitudes . . . 0 6 6
The Sermon on the Mount. Continued. 2 Parts, each 0 6 6

QUARTERLY SERIES—*(selection) continued.*

The Training of the Apostles. Parts I., II., III., IV. each	£0	6	6
The Preaching of the Cross. Part I.	0	6	6
The Preaching of the Cross. Parts II., III. each	0	6	0
Passiontide. Parts I. II. and III., each	0	6	6
Chapters on the Parables of Our Lord	0	7	6

Introductory Volumes.

The Life of our Life. Harmony of the Life of Our Lord, with Introductory Chapters and Indices. Second edition. Two vols.	0	15	0
The Passage of our Lord to the Father. Conclusion of The Life of our Life.	0	7	6
The Works and Words of our Saviour, gathered from the Four Gospels	0	7	6
The Story of the Gospels. Harmonised for Meditation	0	7	6

ROSE, STEWART.

St. Ignatius Loyola and The Early Jesuits, with more than 100 Illustrations by H. W. and H. C. Brewer and L. Wain. The whole produced under the immediate superintendence of the Rev. W. H. Eyre, S.J. Super Royal 8vo. Handsomely bound in Cloth, extra gilt. . . . . . . net.   0 15 0

"This magnificent volume is one of which Catholics have justly reason to be proud. Its historical as well as its literary value is very great, and the illustrations from the pencils of Mr. Louis Wain and Messrs. H. W. and H. C. Brewer are models of what the illustrations of such a book should be. We hope that this book will be found in every Catholic drawing-room, as a proof that 'we Catholics' are in no way behind those around us in the beauty of the illustrated books that issue from our hands, or in the interest which is added to the subject by a skilful pen and finished style."—*Month.*

RYDER, REV. H. I. D. (of the Oratory.)

Catholic Controversy: A Reply to Dr. Littledale's "Plain Reasons." Seventh edition . . .   0 2 6

"Father Ryder of the Birmingham Oratory, has now furnished in a small volume a masterly reply to this assailant from without. The lighter charms of a brilliant and graceful style are added to the solid merits of this handbook of contemporary controversy."—*Irish Monthly.*

STANTON, REV. R. (of the Oratory.)

A Menology of England and Wales; or, Brief Memorials of the British and English Saints, arranged according to the Calendar. Together with the Martyrs of the 16th and 17th centuries. Compiled by order of the Cardinal Archbishop and the Bishops of the Province of Westminster. With Supplement, containing Notes and other additions, together with enlarged Appendices, and a new Index. Demy 8vo, cloth 0 16 0

The Supplement, separately 0 2 0

SWEENEY, RT. REV. ABBOT, (O.S.B.)

Sermons for all Sundays and Festivals of the Year. Fourth Edition. Crown 8vo, handsomely bound in half leather 0 10 6

THOMPSON, EDWARD HEALY, (M.A.)
The Life of Jean-Jacques Olier, Founder of the
Seminary of St. Sulpice. New and Enlarged Edition.
Post 8vo, cloth, pp. xxxvi. 628 . . . . £0 15 0
"It provides us with just what we most need, a model to look up to
and imitate; one whose circumstances and surroundings were sufficiently like our own to admit of an easy and direct application to our
own personal duties and daily occupations."—*Dublin Review.*
The Life and Glories of St. Joseph, Husband of
Mary, Foster-Father of Jesus, and Patron of the
Universal Church. Grounded on the Dissertations of
Canon Antonio Vitalis, Father José Moreno, and other
writers. Second Edition. Crown 8vo, cloth . 0 6 0

ULLATHORNE ARCHBISHOP.
Autobiography of, (*see* Drane, A. T.) . . . 0 7 6
Letters of, do. ,, . . . 0 9 0
Endowments of Man, &c. Popular edition. . . 0 7 0
Groundwork of the Christian Virtues: do. . . 0 7 0
Christian Patience, . . do. do. . . 0 7 0
Memoir of Bishop Willson. 0 2 6

VAUGHAN, ARCHBISHOP, (O.S.B.)
The Life and Labours of St. Thomas of Aquin.
Abridged and edited by Dom Jerome Vaughan,
O.S.B. Second Edition. (Vol. I., Benedictine
Library.) Crown 8vo. Attractively bound . . 0 6 6
"Popularly written, in the best sense of the word, skilfully avoids
all wearisome detail, whilst omitting nothing that is of importance
in the incidents of the Saint's existence, or for a clear understanding
of the nature and the purpose of those sublime theological works
on which so many Pontiffs, and notably Leo XIII., have pronounced
such remarkable and repeated commendations."—*Freeman's Journal.*

WARD, WILFRID.
The Clothes of Religion. A popular Positivism. 0 3 6
"Very witty and interesting."—*Spectator.*
"Really models of what such essays should be."—*Ch.Quart. Review.*

WATERWORTH, REV. J.
The Canons and Decree of the Sacred and Œcumenical
Council of Trent, ed under the Sovereign
Pontiffs, Paul III.,) III., and Pius IV., translated by the Rev. J. WATERWORTH. To which
are prefixed Essays on the External and Internal
History of the Council. A new edition. Demy
8vo, cloth 0 10 6

WESTMINSTER DECREES.
Decreta Quatuor Conciliorum Provincialum Westmonast. : 1853-1873. Adjectis Pluribus Decretis
Rescriptis aliisque Documentis . . . net 0 6 0

WISEMAN, CARDINAL.
Fabiola. A Tale of the Catacombs. . . 3s. 6d. and 0 4 0
Also a new and splendid edition printed on large
quarto paper, embellished with thirty-one full-page
illustrations, and a coloured portrait of St. Agnes.
Handsomely bound. 1 1 0